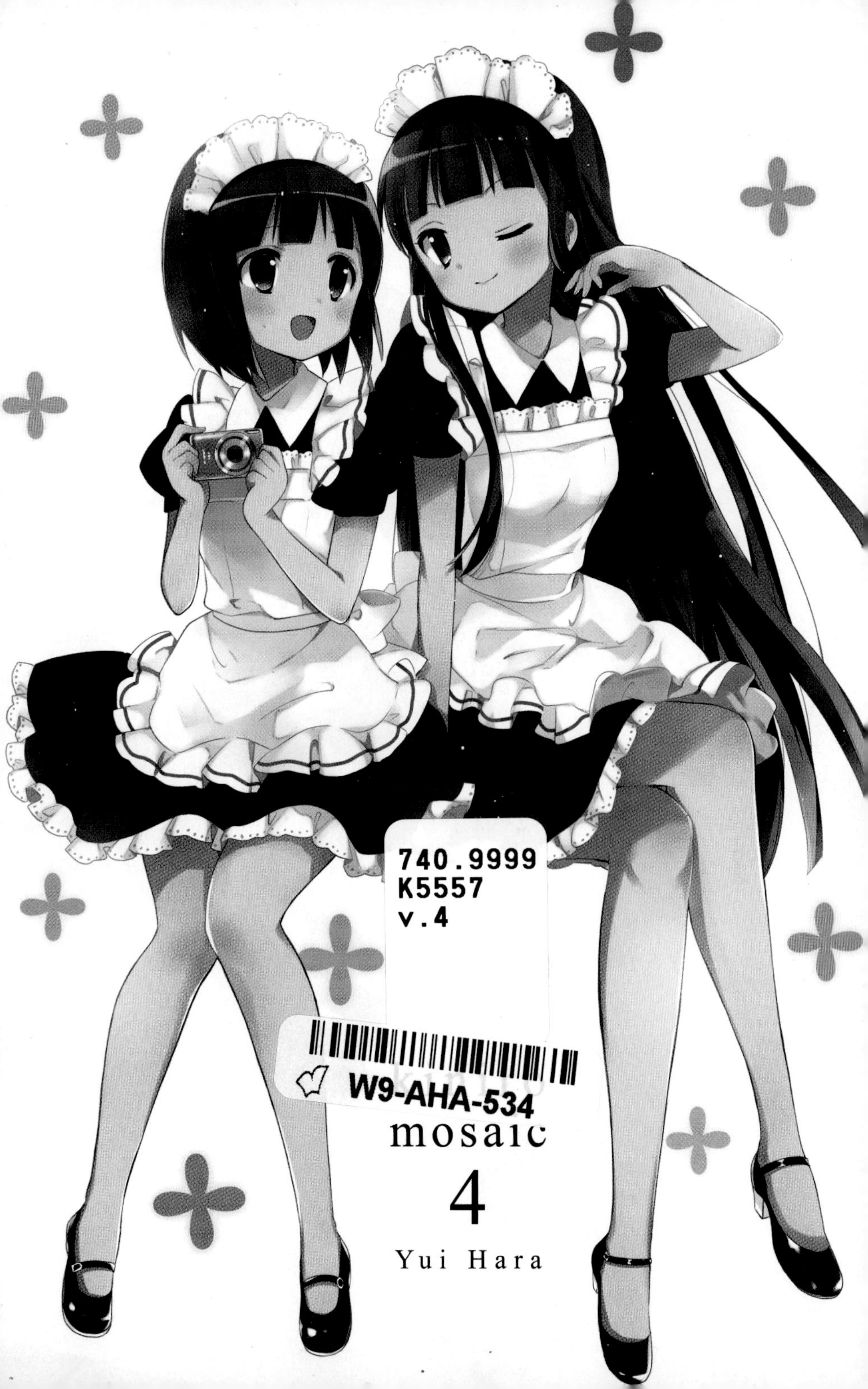

mosaic

4

Yui Hara

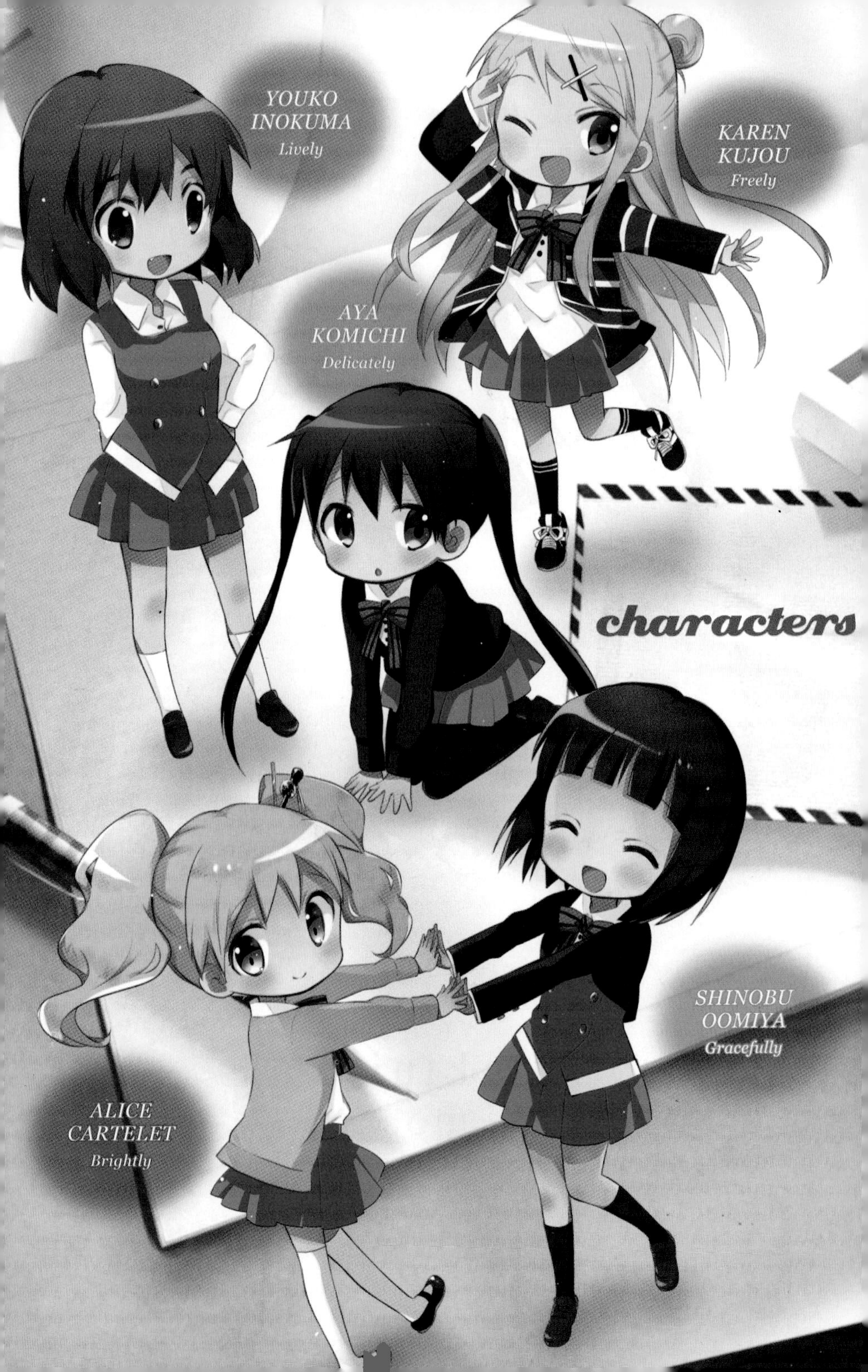
YOUKO
INOKUMA
Lively
KAREN
KUJOU
Freely
AYA
KOMICHI
Delicately
characters
SHINOBU
OOMIYA
Gracefully
ALICE
CARTELET
Brightly

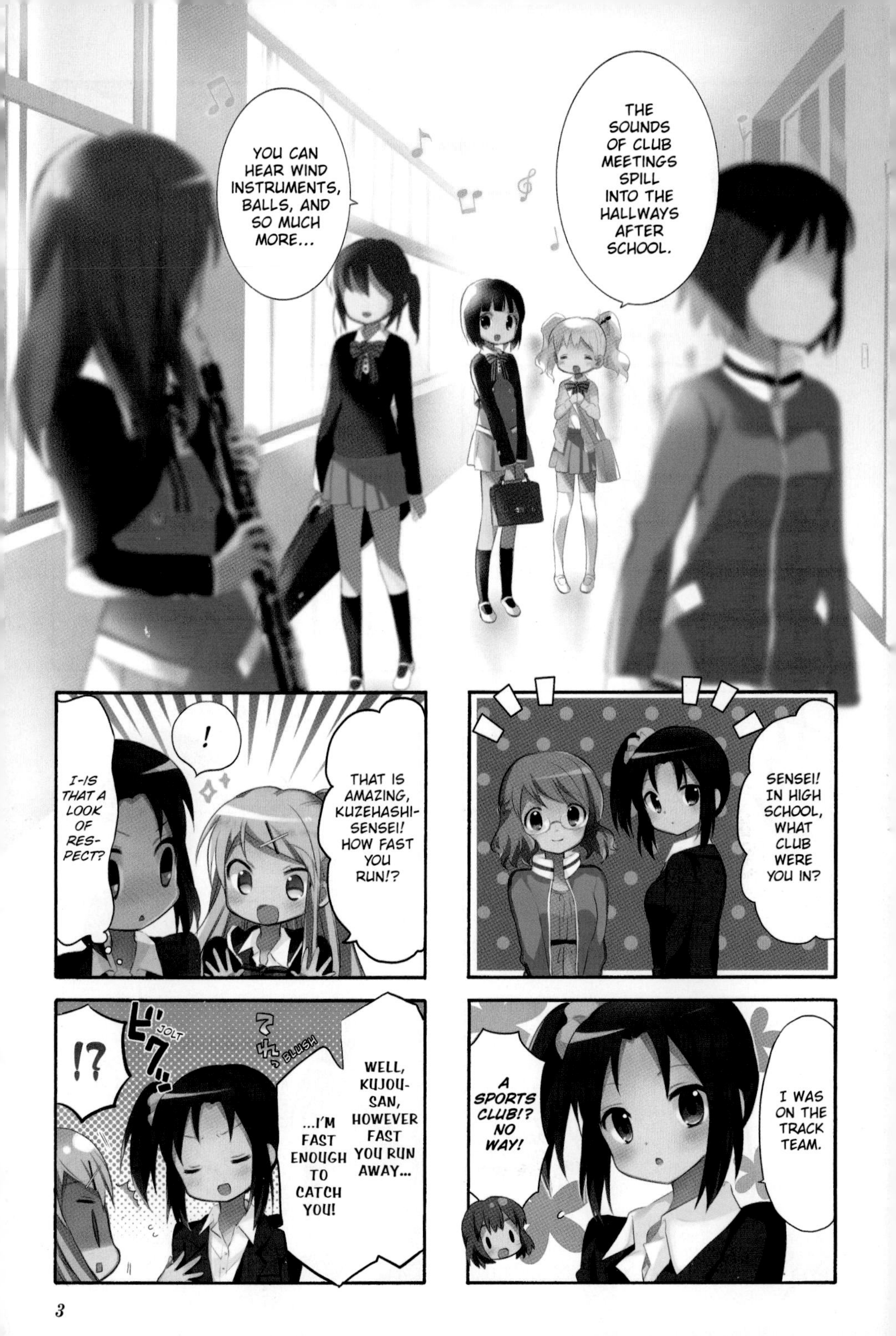
THE SOUNDS OF CLUB MEETINGS SPILL INTO THE HALLWAYS AFTER SCHOOL.
YOU CAN HEAR WIND INSTRUMENTS, BALLS, AND SO MUCH MORE...
SENSEI! IN HIGH SCHOOL, WHAT CLUB WERE YOU IN?
THAT IS AMAZING, KUZEHASHI-SENSEI! HOW FAST YOU RUN!?
!
I-IS THAT A LOOK OF RES-PECT?
I WAS ON THE TRACK TEAM.
A SPORTS CLUB!? NO WAY!
WELL, KUJOU-SAN, HOWEVER FAST YOU RUN AWAY...
...I'M FAST ENOUGH TO CATCH YOU!
BLUSH
JOLT
!?

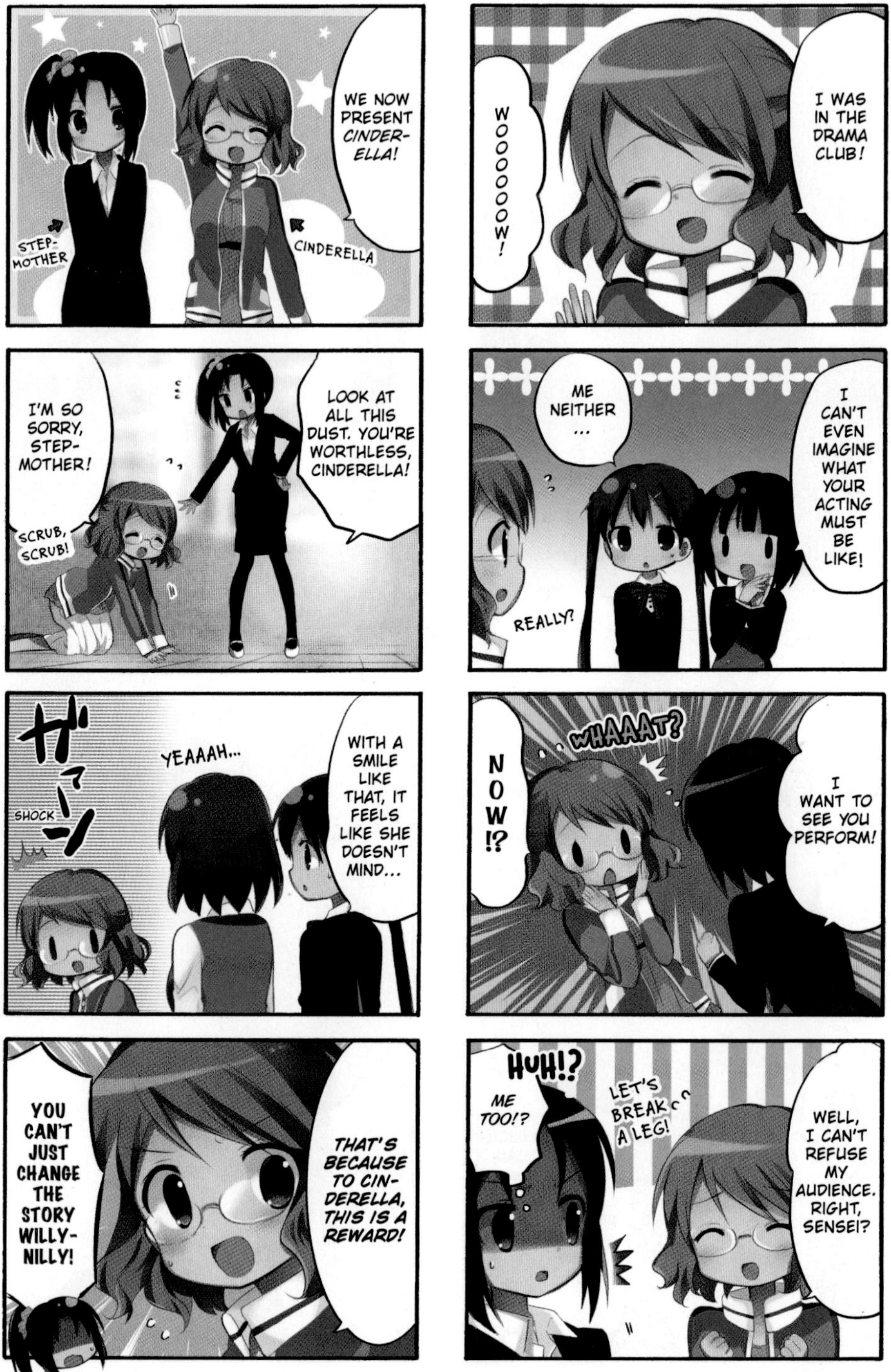
I WAS IN THE DRAMA CLUB!
WOOOOOOOW!
I CAN'T EVEN IMAGINE WHAT YOUR ACTING MUST BE LIKE!
ME NEITHER ...
REALLY?
I WANT TO SEE YOU PERFORM!
NOW!?
WHAAAT?
WELL, I CAN'T REFUSE MY AUDIENCE. RIGHT, SENSEI?
LET'S BREAK A LEG!
HUH!?
ME TOO!?
WE NOW PRESENT CINDERELLA!
CINDERELLA
STEP-MOTHER
LOOK AT ALL THIS DUST. YOU'RE WORTHLESS, CINDERELLA!
I'M SO SORRY, STEP-MOTHER!
SCRUB, SCRUB!
WITH A SMILE LIKE THAT, IT FEELS LIKE SHE DOESN'T MIND...
YEAAAH...
SHOCK
THAT'S BECAUSE TO CINDERELLA, THIS IS A REWARD!
YOU CAN'T JUST CHANGE THE STORY WILLY-NILLY!

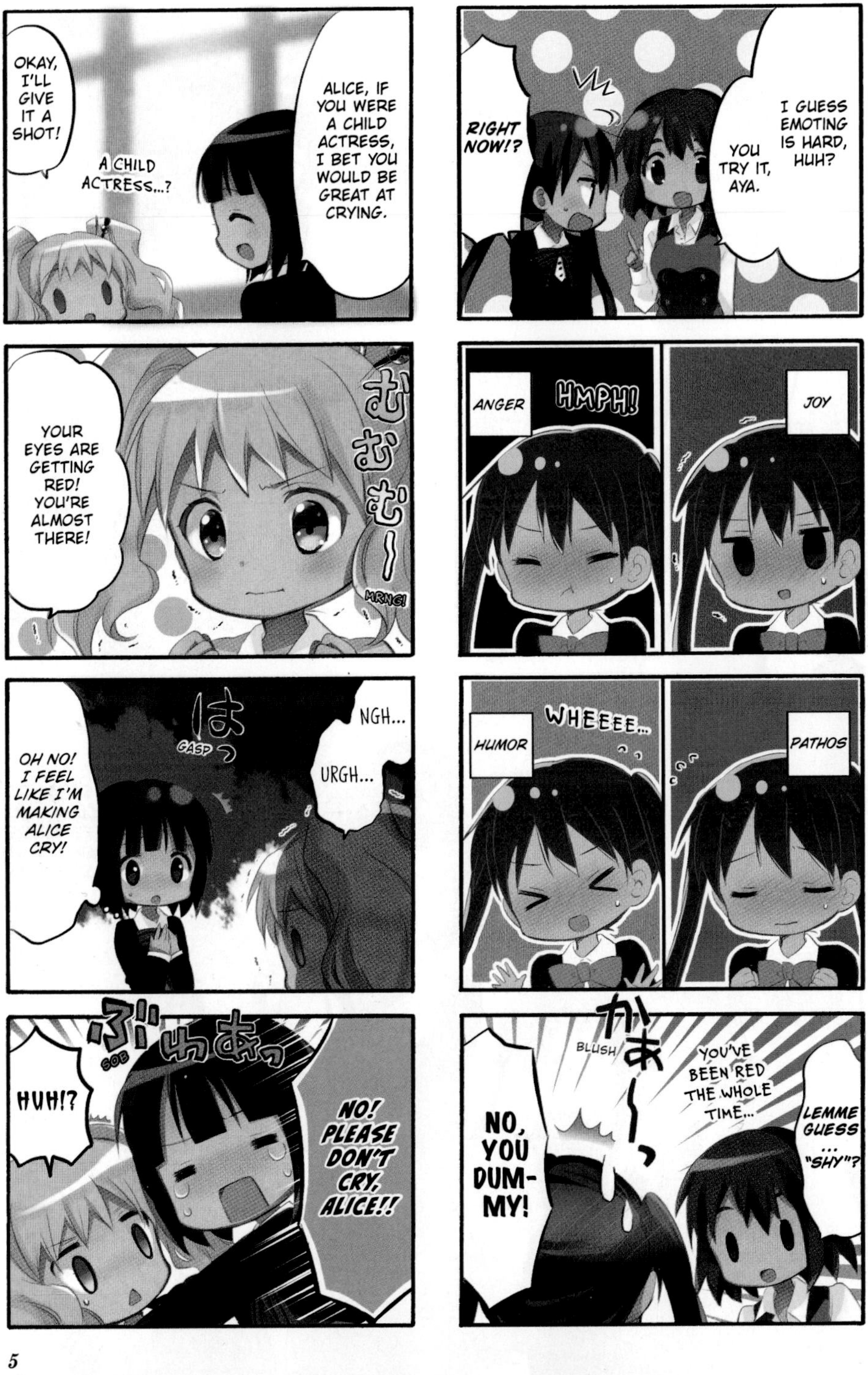
I GUESS EMOTING IS HARD, HUH?
YOU TRY IT, AYA.
RIGHT NOW!?
JOY
ANGER
HMPH!
PATHOS
HUMOR
WHEEEE...
LEMME GUESS... "SHY"?
YOU'VE BEEN RED THE WHOLE TIME...
かぁ~っ
BLUSH
NO, YOU DUM-MY!
ALICE, IF YOU WERE A CHILD ACTRESS, I BET YOU WOULD BE GREAT AT CRYING.
A CHILD ACTRESS...?
OKAY, I'LL GIVE IT A SHOT!
むむむ~
MRNG!
YOUR EYES ARE GETTING RED! YOU'RE ALMOST THERE!
NGH...
URGH...
はっ
GASP
OH NO! I FEEL LIKE I'M MAKING ALICE CRY!
NO! PLEASE DON'T CRY, ALICE!!
ぶわあっ
SOB
HUH!?

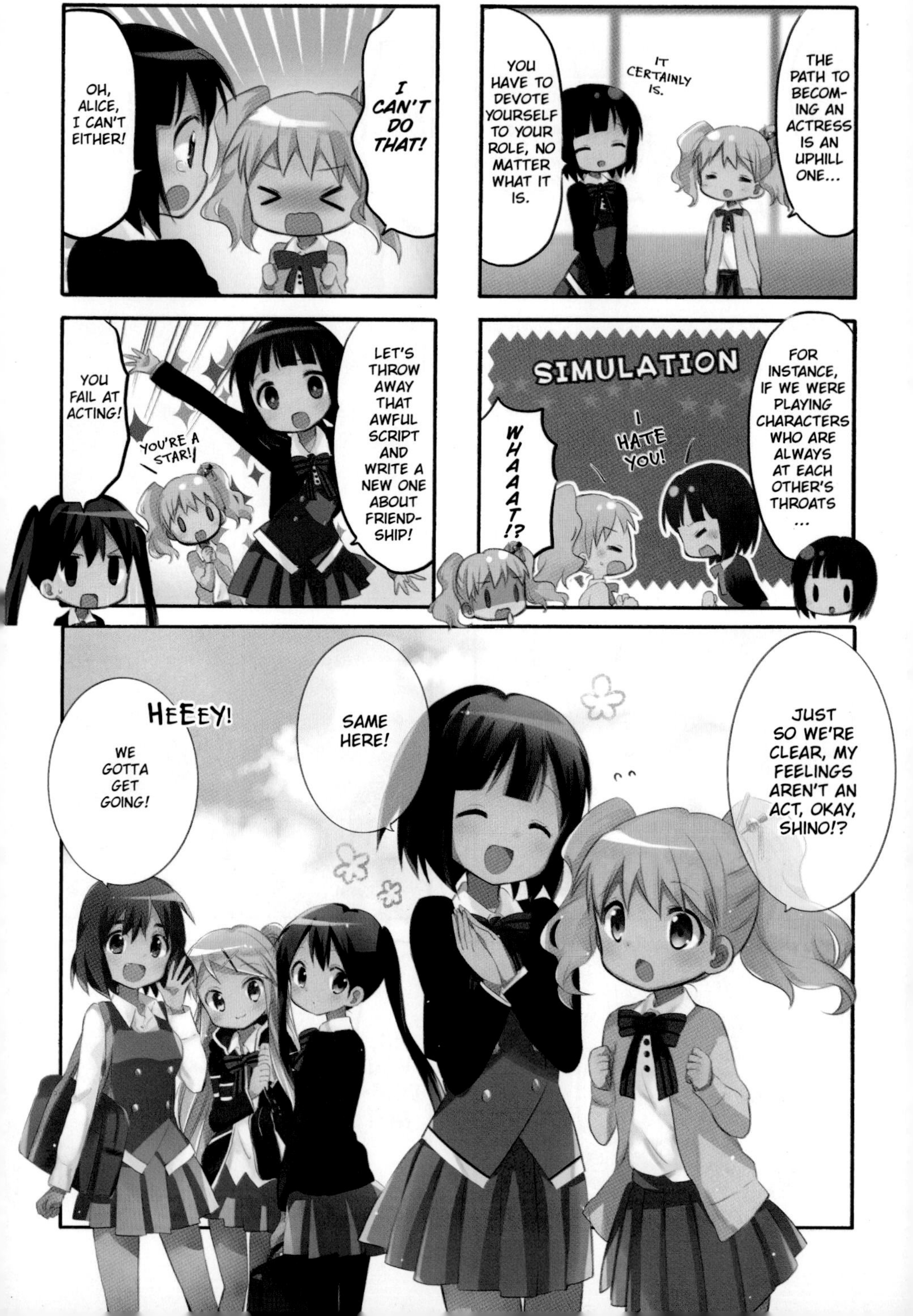
THE PATH TO BECOMING AN ACTRESS IS AN UPHILL ONE...
IT CERTAINLY IS.
YOU HAVE TO DEVOTE YOURSELF TO YOUR ROLE, NO MATTER WHAT IT IS.
I CAN'T DO THAT!
OH, ALICE, I CAN'T EITHER!
FOR INSTANCE, IF WE WERE PLAYING CHARACTERS WHO ARE ALWAYS AT EACH OTHER'S THROATS...
SIMULATION
I HATE YOU!
WHAAAAT!?
LET'S THROW AWAY THAT AWFUL SCRIPT AND WRITE A NEW ONE ABOUT FRIENDSHIP!
YOU'RE A STAR!
YOU FAIL AT ACTING!
JUST SO WE'RE CLEAR, MY FEELINGS AREN'T AN ACT, OKAY, SHINO!?
SAME HERE!
HEEEY!
WE GOTTA GET GOING!

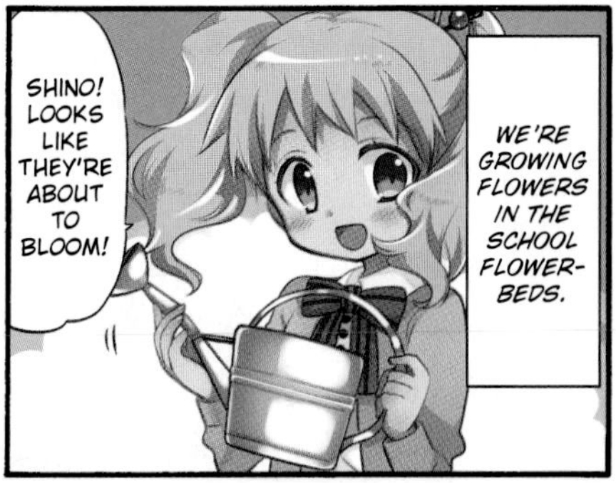
WE'RE GROWING FLOWERS IN THE SCHOOL FLOWER-BEDS.
SHINO! LOOKS LIKE THEY'RE ABOUT TO BLOOM!
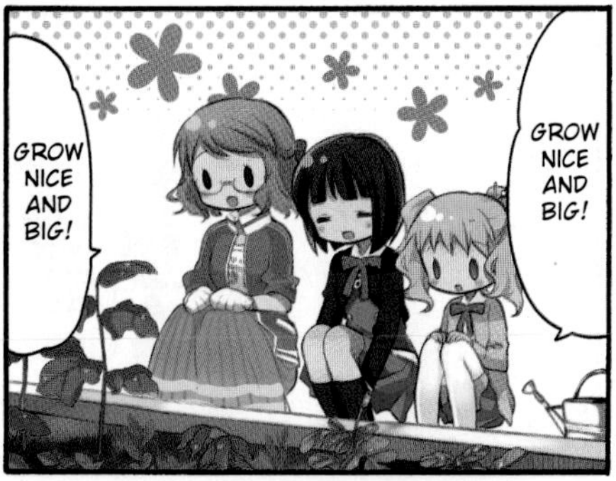
GROW NICE AND BIG!
GROW NICE AND BIG!
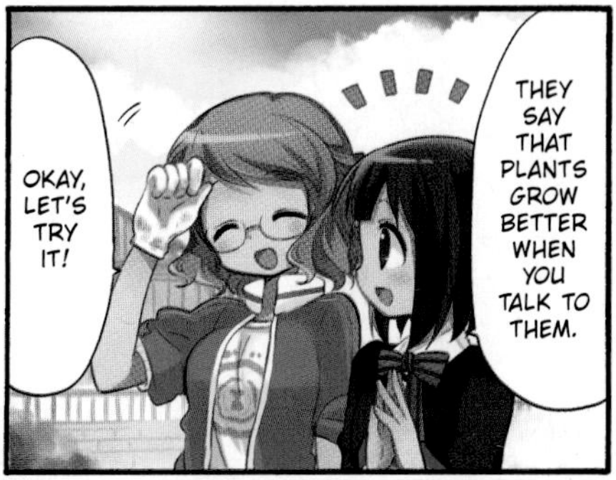
THEY SAY THAT PLANTS GROW BETTER WHEN YOU TALK TO THEM.
OKAY, LET'S TRY IT!
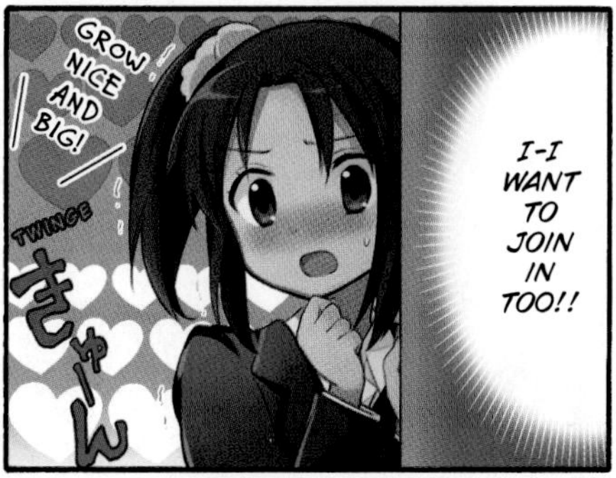
I-I WANT TO JOIN IN TOO!!
GROW NICE AND BIG!
TWINGE
きゅーん
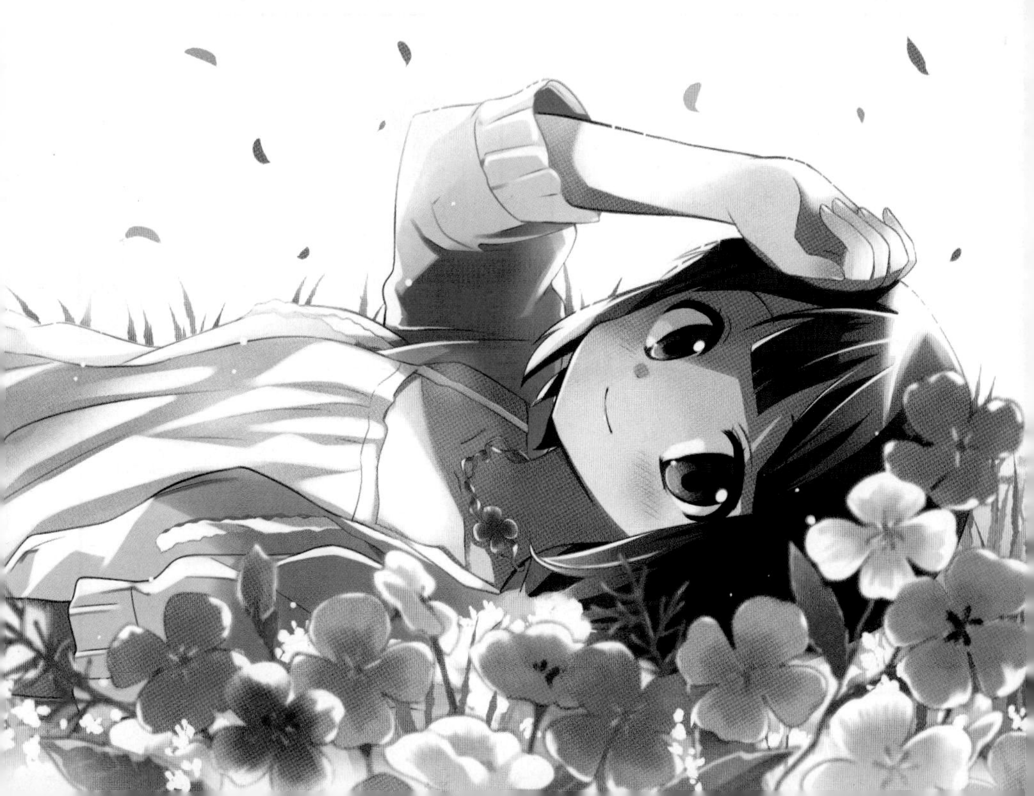

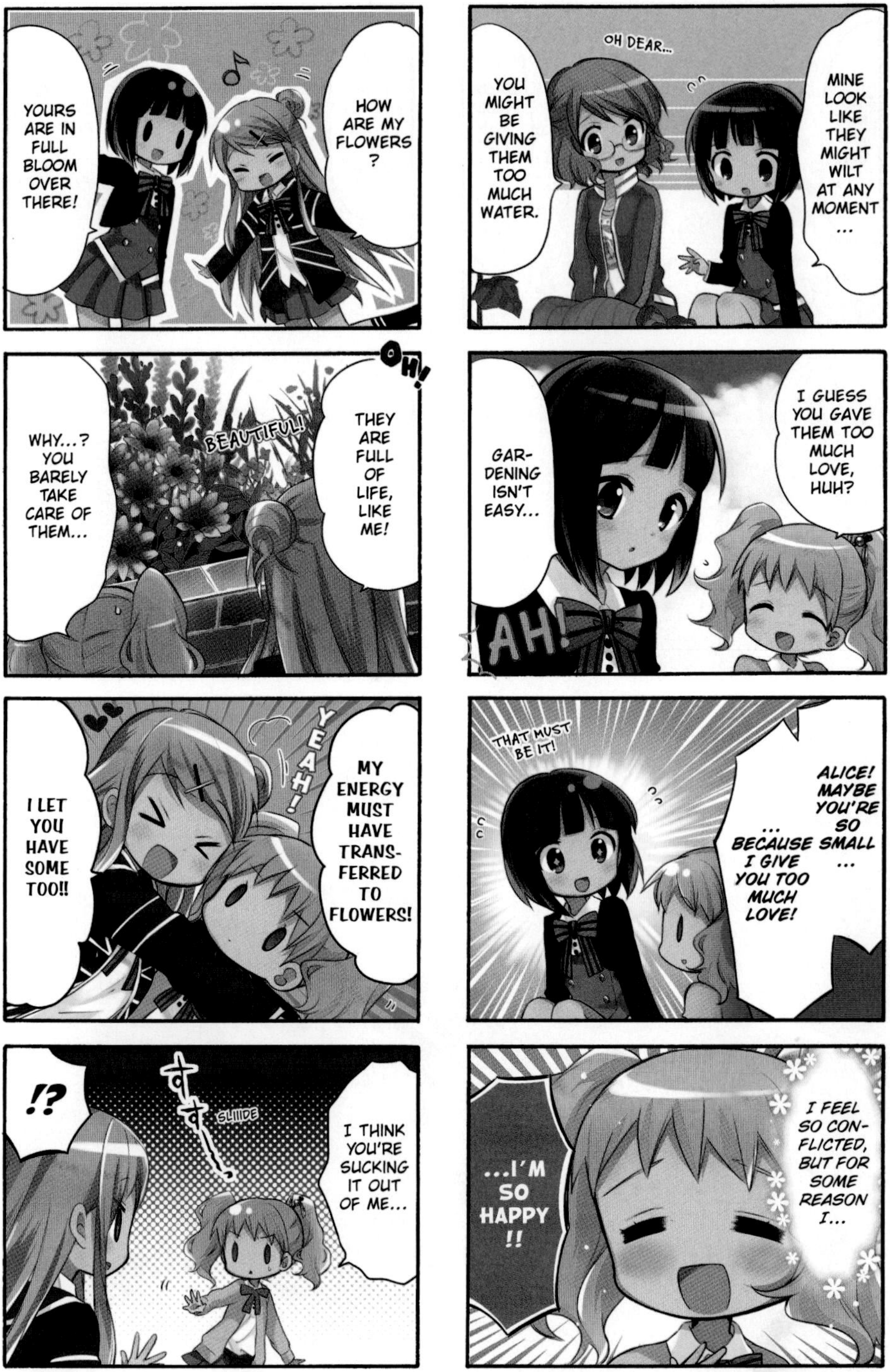
MINE LOOK LIKE THEY MIGHT WILT AT ANY MOMENT…
OH DEAR...
YOU MIGHT BE GIVING THEM TOO MUCH WATER.
I GUESS YOU GAVE THEM TOO MUCH LOVE, HUH?
GAR-DENING ISN'T EASY...
AH!
ALICE! MAYBE YOU'RE SO SMALL…
…BECAUSE I GIVE YOU TOO MUCH LOVE!
THAT MUST BE IT!
I FEEL SO CON-FLICTED, BUT FOR SOME REASON I…
…I'M SO HAPPY!!
HOW ARE MY FLOWERS?
YOURS ARE IN FULL BLOOM OVER THERE!
OH!
THEY ARE FULL OF LIFE, LIKE ME!
BEAUTIFUL!
WHY…? YOU BARELY TAKE CARE OF THEM…
MY ENERGY MUST HAVE TRANS-FERRED TO FLOWERS!
YEAH!
I LET YOU HAVE SOME TOO!!
I THINK YOU'RE SUCKING IT OUT OF ME…
すす
SLIIIDE
!?

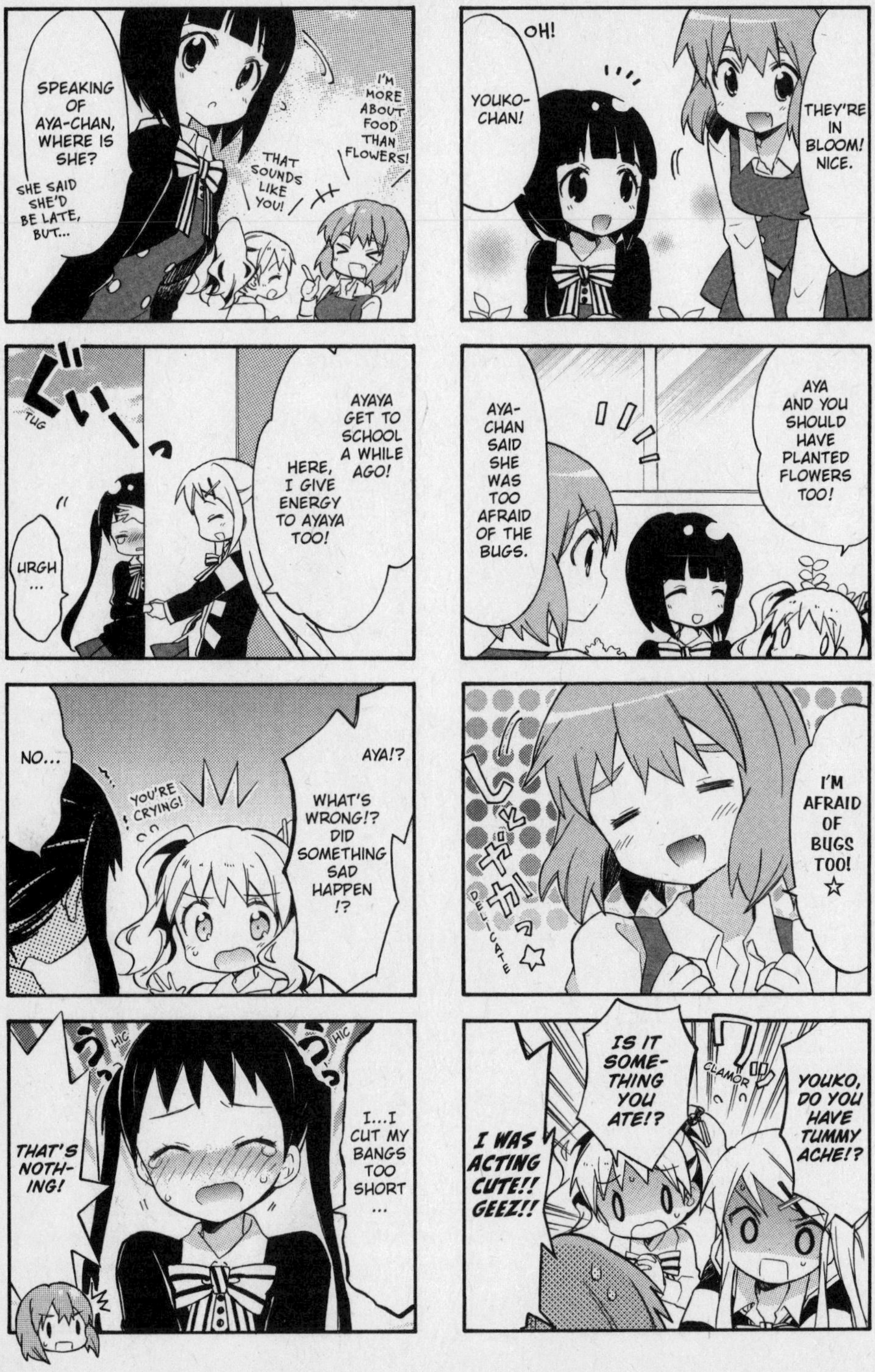
THEY'RE IN BLOOM! NICE.
OH!
YOUKO-CHAN!
AYA AND YOU SHOULD HAVE PLANTED FLOWERS TOO!
AYA-CHAN SAID SHE WAS TOO AFRAID OF THE BUGS.
I'M AFRAID OF BUGS TOO! ☆
DELICATE
YOUKO, DO YOU HAVE TUMMY ACHE!?
CLAMOR
IS IT SOMETHING YOU ATE!?
I WAS ACTING CUTE!! GEEZ!!
I'M MORE ABOUT FOOD THAN FLOWERS!
THAT SOUNDS LIKE YOU!
SPEAKING OF AYA-CHAN, WHERE IS SHE?
SHE SAID SHE'D BE LATE, BUT...
AYAYA GET TO SCHOOL A WHILE AGO!
HERE, I GIVE ENERGY TO AYAYA TOO!
TUG
URGH ...
AYA!?
WHAT'S WRONG!? DID SOMETHING SAD HAPPEN !?
YOU'RE CRYING!
NO...
HIC
I...I CUT MY BANGS TOO SHORT ...
HIC
THAT'S NOTHING!

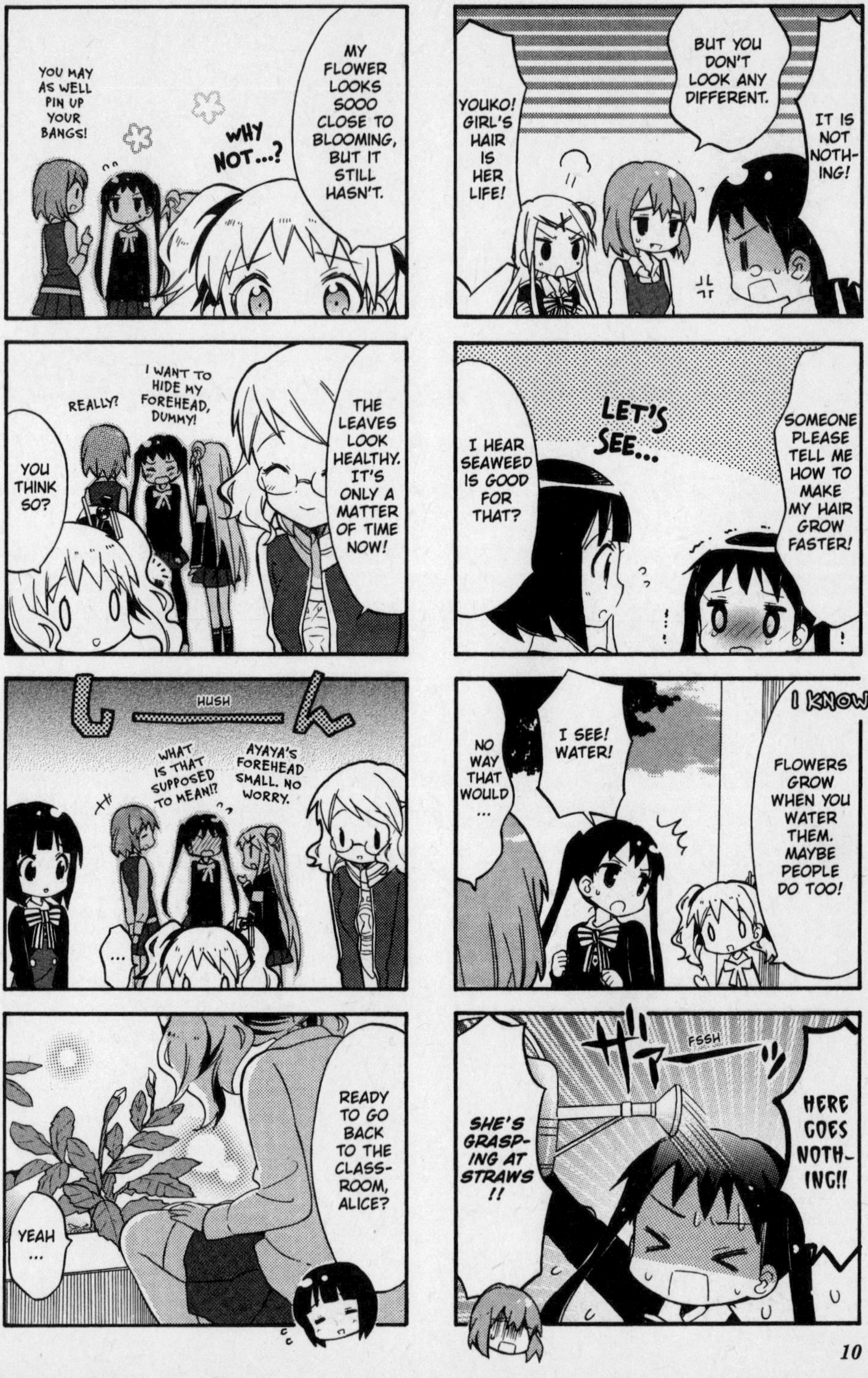
IT IS NOT NOTH-ING!
BUT YOU DON'T LOOK ANY DIFFERENT.
YOUKO! GIRL'S HAIR IS HER LIFE!
SOMEONE PLEASE TELL ME HOW TO MAKE MY HAIR GROW FASTER!
LET'S SEE...
I HEAR SEAWEED IS GOOD FOR THAT?
I KNOW!
FLOWERS GROW WHEN YOU WATER THEM. MAYBE PEOPLE DO TOO!
I SEE! WATER!
NO WAY THAT WOULD ...
HERE GOES NOTH-ING!!
FSSH
SHE'S GRASP-ING AT STRAWS !!
MY FLOWER LOOKS SOOO CLOSE TO BLOOMING, BUT IT STILL HASN'T.
WHY NOT...?
YOU MAY AS WELL PIN UP YOUR BANGS!
THE LEAVES LOOK HEALTHY. IT'S ONLY A MATTER OF TIME NOW!
I WANT TO HIDE MY FOREHEAD, DUMMY!
REALLY?
YOU THINK SO?
HUSH
AYAYA'S FOREHEAD SMALL. NO WORRY.
WHAT IS THAT SUPPOSED TO MEAN!?
...
READY TO GO BACK TO THE CLASS-ROOM, ALICE?
YEAH ...

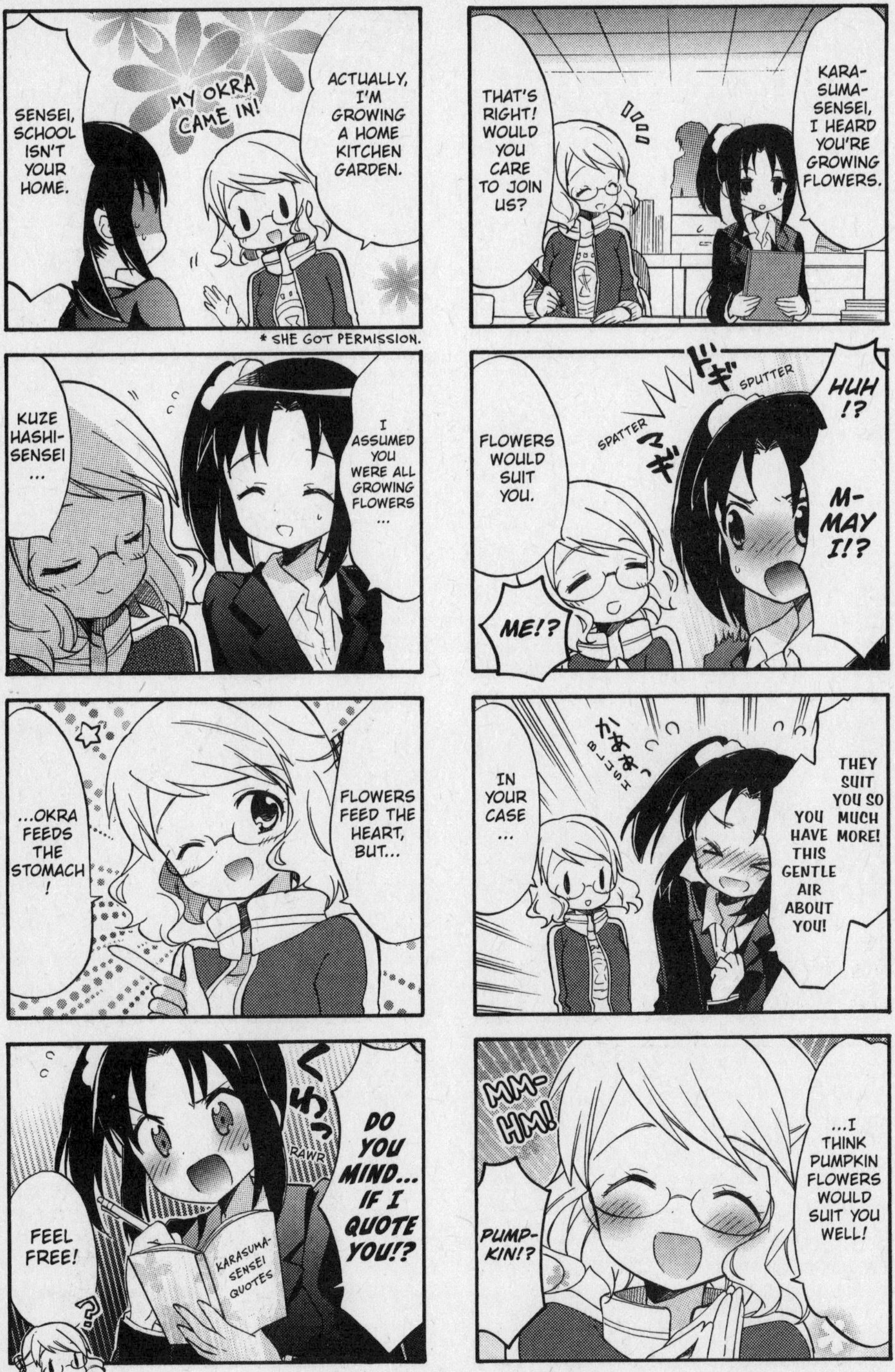
KARA-SUMA-SENSEI, I HEARD YOU'RE GROWING FLOWERS.
THAT'S RIGHT! WOULD YOU CARE TO JOIN US?
HUH!?
ドギ
SPUTTER
マギ
SPATTER
M-MAY I!?
FLOWERS WOULD SUIT YOU.
ME!?
THEY SUIT YOU SO MUCH MORE!
YOU HAVE THIS GENTLE AIR ABOUT YOU!
かあぁっ
BLUSH
IN YOUR CASE ...
...I THINK PUMPKIN FLOWERS WOULD SUIT YOU WELL!
MM-HM!
PUMP-KIN!?
ACTUALLY, I'M GROWING A HOME KITCHEN GARDEN.
MY OKRA CAME IN!
SENSEI, SCHOOL ISN'T YOUR HOME.
* SHE GOT PERMISSION.
I ASSUMED YOU WERE ALL GROWING FLOWERS ...
KUZE HASHI-SENSEI ...
FLOWERS FEED THE HEART, BUT...
...OKRA FEEDS THE STOMACH!
DO YOU MIND... IF I QUOTE YOU!?
くわっ
RAWR
KARASUMA-SENSEI QUOTES
FEEL FREE!

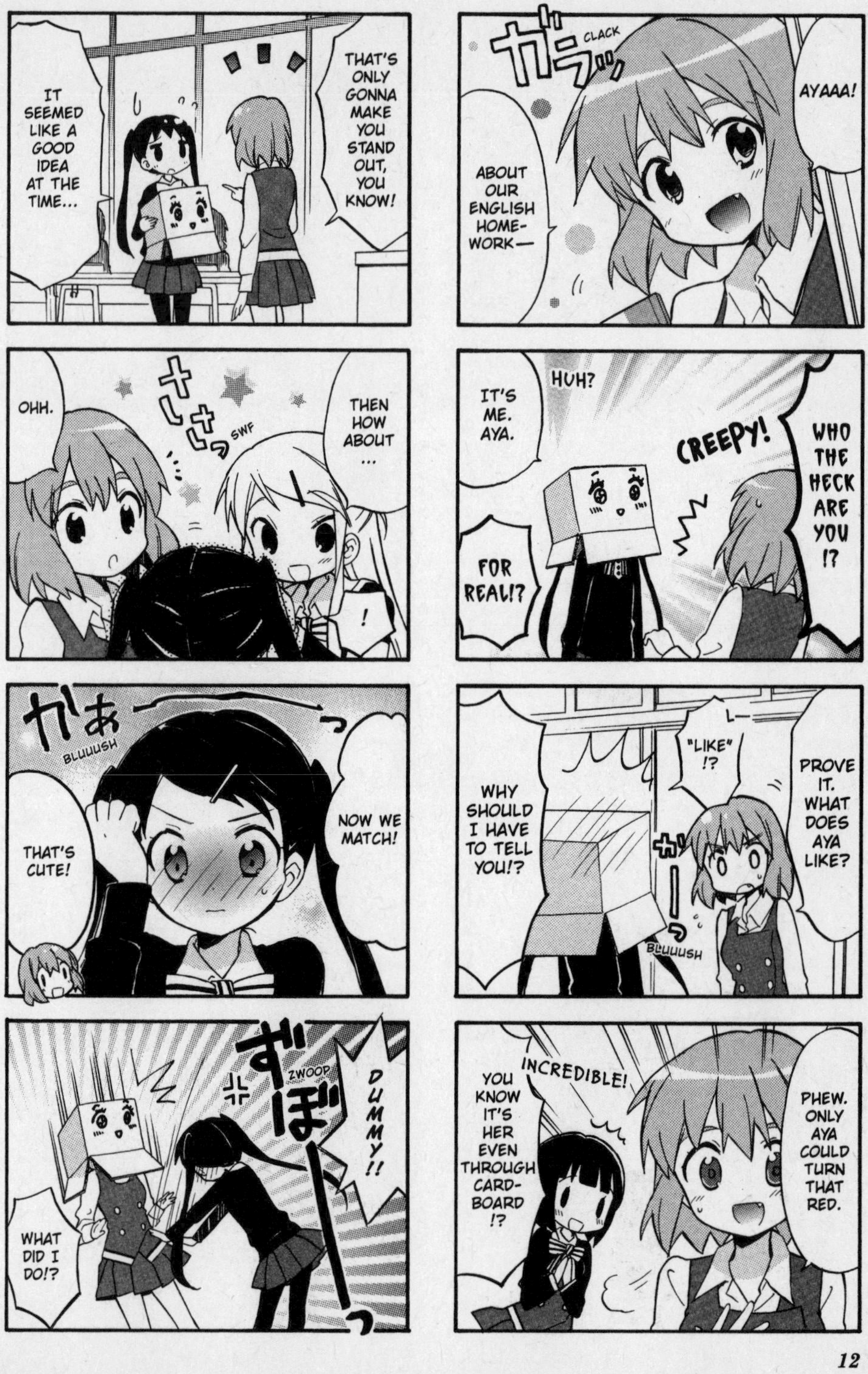

AYAAA!
CLACK
ABOUT OUR ENGLISH HOME-WORK—
WHO THE HECK ARE YOU !?
CREEPY!
HUH?
IT'S ME. AYA.
FOR REAL!?
PROVE IT. WHAT DOES AYA LIKE?
L—
"LIKE" !?
WHY SHOULD I HAVE TO TELL YOU!?
BLUUUSH
PHEW. ONLY AYA COULD TURN THAT RED.
INCREDIBLE!
YOU KNOW IT'S HER EVEN THROUGH CARD-BOARD !?
THAT'S ONLY GONNA MAKE YOU STAND OUT, YOU KNOW!
IT SEEMED LIKE A GOOD IDEA AT THE TIME...
THEN HOW ABOUT ...
SWF
OHH.
!
NOW WE MATCH!
BLUUUSH
THAT'S CUTE!
DUMMY!!
ZWOOP
WHAT DID I DO!?

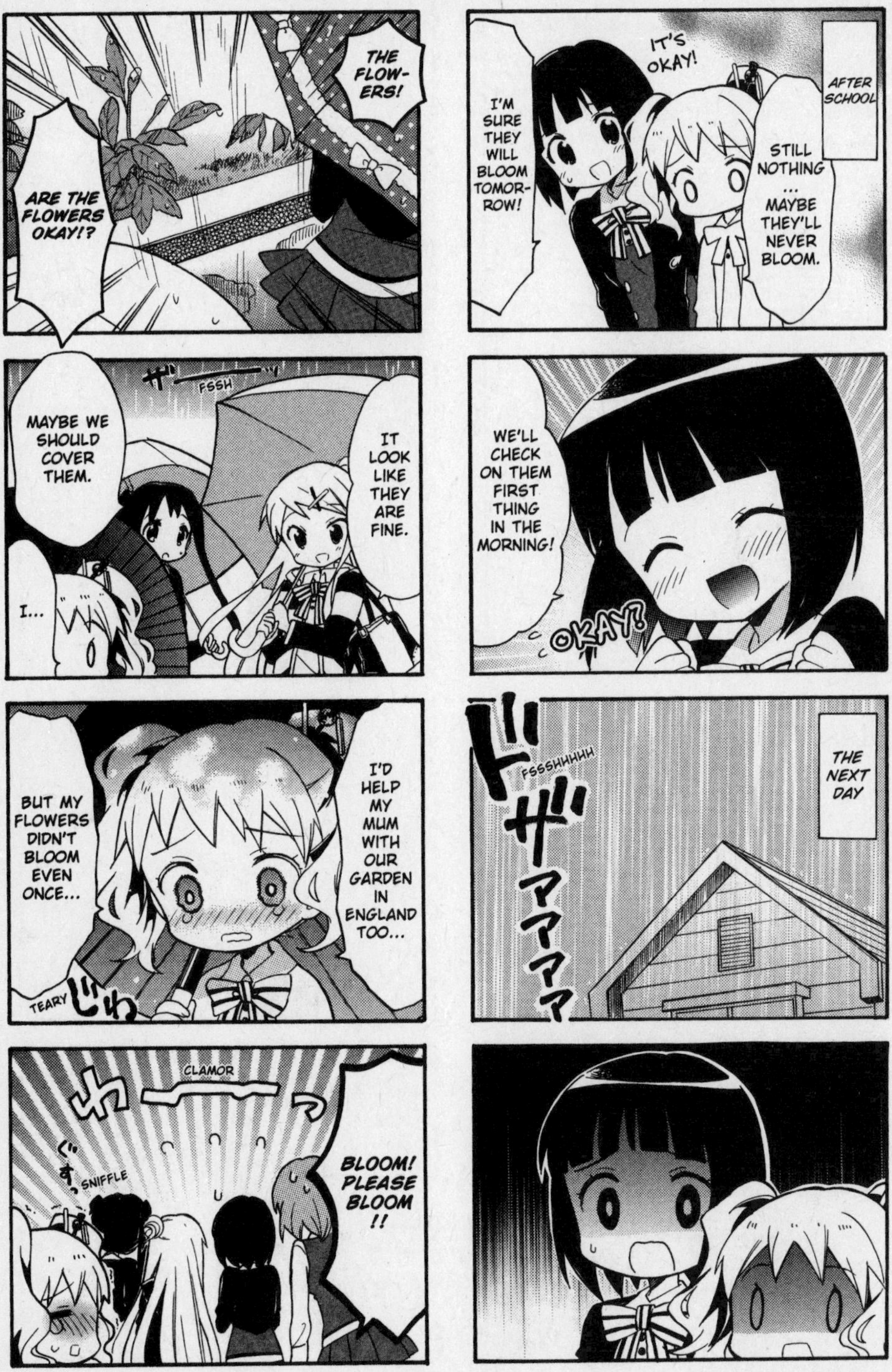
AFTER SCHOOL
STILL NOTHING ... MAYBE THEY'LL NEVER BLOOM.
IT'S OKAY!
I'M SURE THEY WILL BLOOM TOMORROW!
WE'LL CHECK ON THEM FIRST THING IN THE MORNING!
OKAY!?
THE NEXT DAY
ド
FSSSHHHHH
ザァァァァ
THE FLOWERS!
ARE THE FLOWERS OKAY!?
ザーーッ
FSSH
IT LOOK LIKE THEY ARE FINE.
MAYBE WE SHOULD COVER THEM.
I...
I'D HELP MY MUM WITH OUR GARDEN IN ENGLAND TOO...
BUT MY FLOWERS DIDN'T BLOOM EVEN ONCE...
じわ
TEARY
わーーっ
CLAMOR
BLOOM! PLEASE BLOOM !!
ぐすっ
SNIFFLE

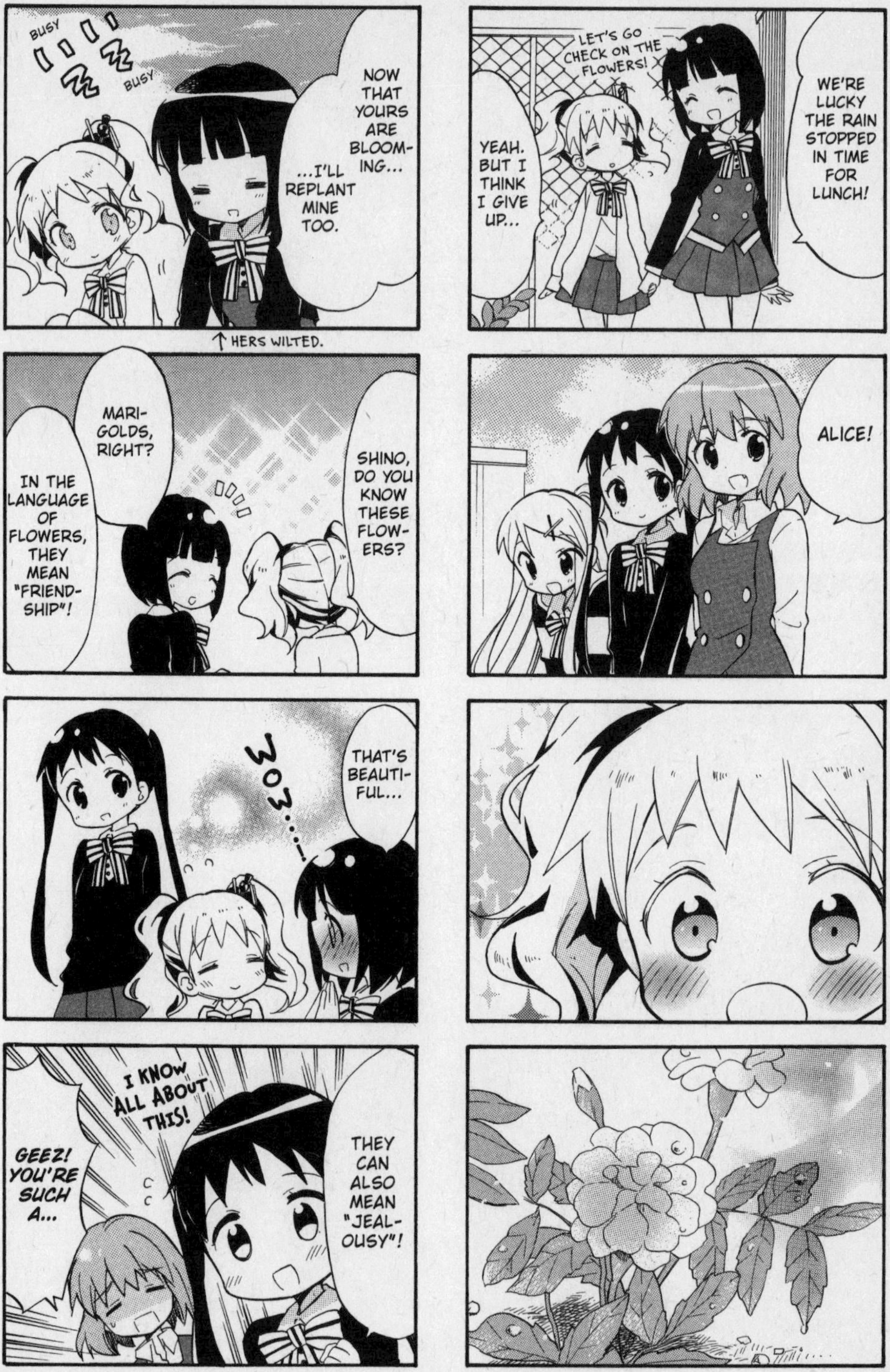
WE'RE LUCKY THE RAIN STOPPED IN TIME FOR LUNCH!
LET'S GO CHECK ON THE FLOWERS!
YEAH. BUT I THINK I GIVE UP...
NOW THAT YOURS ARE BLOOMING...
...I'LL REPLANT MINE TOO.
BUSY
BUSY
↑HERS WILTED.
ALICE!
SHINO, DO YOU KNOW THESE FLOWERS?
MARIGOLDS, RIGHT?
IN THE LANGUAGE OF FLOWERS, THEY MEAN "FRIENDSHIP"!
THAT'S BEAUTIFUL...
WOW...!
THEY CAN ALSO MEAN "JEALOUSY"!
I KNOW ALL ABOUT THIS!
GEEZ! YOU'RE SUCH A...

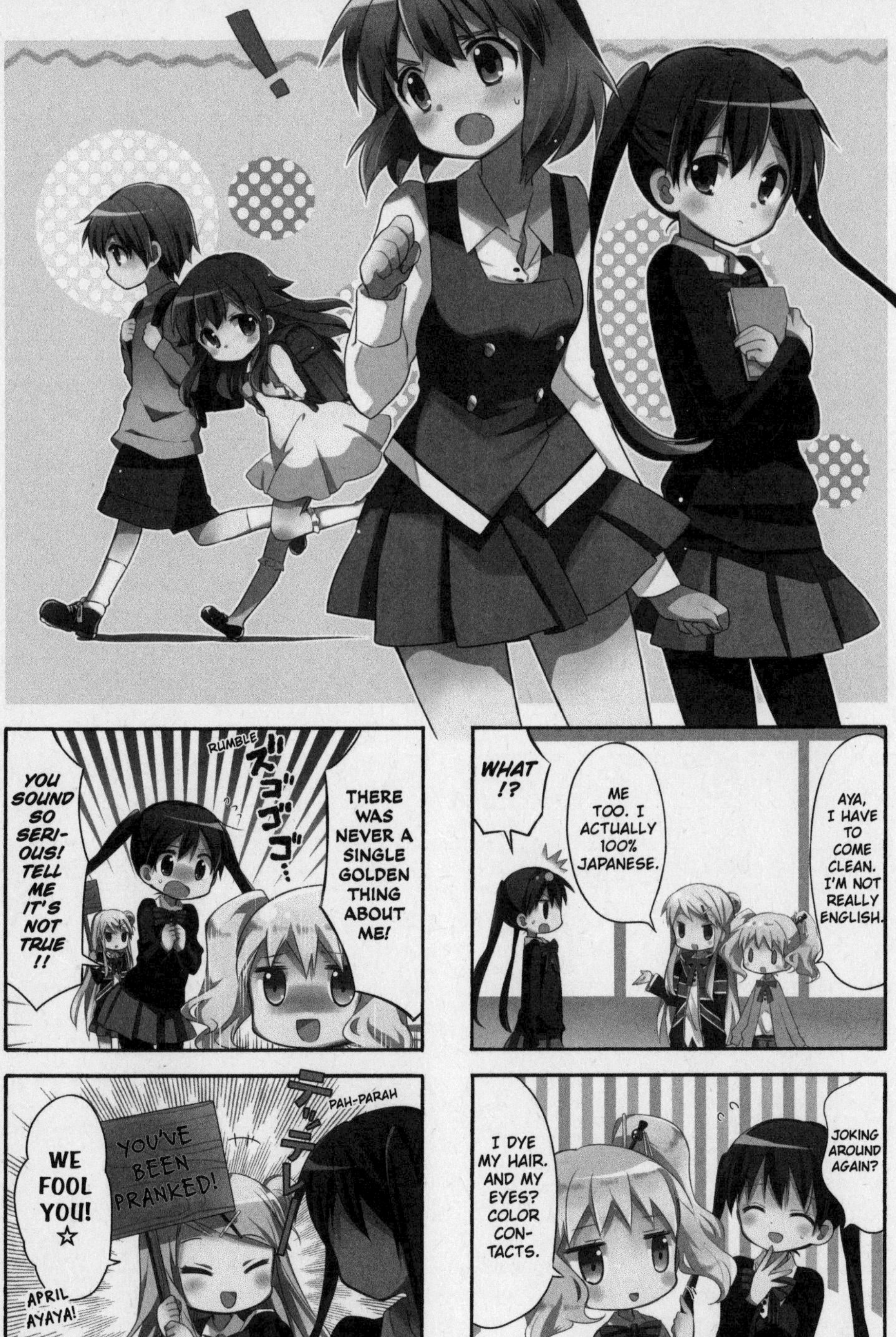
!
AYA, I HAVE TO COME CLEAN. I'M NOT REALLY ENGLISH.
ME TOO. I ACTUALLY 100% JAPANESE.
WHAT!?
THERE WAS NEVER A SINGLE GOLDEN THING ABOUT ME!
RUMBLE
ズゴゴゴ…
YOU SOUND SO SERI-OUS! TELL ME IT'S NOT TRUE!!
JOKING AROUND AGAIN?
I DYE MY HAIR. AND MY EYES? COLOR CON-TACTS.
PAH-PARAH
WE FOOL YOU! ☆
YOU'VE BEEN PRANKED!
APRIL AYAYA!

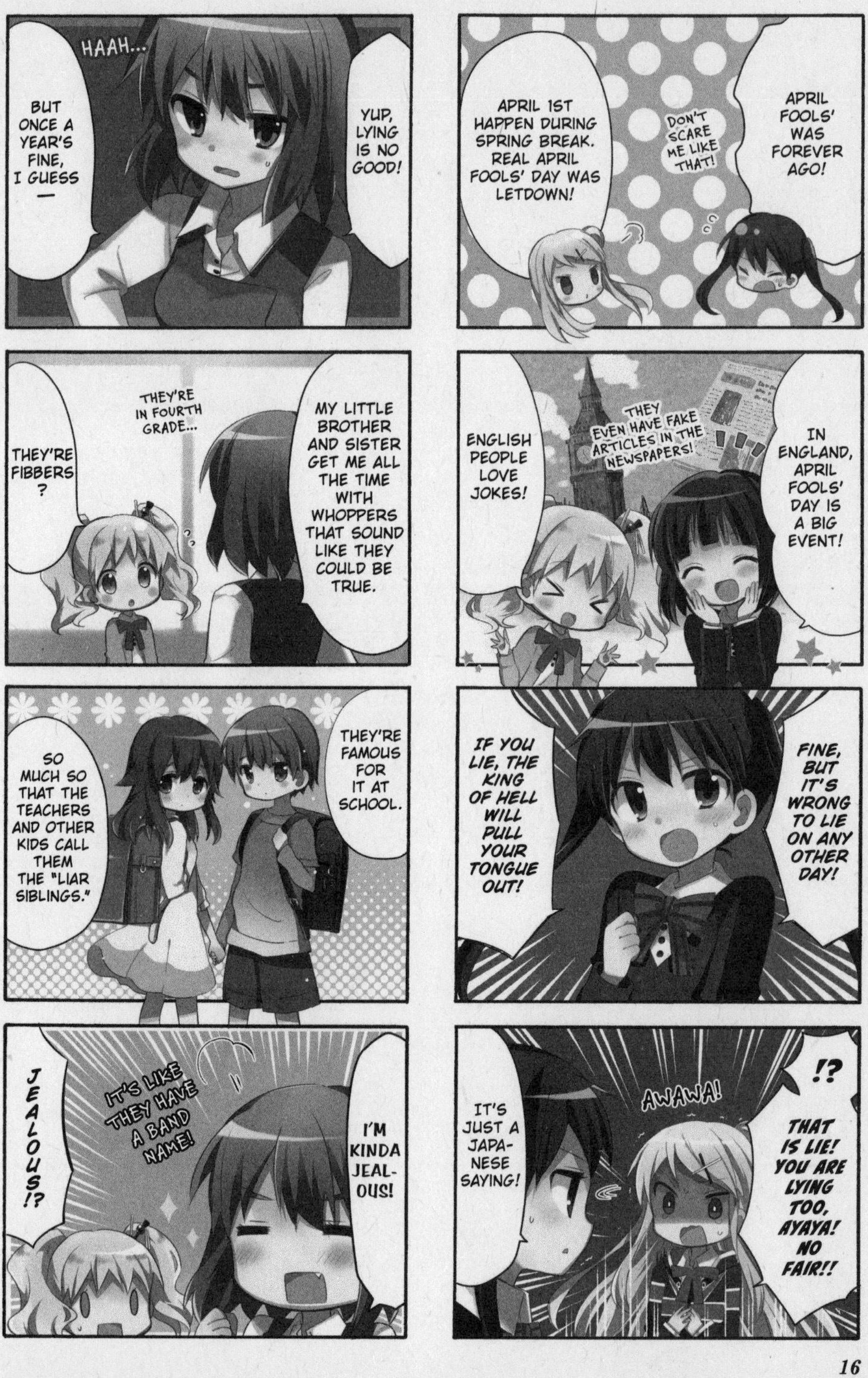
APRIL FOOLS' WAS FOREVER AGO!
DON'T SCARE ME LIKE THAT!
APRIL 1ST HAPPEN DURING SPRING BREAK. REAL APRIL FOOLS' DAY WAS LETDOWN!
IN ENGLAND, APRIL FOOLS' DAY IS A BIG EVENT!
THEY EVEN HAVE FAKE ARTICLES IN THE NEWSPAPERS!
ENGLISH PEOPLE LOVE JOKES!
FINE, BUT IT'S WRONG TO LIE ON ANY OTHER DAY!
IF YOU LIE, THE KING OF HELL WILL PULL YOUR TONGUE OUT!
!?
THAT IS LIE! YOU ARE LYING TOO, AYAYA! NO FAIR!!
AWAWA!
IT'S JUST A JAPANESE SAYING!
YUP, LYING IS NO GOOD!
HAAH...
BUT ONCE A YEAR'S FINE, I GUESS—
MY LITTLE BROTHER AND SISTER GET ME ALL THE TIME WITH WHOPPERS THAT SOUND LIKE THEY COULD BE TRUE.
THEY'RE IN FOURTH GRADE...
THEY'RE FIBBERS?
THEY'RE FAMOUS FOR IT AT SCHOOL.
SO MUCH SO THAT THE TEACHERS AND OTHER KIDS CALL THEM THE "LIAR SIBLINGS."
I'M KINDA JEALOUS!
IT'S LIKE THEY HAVE A BAND NAME!
JEALOUS!?

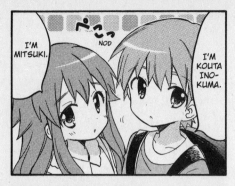

THEY'RE TWINS NAMED KOUTA-KUN AND MITSUKI-CHAN!
I MET THEM ONCE, WHEN THEY WERE TINY!
I WISH I HAD SIB-LINGS.
YOUKO, AS THEIR BIG SISTER, YOU HAVE TO WHIP THEM INTO SHAPE!
BIG SISTER WIND
ビュンビュン
WHOOSH
WHOOSH
WHAT'S WITH THE WIND...?
I DUNNO ...
EACH TIME THEY LIE...
...TELL THEM "NO!"
WHOA!
NOT "WHOA." "NO!"
ちょこーん
POP
WHY ARE YOU HERE !?
I'M KOUTA INO-KUMA.
ぺこっ
NOD
I'M MITSUKI.
WE'RE NEW TRANSFER STUDENTS IN FIRST YEAR—YOUR KOUHAI.
NICE TO MEET YOU.
DON'T LIE SO SMOOTH-LY!
SO CUTE!
AH!
THAT TIME I CALLED ...
わらわら
CROWD
CROWD
YOU DO NOT LOOK LIKE YOUKO AT ALL!
ビクッ
FLINCH
IF...
IF YOU STARE AT US TOO MUCH, WE'LL EX-PLODE!
かあっ
BLUSH
EX-PLODE !?
ARE THEY REALLY LIARS, OR ARE THEY JUST SHY...?

⇧ AYA'S FIRST TIME MEETING THEM TOO.

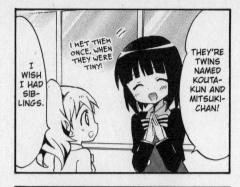

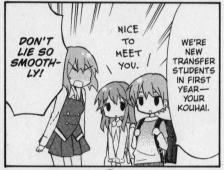

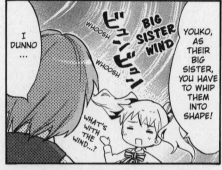

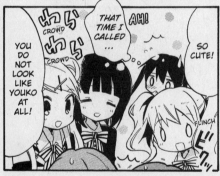

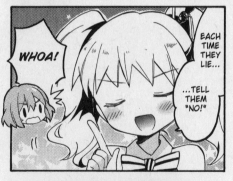

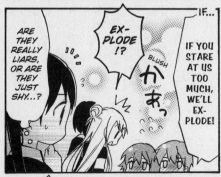

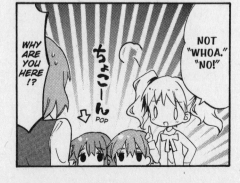

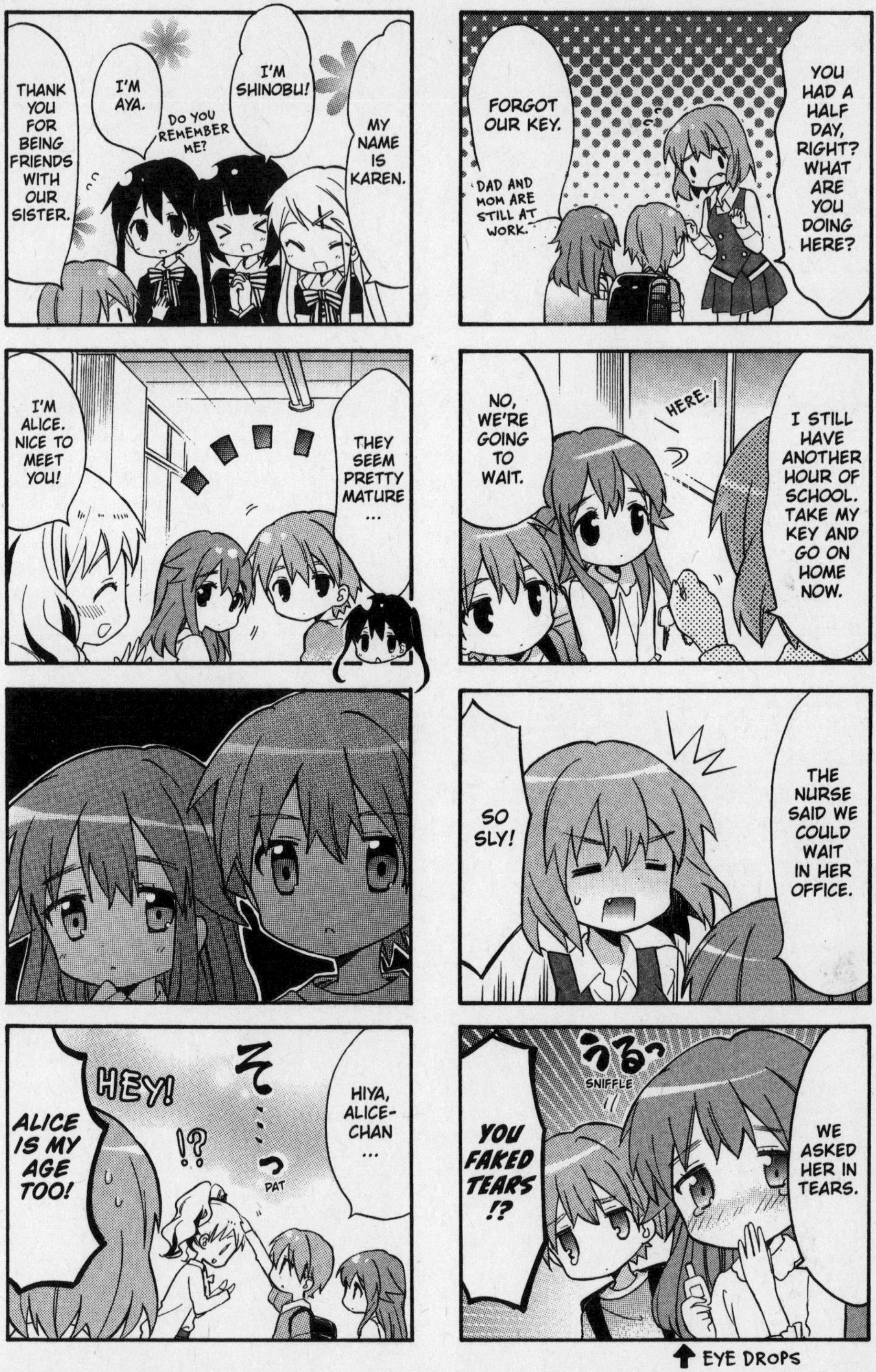

YOU HAD A HALF DAY, RIGHT? WHAT ARE YOU DOING HERE?
FORGOT OUR KEY.
DAD AND MOM ARE STILL AT WORK.
I STILL HAVE ANOTHER HOUR OF SCHOOL. TAKE MY KEY AND GO ON HOME NOW.
HERE.
NO, WE'RE GOING TO WAIT.
THE NURSE SAID WE COULD WAIT IN HER OFFICE.
SO SLY!
WE ASKED HER IN TEARS.
うるっ
SNIFFLE
YOU FAKED TEARS!?
MY NAME IS KAREN.
I'M SHINOBU!
DO YOU REMEMBER ME?
I'M AYA.
THANK YOU FOR BEING FRIENDS WITH OUR SISTER.
THEY SEEM PRETTY MATURE ...
I'M ALICE. NICE TO MEET YOU!
HIYA, ALICE-CHAN ...
そ…っ
PAT
!?
HEY!
ALICE IS MY AGE TOO!

↑ EYE DROPS

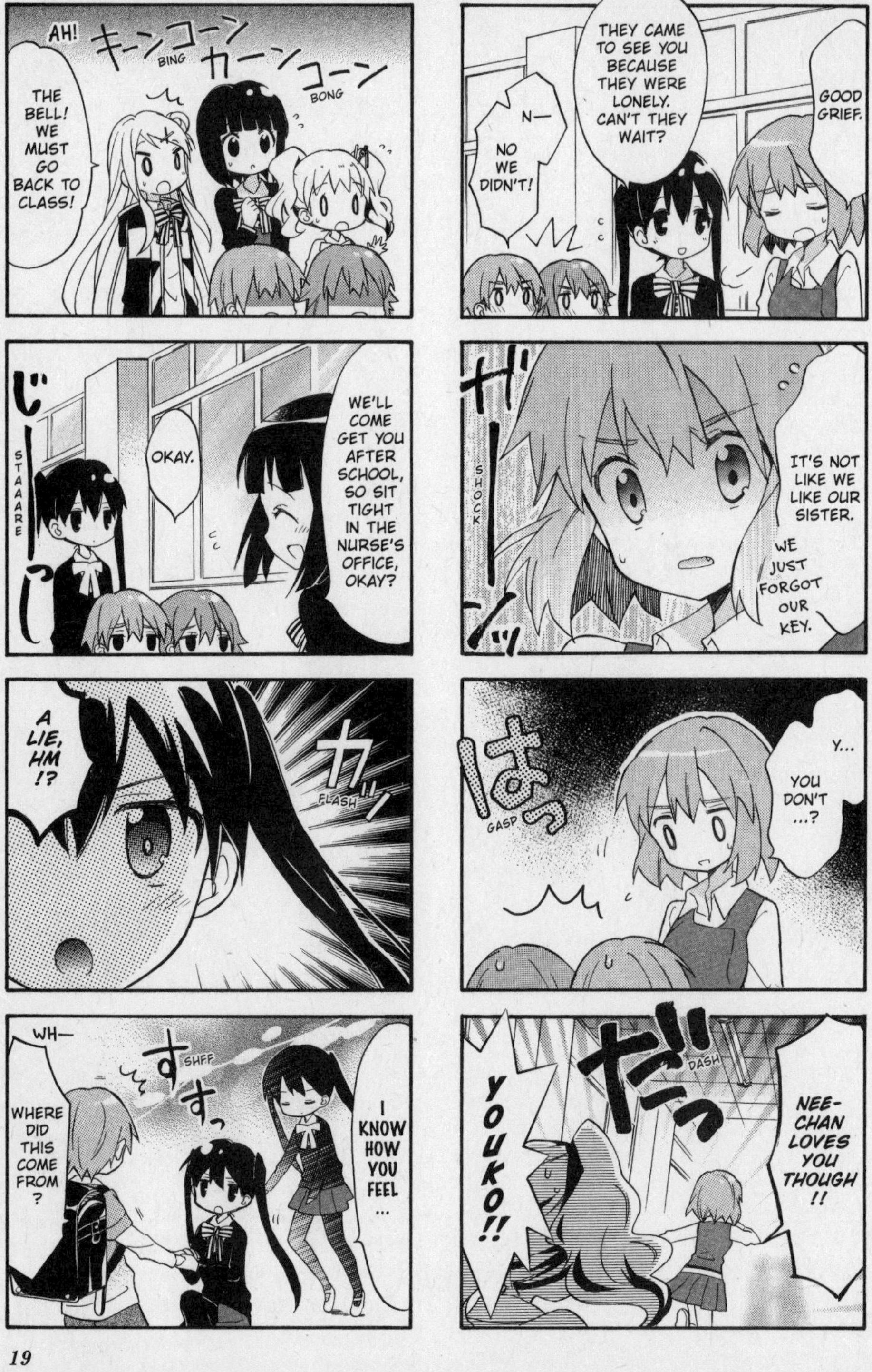
GOOD GRIEF.
THEY CAME TO SEE YOU BECAUSE THEY WERE LONELY. CAN'T THEY WAIT?
N— NO WE DIDN'T!
IT'S NOT LIKE WE LIKE OUR SISTER.
WE JUST FORGOT OUR KEY.
SHOCK
Y... YOU DON'T ...?
はっ
GASP
NEE-CHAN LOVES YOU THOUGH!!
だっ
DASH
YOUKO!!
キーンコーン
BING
カーンコーン
BONG
AH!
THE BELL! WE MUST GO BACK TO CLASS!
WE'LL COME GET YOU AFTER SCHOOL, SO SIT TIGHT IN THE NURSE'S OFFICE, OKAY?
OKAY.
じーっ
STAAARE
カッ
FLASH
A LIE, HM!?
I KNOW HOW YOU FEEL ...
すすっ
SHFF
WH—
WHERE DID THIS COME FROM?

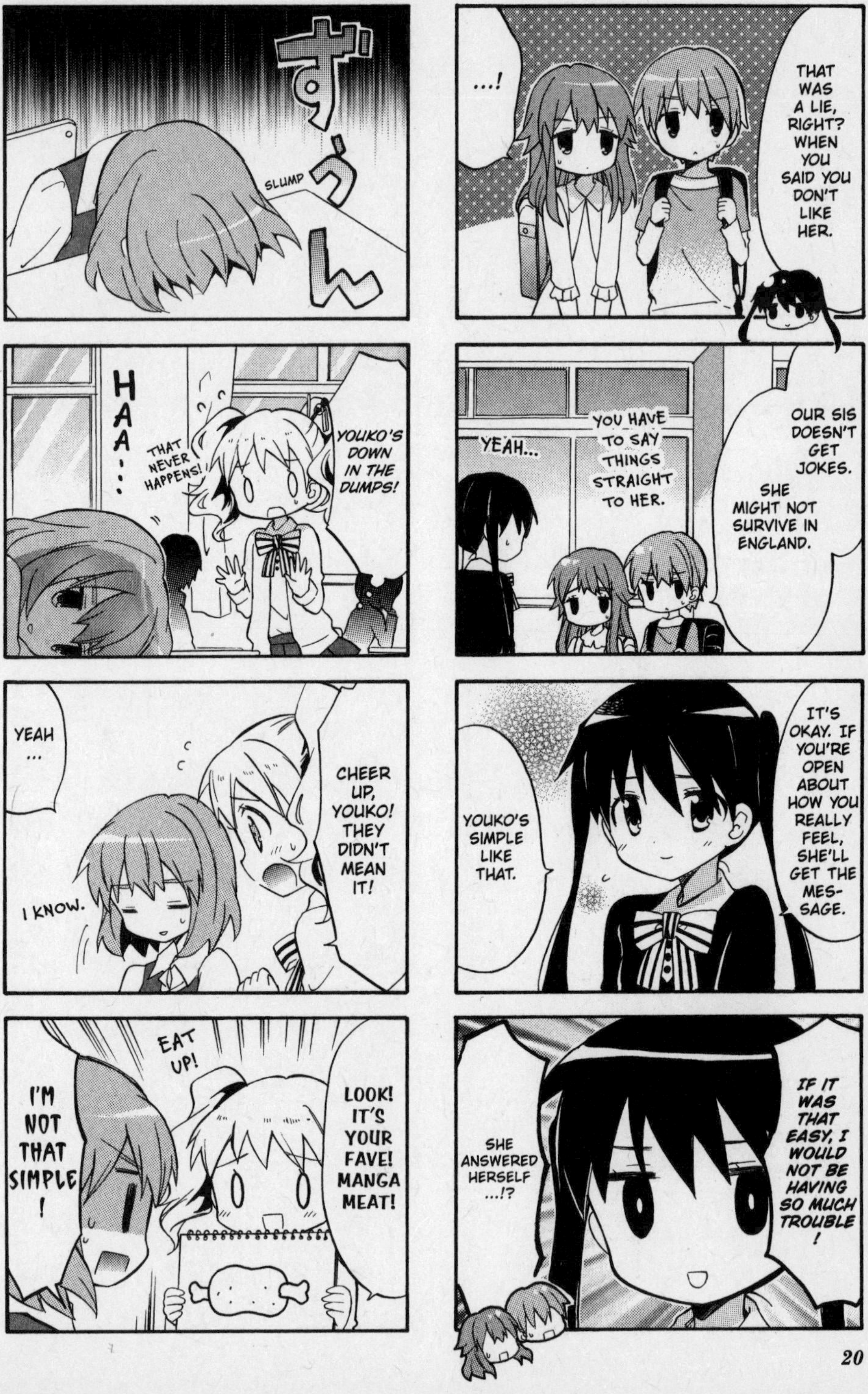
THAT WAS A LIE, RIGHT? WHEN YOU SAID YOU DON'T LIKE HER.
...!
ずぅん
SLUMP
OUR SIS DOESN'T GET JOKES.
SHE MIGHT NOT SURVIVE IN ENGLAND.
YOU HAVE TO SAY THINGS STRAIGHT TO HER.
YEAH...
YOUKO'S DOWN IN THE DUMPS!
THAT NEVER HAPPENS!
HAA...
IT'S OKAY. IF YOU'RE OPEN ABOUT HOW YOU REALLY FEEL, SHE'LL GET THE MES-SAGE.
YOUKO'S SIMPLE LIKE THAT.
CHEER UP, YOUKO! THEY DIDN'T MEAN IT!
YEAH ...
I KNOW.
IF IT WAS THAT EASY, I WOULD NOT BE HAVING SO MUCH TROUBLE!
SHE ANSWERED HERSELF ...!?
LOOK! IT'S YOUR FAVE! MANGA MEAT!
EAT UP!
I'M NOT THAT SIMPLE!

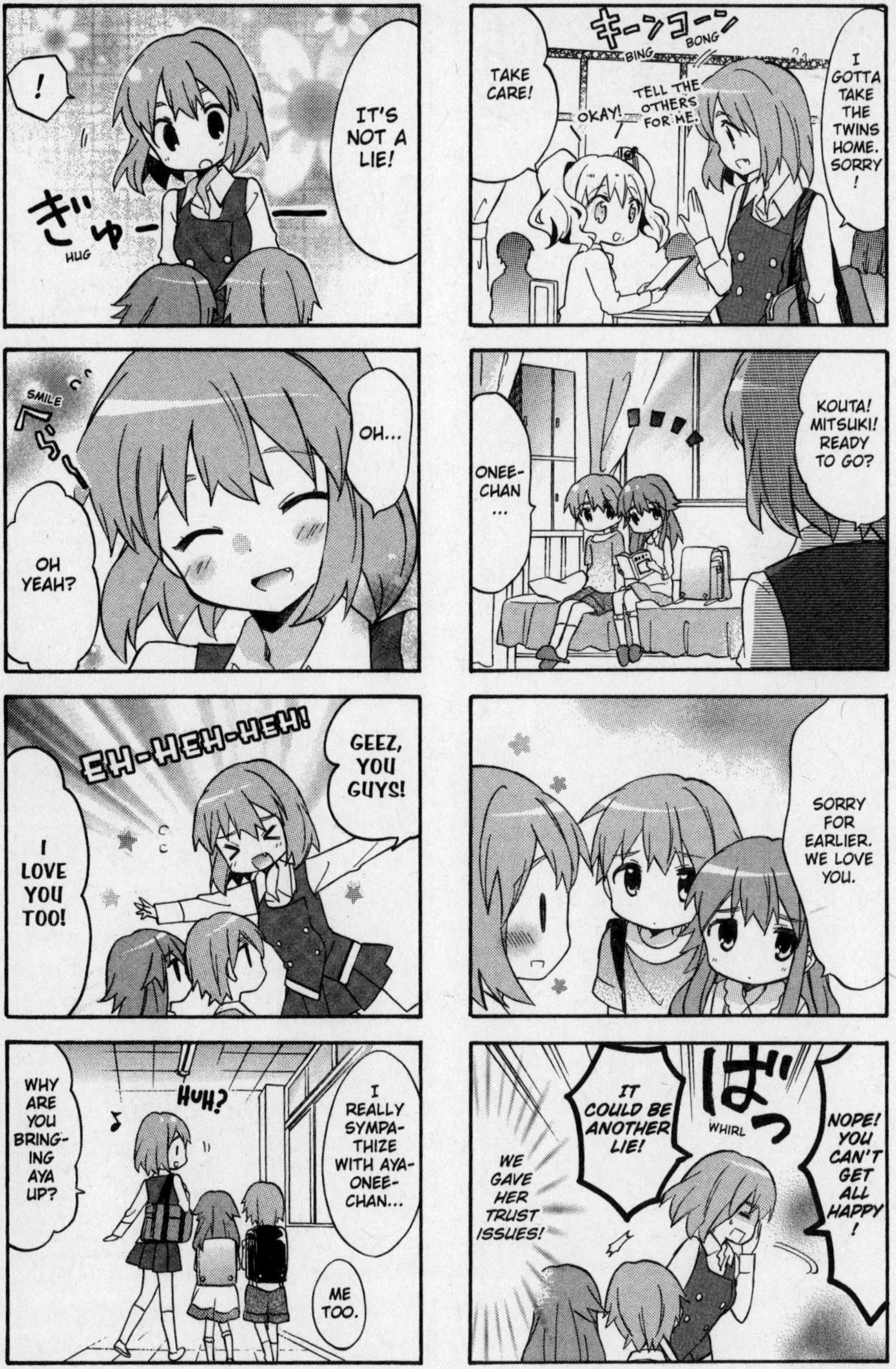
キーンコーン
BING
BONG
I GOTTA TAKE THE TWINS HOME. SORRY!
TELL THE OTHERS FOR ME.
OKAY!
TAKE CARE!
KOUTA! MITSUKI! READY TO GO?
ONEE-CHAN...
SORRY FOR EARLIER. WE LOVE YOU.
NOPE! YOU CAN'T GET ALL HAPPY!
ばっ
WHIRL
IT COULD BE ANOTHER LIE!
WE GAVE HER TRUST ISSUES!
IT'S NOT A LIE!
!
ぎゅー
HUG
OH...
SMILE
OH YEAH?
GEEZ, YOU GUYS!
EH-HEH-HEH!
I LOVE YOU TOO!
I REALLY SYMPATHIZE WITH AYA-ONEE-CHAN...
ME TOO.
HUH?
WHY ARE YOU BRINGING AYA UP?

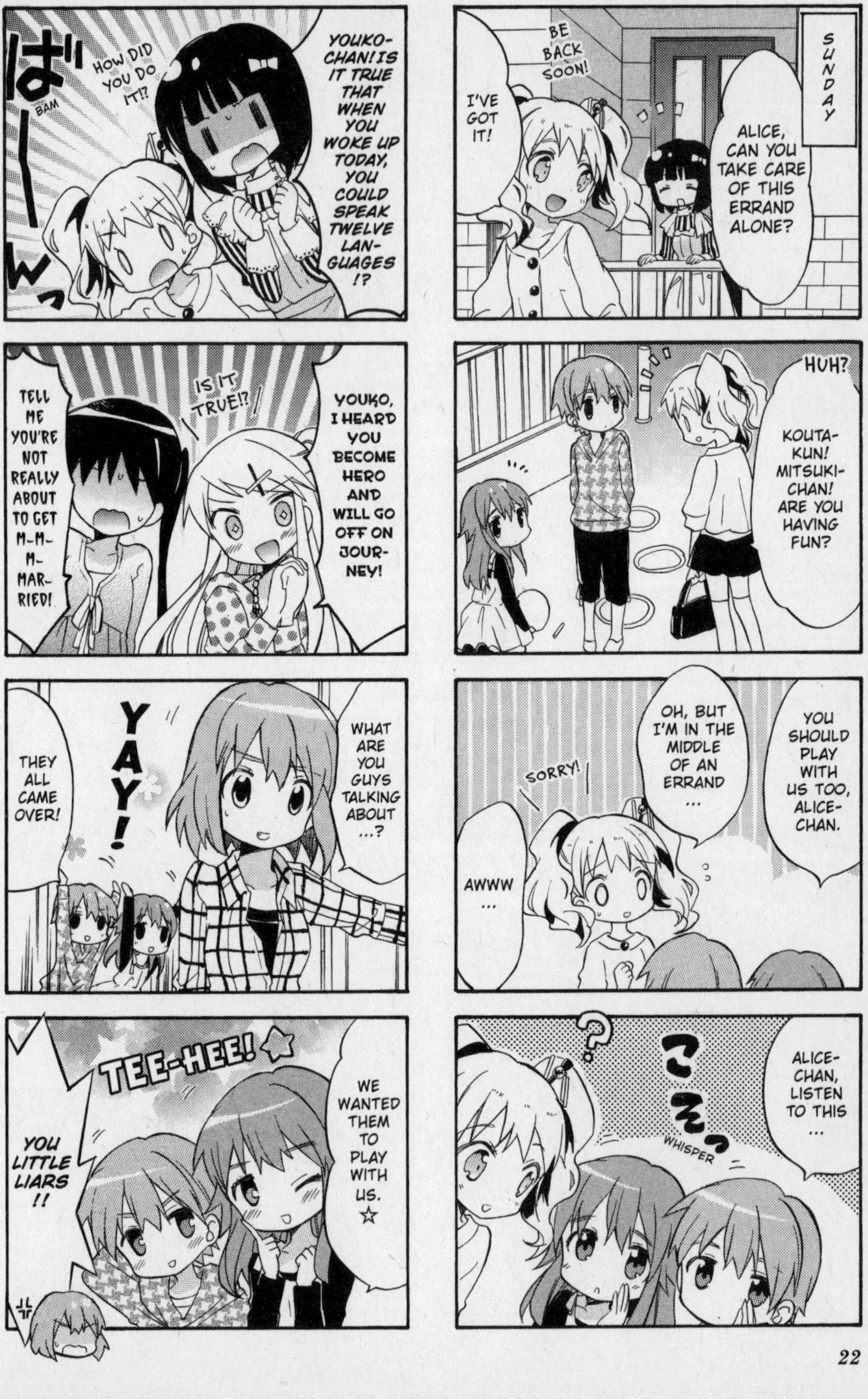

SUNDAY
ALICE, CAN YOU TAKE CARE OF THIS ERRAND ALONE?
BE BACK SOON!
I'VE GOT IT!
HUH?
KOUTA-KUN! MITSUKI-CHAN! ARE YOU HAVING FUN?
YOU SHOULD PLAY WITH US TOO, ALICE-CHAN.
OH, BUT I'M IN THE MIDDLE OF AN ERRAND ...
SORRY!
AWWW ...
ALICE-CHAN, LISTEN TO THIS ...
WHISPER
YOUKO-CHAN! IS IT TRUE THAT WHEN YOU WOKE UP TODAY, YOU COULD SPEAK TWELVE LANGUAGES !?
HOW DID YOU DO IT!?
BAM
YOUKO, I HEARD YOU BECOME HERO AND WILL GO OFF ON JOURNEY!
IS IT TRUE!?
TELL ME YOU'RE NOT REALLY ABOUT TO GET M-M-M-MARRIED!
WHAT ARE YOU GUYS TALKING ABOUT ...?
YAY!
THEY ALL CAME OVER!
WE WANTED THEM TO PLAY WITH US. ☆
TEE-HEE!
YOU LITTLE LIARS !!

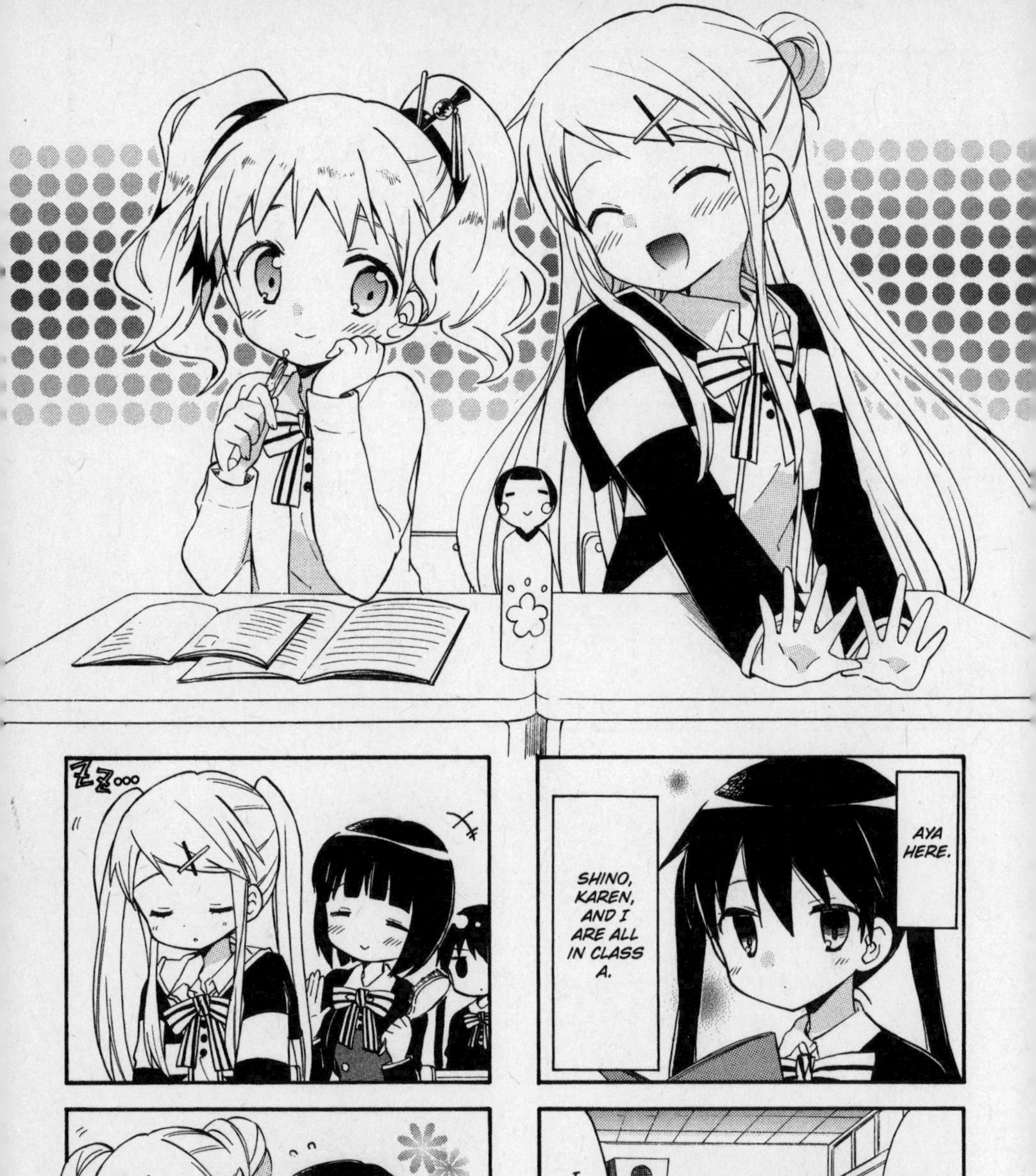
AYA HERE.
SHINO, KAREN, AND I ARE ALL IN CLASS A.
Zzz...
THOSE TWO ARE POOR STU-DENTS.
I HAVE TO KEEP AN EYE ON THEM.
MRM MRM ...

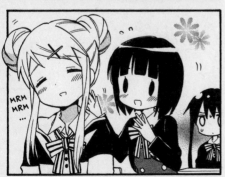

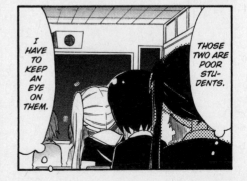

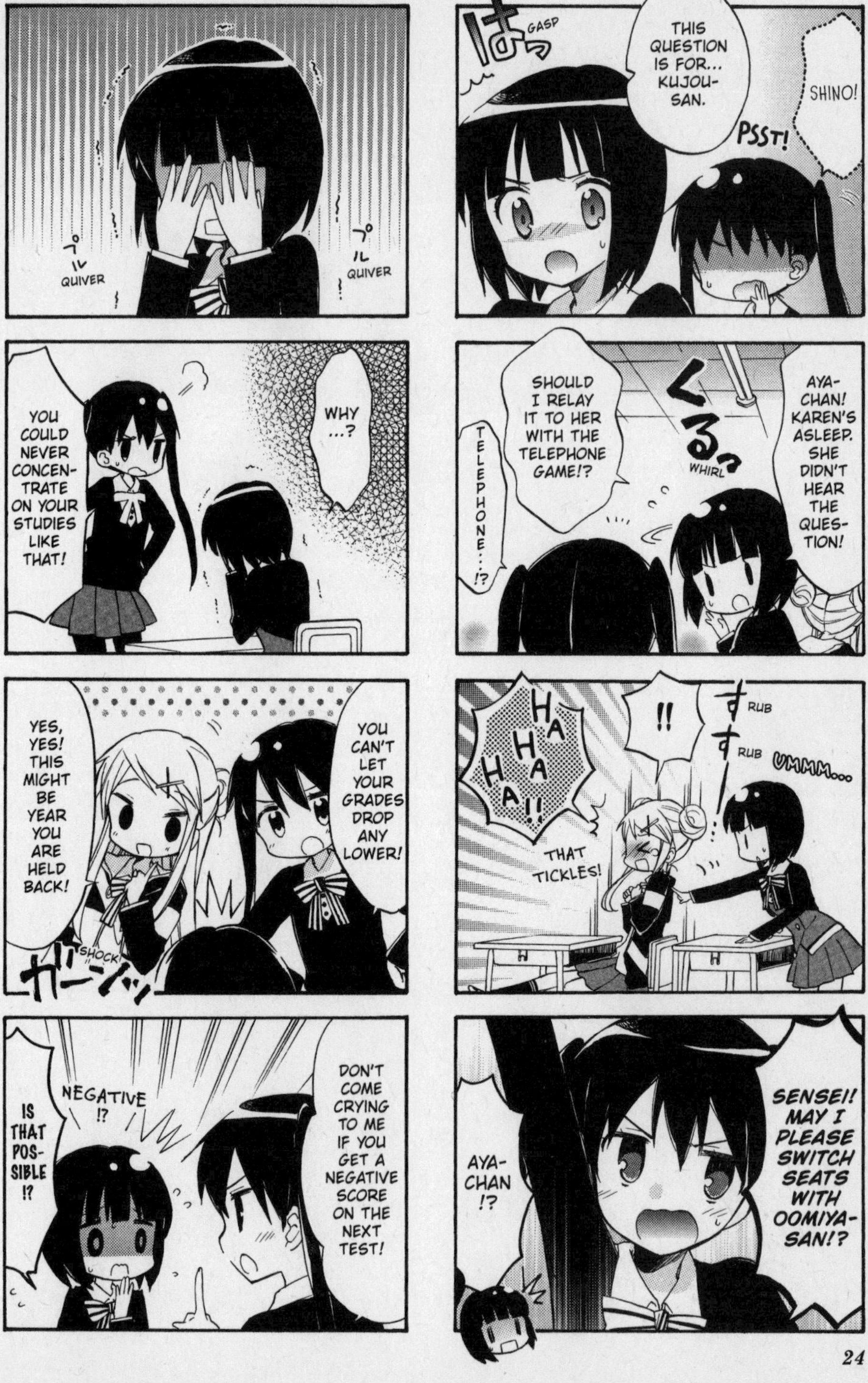
GASP
THIS QUESTION IS FOR... KUJOU-SAN.
SHINO!
PSST!
QUIVER
QUIVER
AYA-CHAN! KAREN'S ASLEEP. SHE DIDN'T HEAR THE QUESTION!
WHIRL
SHOULD I RELAY IT TO HER WITH THE TELEPHONE GAME!?
TELEPHONE...!?
WHY ...?
YOU COULD NEVER CONCENTRATE ON YOUR STUDIES LIKE THAT!
RUB
RUB
!!
UMMM...
HA HA HA HA!!
THAT TICKLES!
YOU CAN'T LET YOUR GRADES DROP ANY LOWER!
YES, YES! THIS MIGHT BE YEAR YOU ARE HELD BACK!
SHOCK!
SENSEI!! MAY I PLEASE SWITCH SEATS WITH OOMIYA-SAN!?
AYA-CHAN!?
DON'T COME CRYING TO ME IF YOU GET A NEGATIVE SCORE ON THE NEXT TEST!
NEGATIVE !?
IS THAT POSSIBLE !?

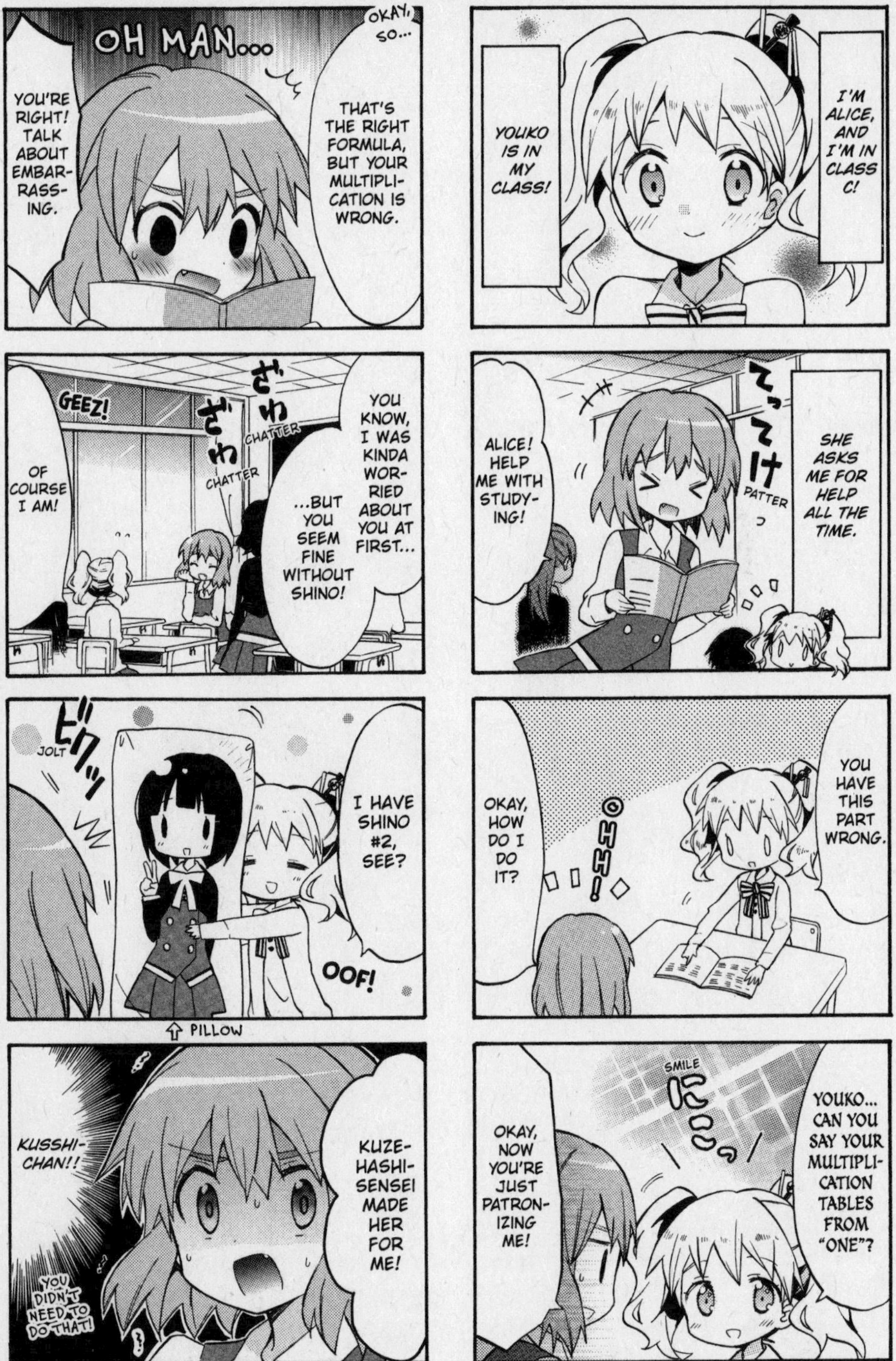
I'M ALICE, AND I'M IN CLASS C!
YOUKO IS IN MY CLASS!
OKAY, SO...
THAT'S THE RIGHT FORMULA, BUT YOUR MULTIPLICATION IS WRONG.
OH MAN...
YOU'RE RIGHT! TALK ABOUT EMBARRASSING.
SHE ASKS ME FOR HELP ALL THE TIME.
PATTER
ALICE! HELP ME WITH STUDYING!
YOU KNOW, I WAS KINDA WORRIED ABOUT YOU AT FIRST...
...BUT YOU SEEM FINE WITHOUT SHINO!
CHATTER
CHATTER
GEEZ!
OF COURSE I AM!
YOU HAVE THIS PART WRONG.
OHH!
OKAY, HOW DO I DO IT?
I HAVE SHINO #2, SEE?
OOF!
JOLT
PILLOW
YOUKO... CAN YOU SAY YOUR MULTIPLICATION TABLES FROM "ONE"?
SMILE
OKAY, NOW YOU'RE JUST PATRONIZING ME!
PURE EYES
KUZEHASHI-SENSEI MADE HER FOR ME!
KUSSHI-CHAN!!
YOU DIDN'T NEED TO DO THAT!

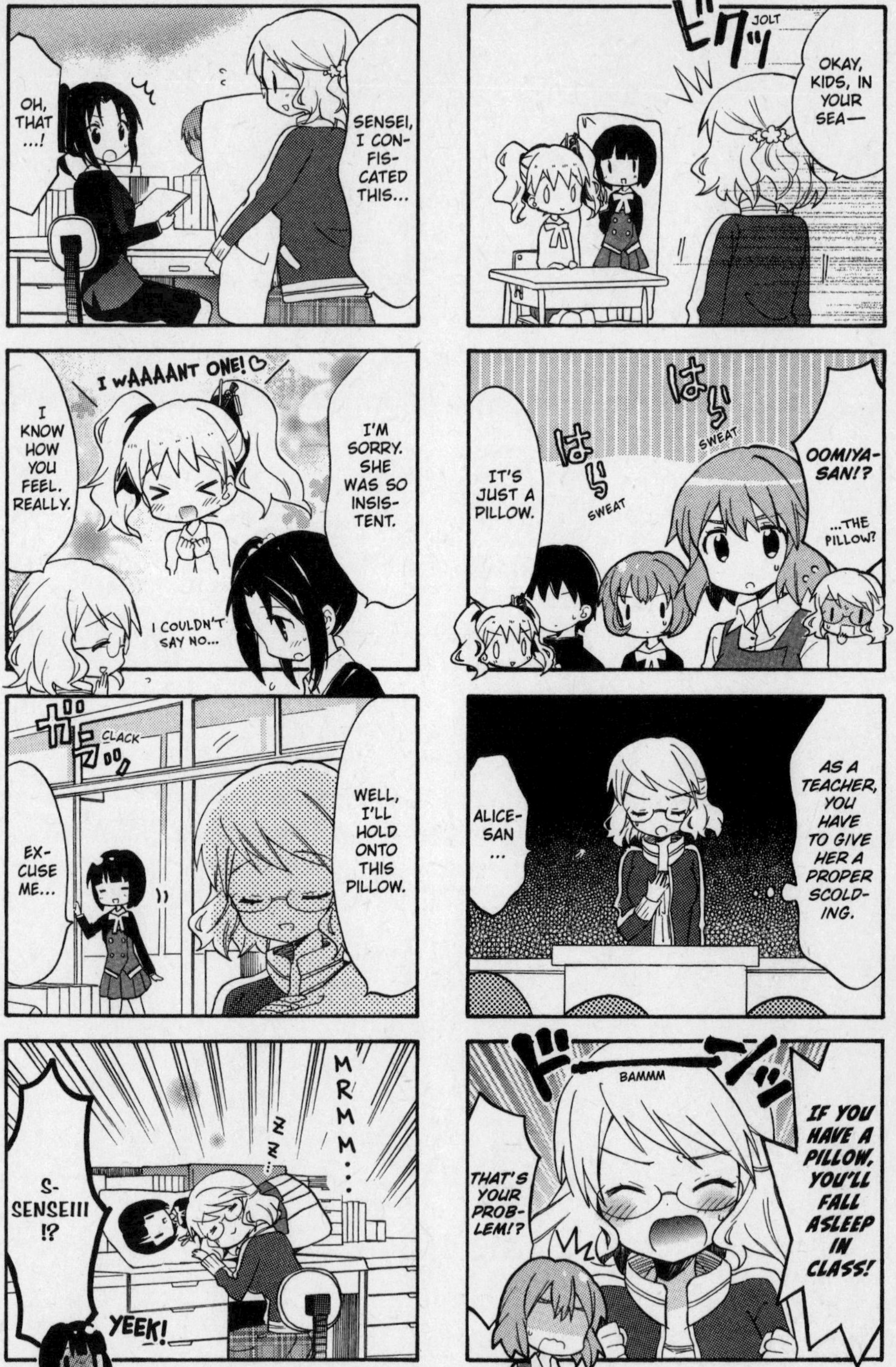

ビクッ
JOLT
OKAY, KIDS, IN YOUR SEA—
はら はら
SWEAT SWEAT
OOMIYA-SAN!?
...THE PILLOW?
IT'S JUST A PILLOW.
AS A TEACHER, YOU HAVE TO GIVE HER A PROPER SCOLDING.
ALICE-SAN ...
ドーーンッ
BAMMM
IF YOU HAVE A PILLOW, YOU'LL FALL ASLEEP IN CLASS!
THAT'S YOUR PROBLEM!?
SENSEI, I CONFISCATED THIS...
OH, THAT ...!
I'M SORRY. SHE WAS SO INSISTENT.
I wAAAANT ONE! ♡
I KNOW HOW YOU FEEL. REALLY.
I COULDN'T SAY NO...
ガラッ
CLACK
WELL, I'LL HOLD ONTO THIS PILLOW.
EXCUSE ME...
MRMMM...
Z Z
S-SENSEIII!?
YEEK!

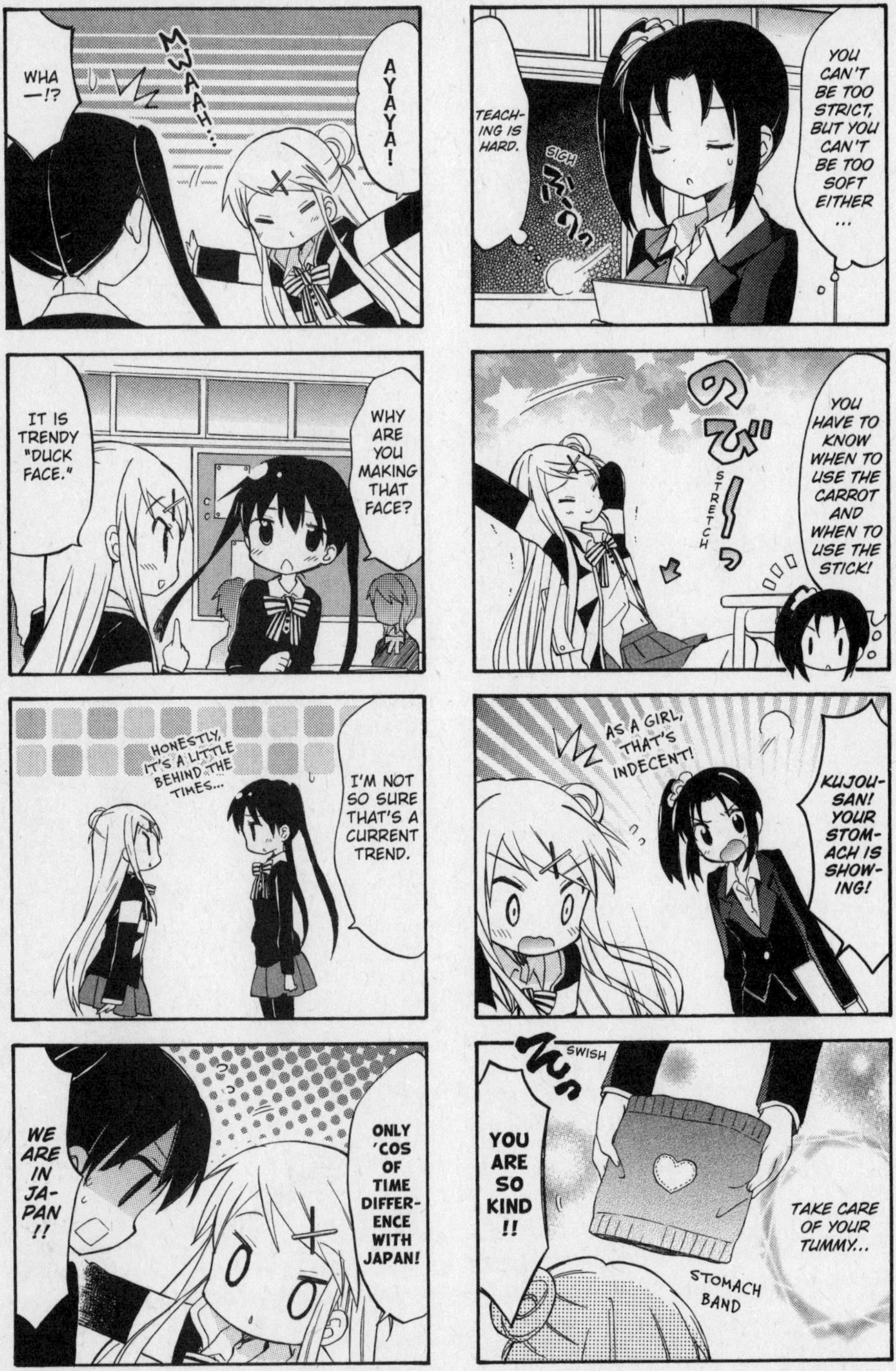
YOU CAN'T BE TOO STRICT, BUT YOU CAN'T BE TOO SOFT EITHER...
TEACHING IS HARD.
SIGH
YOU HAVE TO KNOW WHEN TO USE THE CARROT AND WHEN TO USE THE STICK!
STRETCH
KUJOU-SAN! YOUR STOMACH IS SHOWING!
AS A GIRL, THAT'S INDECENT!
SWISH
TAKE CARE OF YOUR TUMMY...
YOU ARE SO KIND!!
STOMACH BAND
AYAYA!
MWAAH...
WHA—!?
WHY ARE YOU MAKING THAT FACE?
IT IS TRENDY "DUCK FACE."
I'M NOT SO SURE THAT'S A CURRENT TREND.
HONESTLY, IT'S A LITTLE BEHIND THE TIMES...
ONLY 'COS OF TIME DIFFERENCE WITH JAPAN!
WE ARE IN JAPAN!!

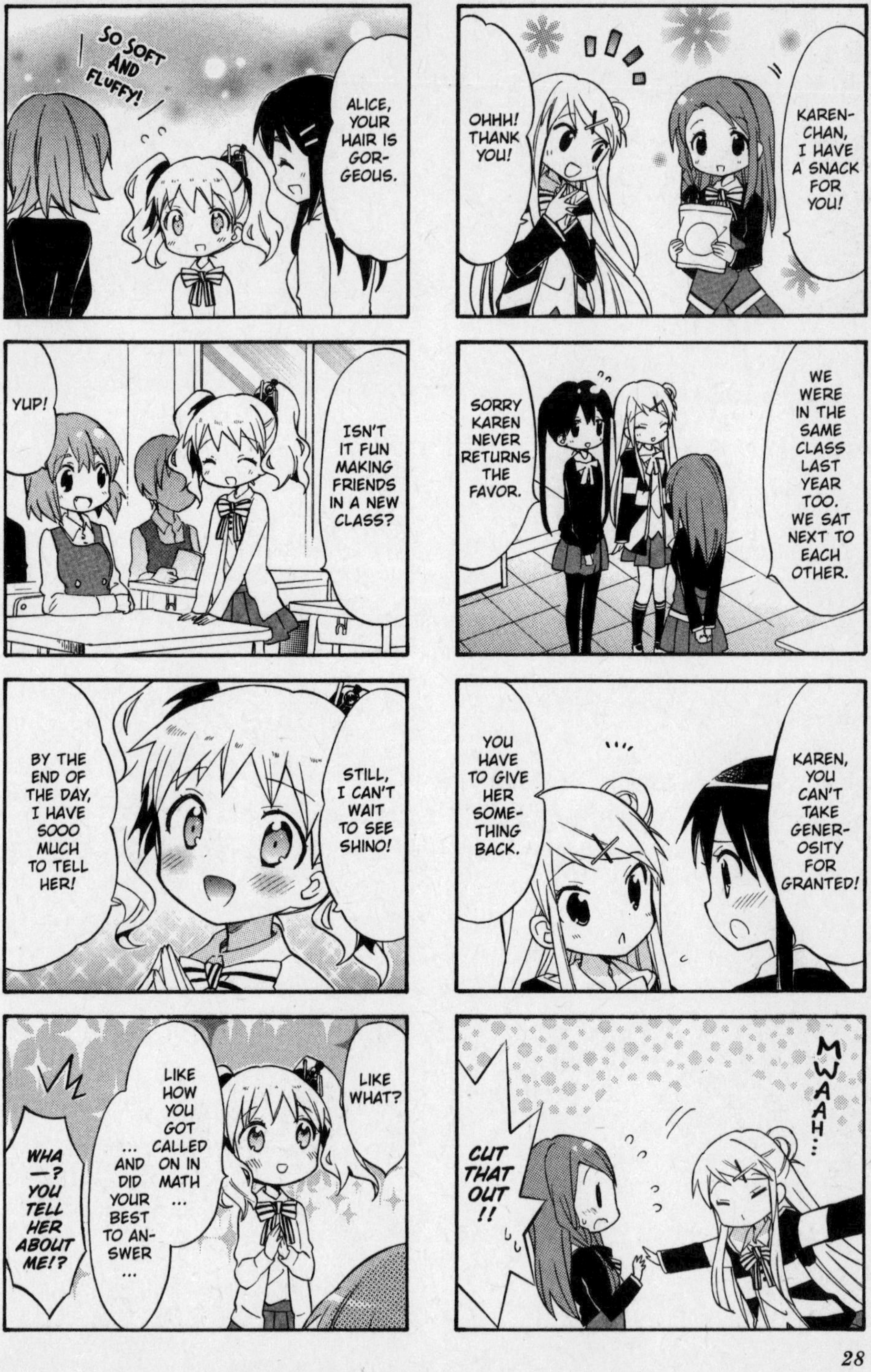
KAREN-CHAN, I HAVE A SNACK FOR YOU!
OHHH! THANK YOU!
WE WERE IN THE SAME CLASS LAST YEAR TOO. WE SAT NEXT TO EACH OTHER.
SORRY KAREN NEVER RETURNS THE FAVOR.
KAREN, YOU CAN'T TAKE GENEROSITY FOR GRANTED!
YOU HAVE TO GIVE HER SOMETHING BACK.
MWAAH...
CUT THAT OUT!!
ALICE, YOUR HAIR IS GORGEOUS.
SO SOFT AND FLUFFY!
ISN'T IT FUN MAKING FRIENDS IN A NEW CLASS?
YUP!
STILL, I CAN'T WAIT TO SEE SHINO!
BY THE END OF THE DAY, I HAVE SOOO MUCH TO TELL HER!
LIKE WHAT?
LIKE HOW YOU GOT CALLED ON IN MATH...
...AND DID YOUR BEST TO ANSWER...
WHA—? YOU TELL HER ABOUT ME!?

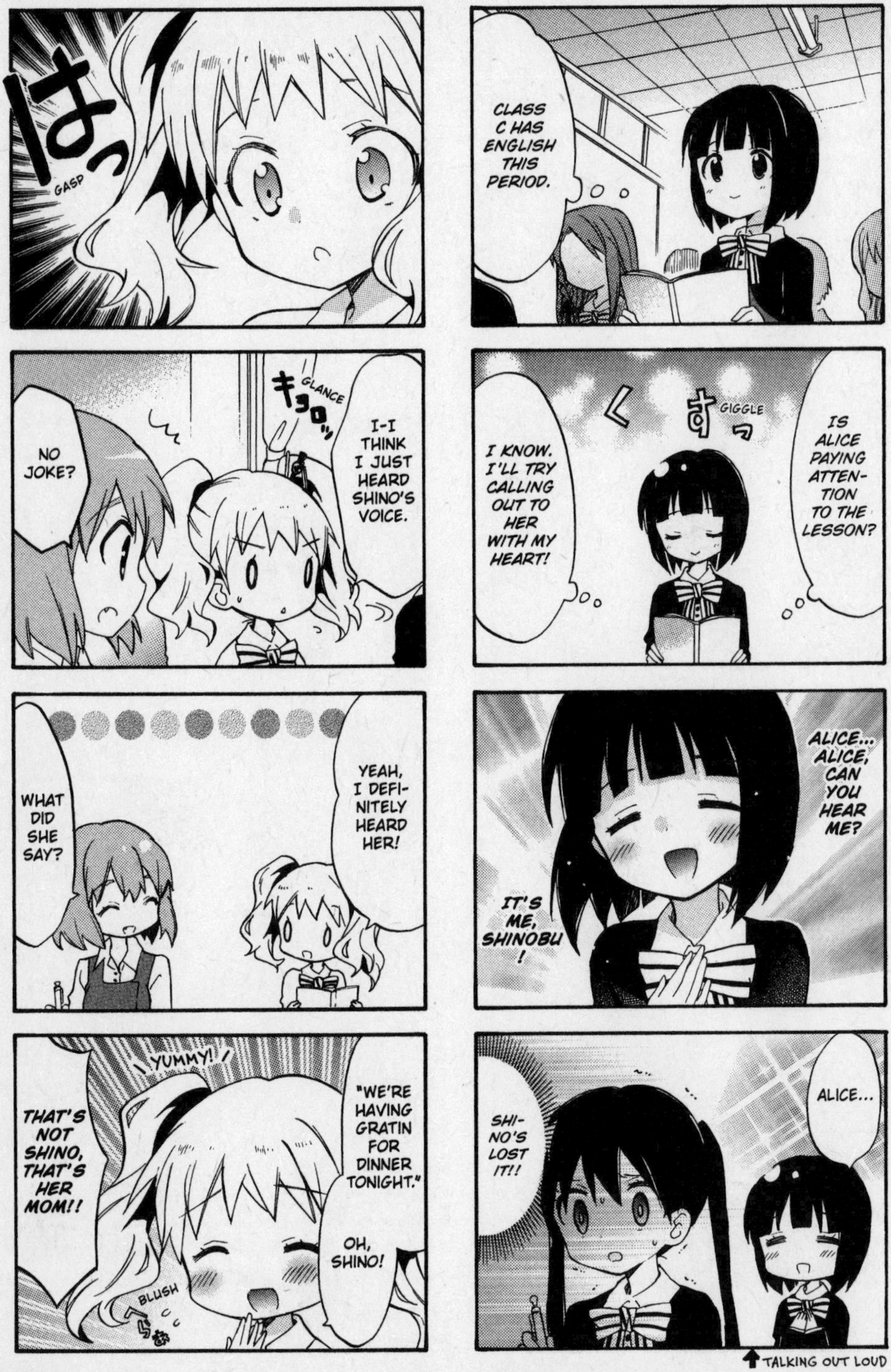
CLASS C HAS ENGLISH THIS PERIOD.
IS ALICE PAYING ATTENTION TO THE LESSON?
くすっ
GIGGLE
I KNOW. I'LL TRY CALLING OUT TO HER WITH MY HEART!
ALICE... ALICE, CAN YOU HEAR ME?
IT'S ME, SHINOBU!
ALICE...
SHI-NO'S LOST IT!!
TALKING OUT LOUD
はっ
GASP
キョロッ
GLANCE
I-I THINK I JUST HEARD SHINO'S VOICE.
NO JOKE?
YEAH, I DEFI-NITELY HEARD HER!
WHAT DID SHE SAY?
"WE'RE HAVING GRATIN FOR DINNER TONIGHT."
OH, SHINO!
YUMMY!
BLUSH
THAT'S NOT SHINO, THAT'S HER MOM!!

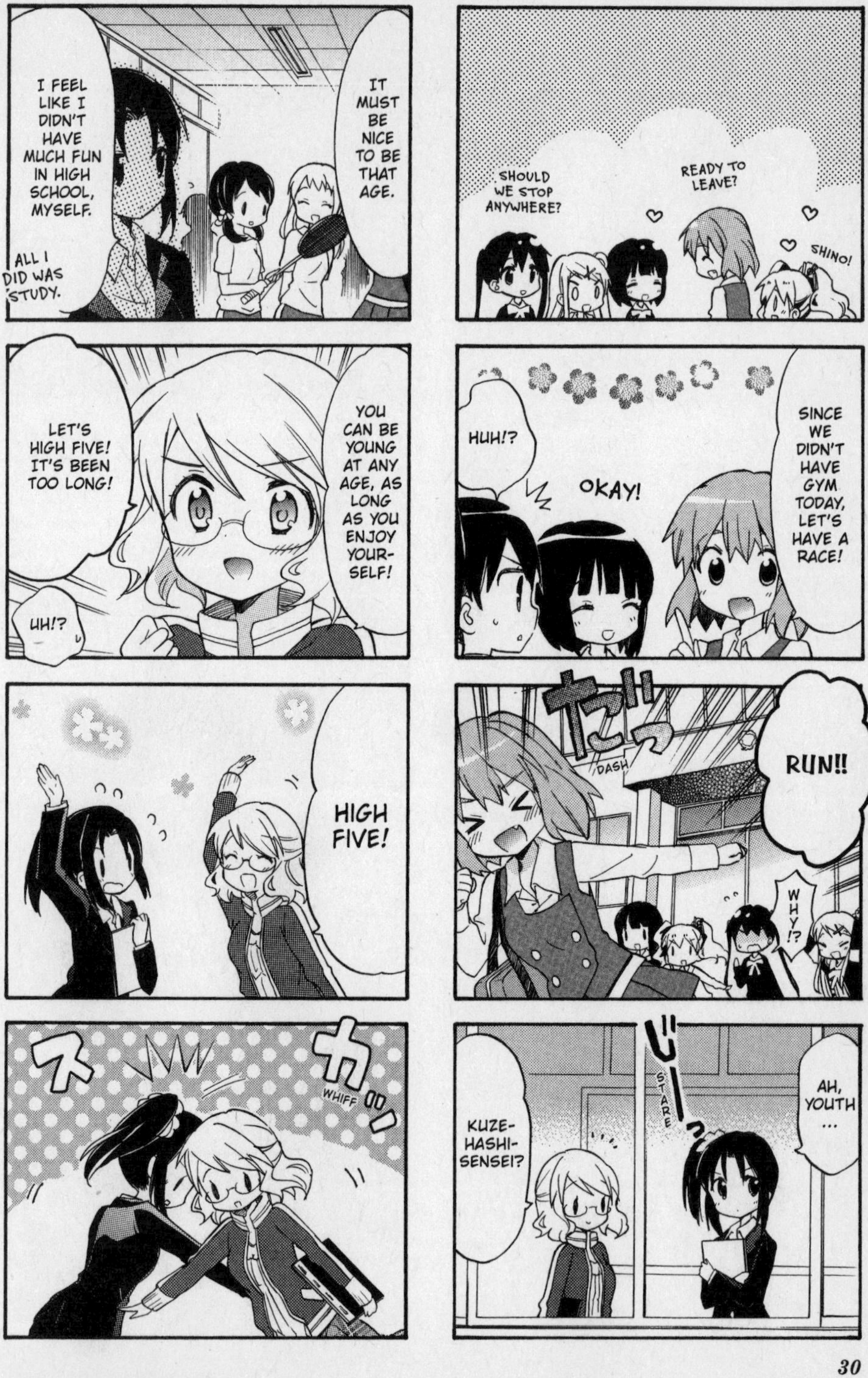
READY TO LEAVE?
SHINO!
SHOULD WE STOP ANYWHERE?
SINCE WE DIDN'T HAVE GYM TODAY, LET'S HAVE A RACE!
OKAY!
HUH!?
RUN!!
DASH
WHY!?
AH, YOUTH ...
STARE
KUZE-HASHI-SENSEI?
IT MUST BE NICE TO BE THAT AGE.
I FEEL LIKE I DIDN'T HAVE MUCH FUN IN HIGH SCHOOL, MYSELF.
ALL I DID WAS STUDY.
YOU CAN BE YOUNG AT ANY AGE, AS LONG AS YOU ENJOY YOUR-SELF!
LET'S HIGH FIVE! IT'S BEEN TOO LONG!
UH!?
HIGH FIVE!
WHIFF

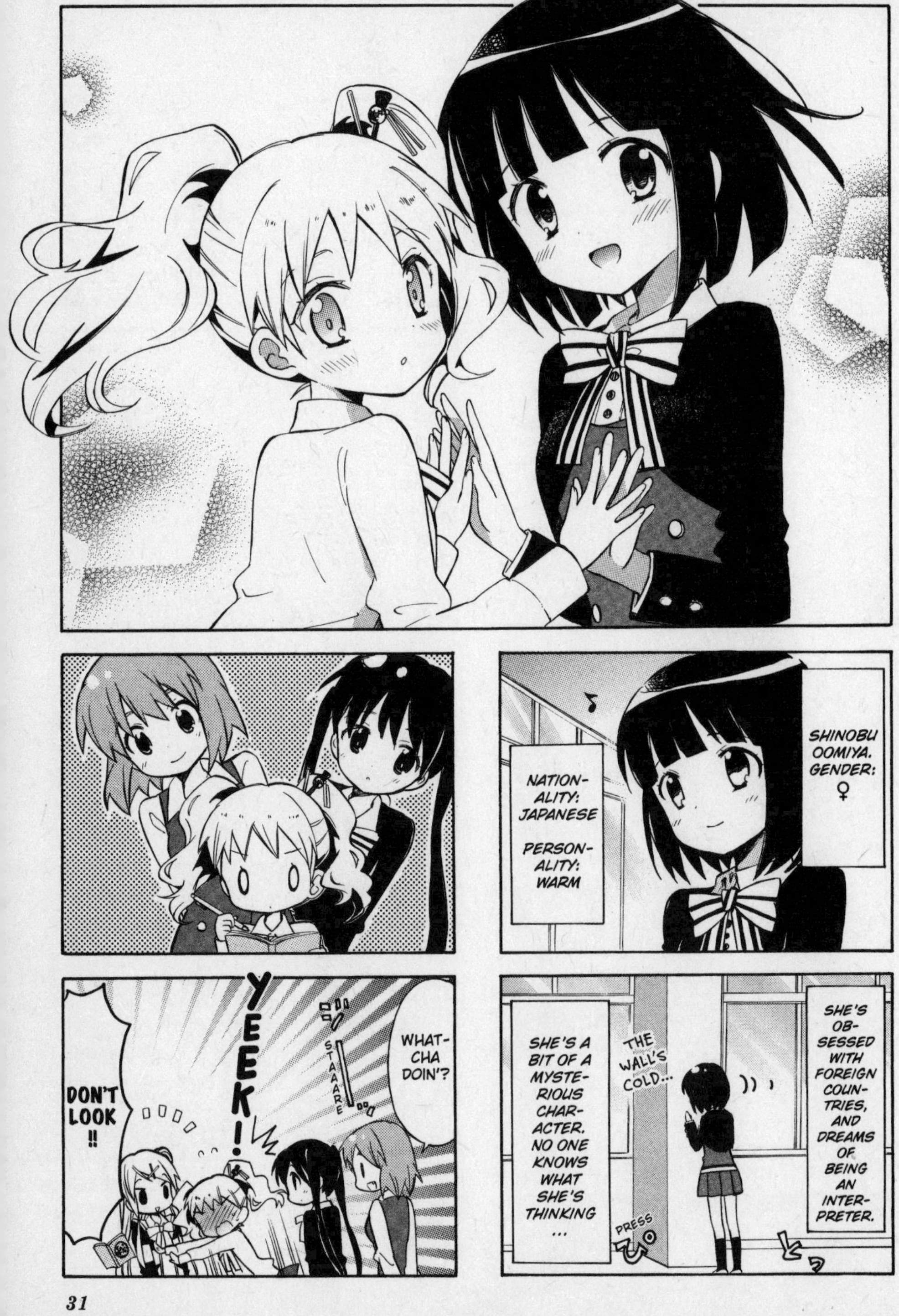
SHINOBU OOMIYA. GENDER: ♀
NATION-ALITY: JAPANESE
PERSON-ALITY: WARM
SHE'S OB-SESSED WITH FOREIGN COUN-TRIES, AND DREAMS OF BEING AN INTER-PRETER.
THE WALL'S COLD...
SHE'S A BIT OF A MYSTE-RIOUS CHAR-ACTER. NO ONE KNOWS WHAT SHE'S THINKING ...
PRESS
WHAT-CHA DOIN'?
STAAARE
YEEEK!
DON'T LOOK!!

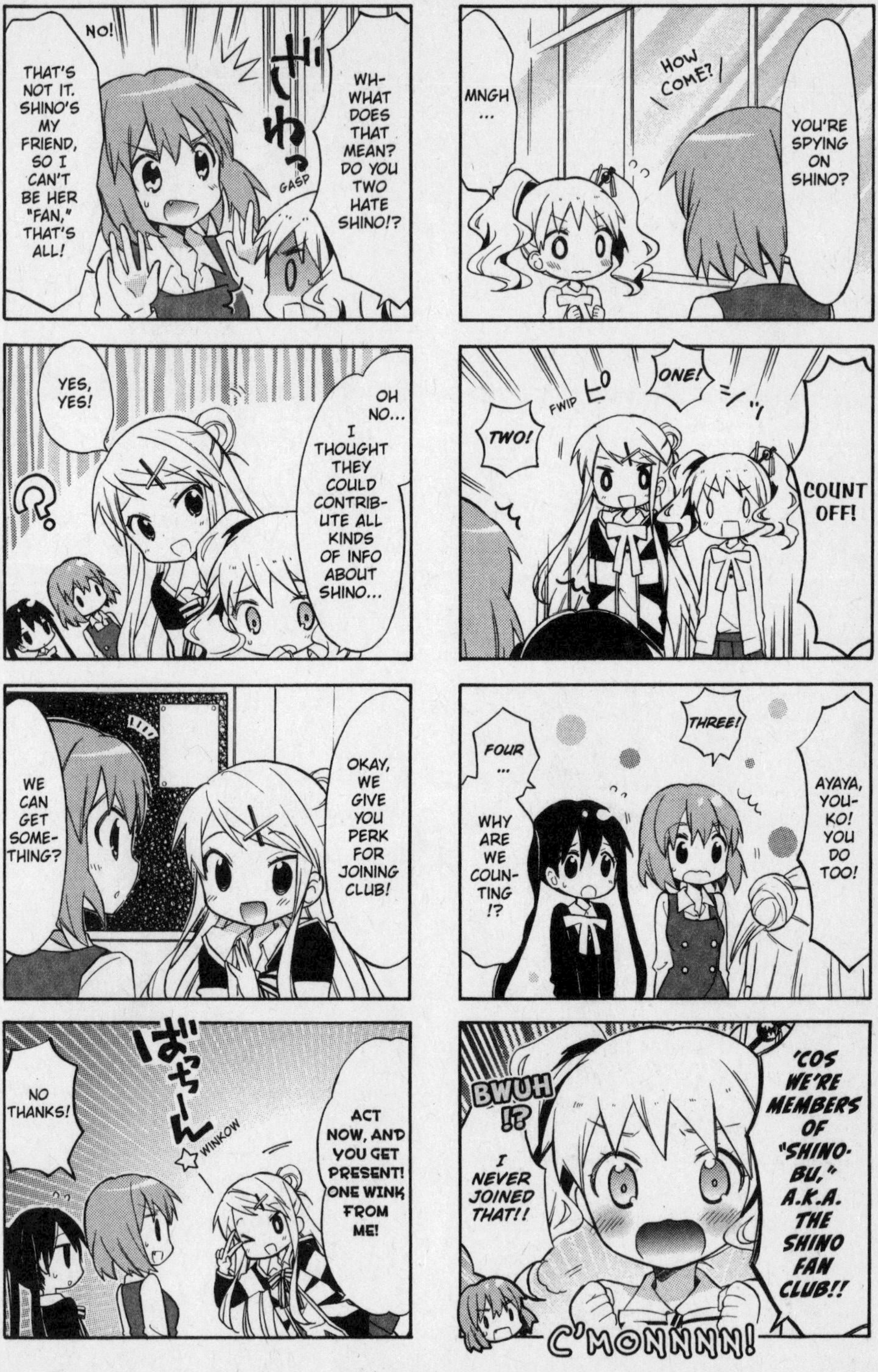
YOU'RE SPYING ON SHINO?
HOW COME?
MNGH ...
COUNT OFF!
ONE!
FWIP
TWO!
AYAYA, YOU-KO! YOU DO TOO!
THREE!
FOUR ...
WHY ARE WE COUNTING !?
'COS WE'RE MEMBERS OF "SHINO-BU," A.K.A. THE SHINO FAN CLUB!!
BWUH !?
I NEVER JOINED THAT!!
C'MONNNNN!
WH-WHAT DOES THAT MEAN? DO YOU TWO HATE SHINO!?
ざわっ
GASP
NO!
THAT'S NOT IT. SHINO'S MY FRIEND, SO I CAN'T BE HER "FAN," THAT'S ALL!
OH NO... I THOUGHT THEY COULD CONTRIBUTE ALL KINDS OF INFO ABOUT SHINO...
YES, YES!
OKAY, WE GIVE YOU PERK FOR JOINING CLUB!
WE CAN GET SOMETHING?
ACT NOW, AND YOU GET PRESENT! ONE WINK FROM ME!
ばっちーん
WINKOW
NO THANKS!

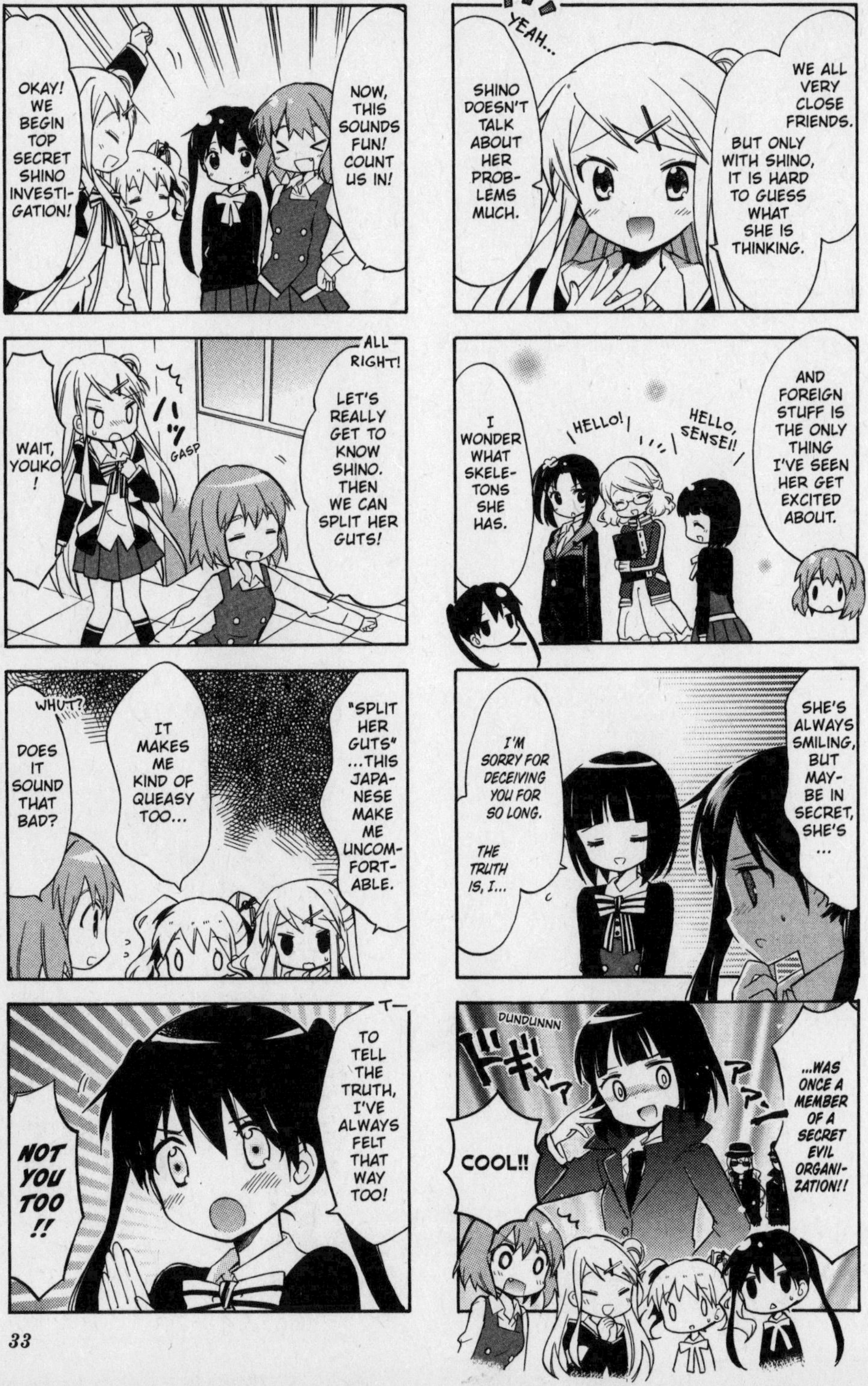
YEAH...
WE ALL VERY CLOSE FRIENDS. BUT ONLY WITH SHINO, IT IS HARD TO GUESS WHAT SHE IS THINKING.
SHINO DOESN'T TALK ABOUT HER PROB-LEMS MUCH.
NOW, THIS SOUNDS FUN! COUNT US IN!
OKAY! WE BEGIN TOP SECRET SHINO INVESTI-GATION!
AND FOREIGN STUFF IS THE ONLY THING I'VE SEEN HER GET EXCITED ABOUT.
HELLO, SENSEI!
HELLO!
I WONDER WHAT SKELE-TONS SHE HAS.
ALL RIGHT!
LET'S REALLY GET TO KNOW SHINO. THEN WE CAN SPLIT HER GUTS!
ハッ
GASP
WAIT, YOUKO!
SHE'S ALWAYS SMILING, BUT MAY-BE IN SECRET, SHE'S...
I'M SORRY FOR DECEIVING YOU FOR SO LONG.
THE TRUTH IS, I...
"SPLIT HER GUTS" ...THIS JAPA-NESE MAKE ME UNCOM-FORT-ABLE.
IT MAKES ME KIND OF QUEASY TOO...
WHUT?
DOES IT SOUND THAT BAD?
...WAS ONCE A MEMBER OF A SECRET EVIL ORGANI-ZATION!!
アァ
ドギャア
DUNDUNNN
COOL!!
T—
TO TELL THE TRUTH, I'VE ALWAYS FELT THAT WAY TOO!
NOT YOU TOO!!

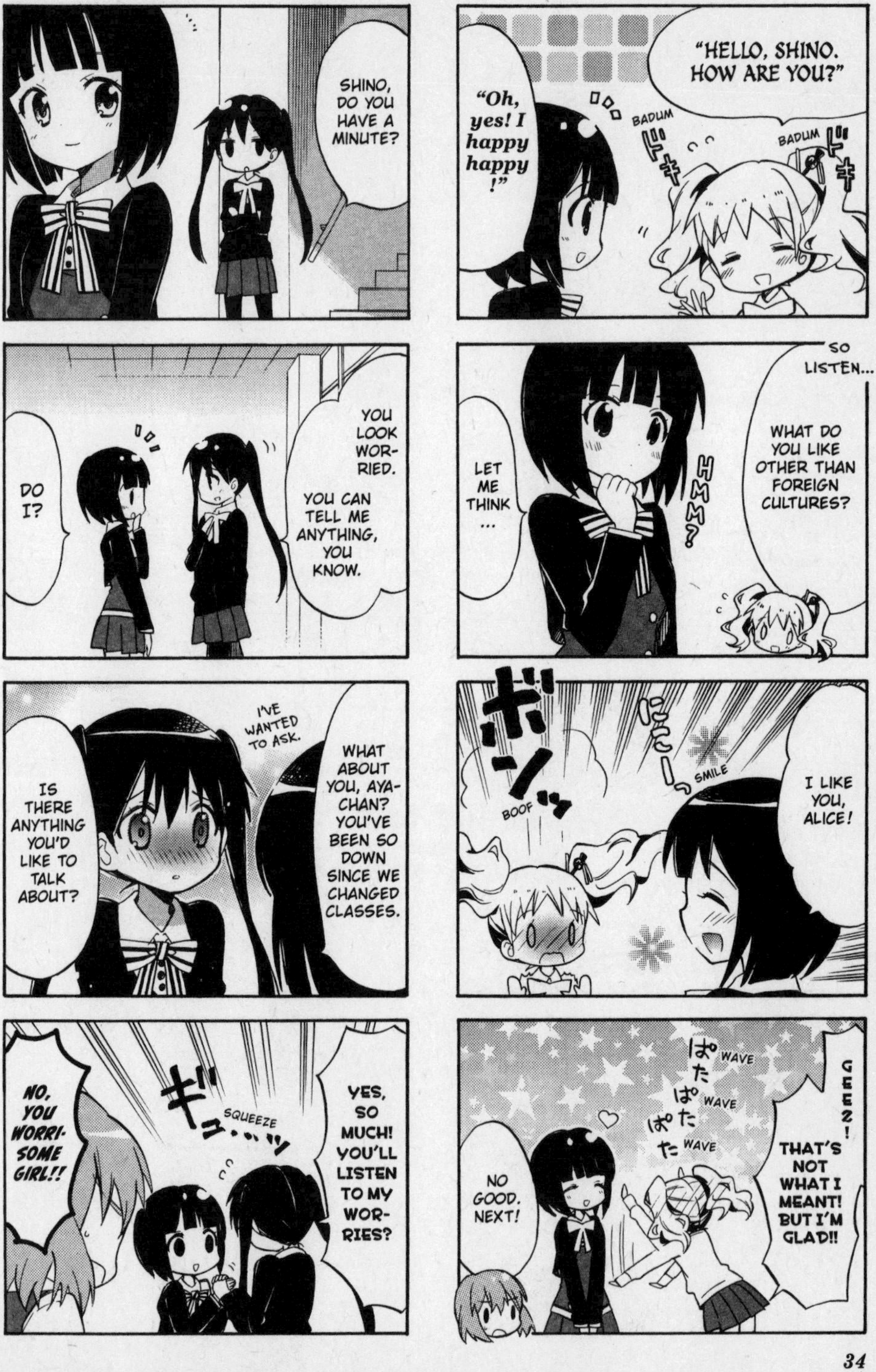
"HELLO, SHINO. HOW ARE YOU?"
BADUM ドキ
BADUM ドキ
"Oh, yes! I happy happy!"
SO LISTEN...
WHAT DO YOU LIKE OTHER THAN FOREIGN CULTURES?
HMMM?
LET ME THINK...
ボンッ
BOOF
にこー
SMILE
I LIKE YOU, ALICE!
GEEZ!
THAT'S NOT WHAT I MEANT! BUT I'M GLAD!!
ぱた WAVE
ぱた WAVE
ぱた WAVE
NO GOOD. NEXT!
SHINO, DO YOU HAVE A MINUTE?
YOU LOOK WORRIED.
YOU CAN TELL ME ANYTHING, YOU KNOW.
DO I?
WHAT ABOUT YOU, AYA-CHAN? YOU'VE BEEN SO DOWN SINCE WE CHANGED CLASSES.
I'VE WANTED TO ASK.
IS THERE ANYTHING YOU'D LIKE TO TALK ABOUT?
YES, SO MUCH! YOU'LL LISTEN TO MY WORRIES?
ギュッ
SQUEEZE
NO, YOU WORRISOME GIRL!!

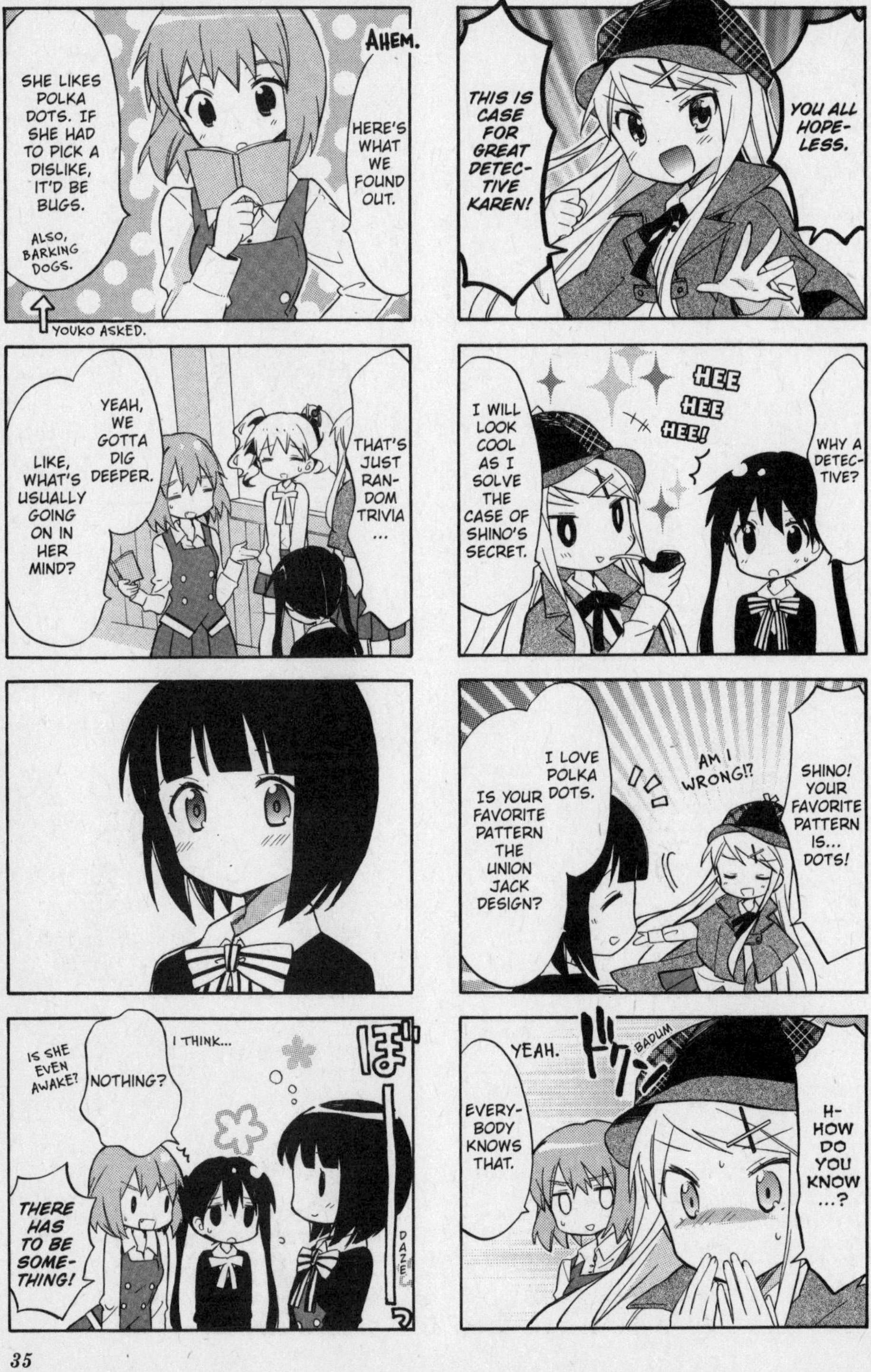

YOU ALL HOPELESS.
THIS IS CASE FOR GREAT DETECTIVE KAREN!
WHY A DETECTIVE?
HEE HEE HEE!
I WILL LOOK COOL AS I SOLVE THE CASE OF SHINO'S SECRET.
SHINO! YOUR FAVORITE PATTERN IS... DOTS!
AM I WRONG!?
I LOVE POLKA DOTS.
IS YOUR FAVORITE PATTERN THE UNION JACK DESIGN?
H-HOW DO YOU KNOW...?
BADUM
YEAH.
EVERYBODY KNOWS THAT.
AHEM.
HERE'S WHAT WE FOUND OUT.
SHE LIKES POLKA DOTS. IF SHE HAD TO PICK A DISLIKE, IT'D BE BUGS.
ALSO, BARKING DOGS.
YOUKO ASKED.
THAT'S JUST RANDOM TRIVIA...
YEAH, WE GOTTA DIG DEEPER.
LIKE, WHAT'S USUALLY GOING ON IN HER MIND?
ぽーっ
DAZE
I THINK...
NOTHING?
IS SHE EVEN AWAKE?
THERE HAS TO BE SOMETHING!

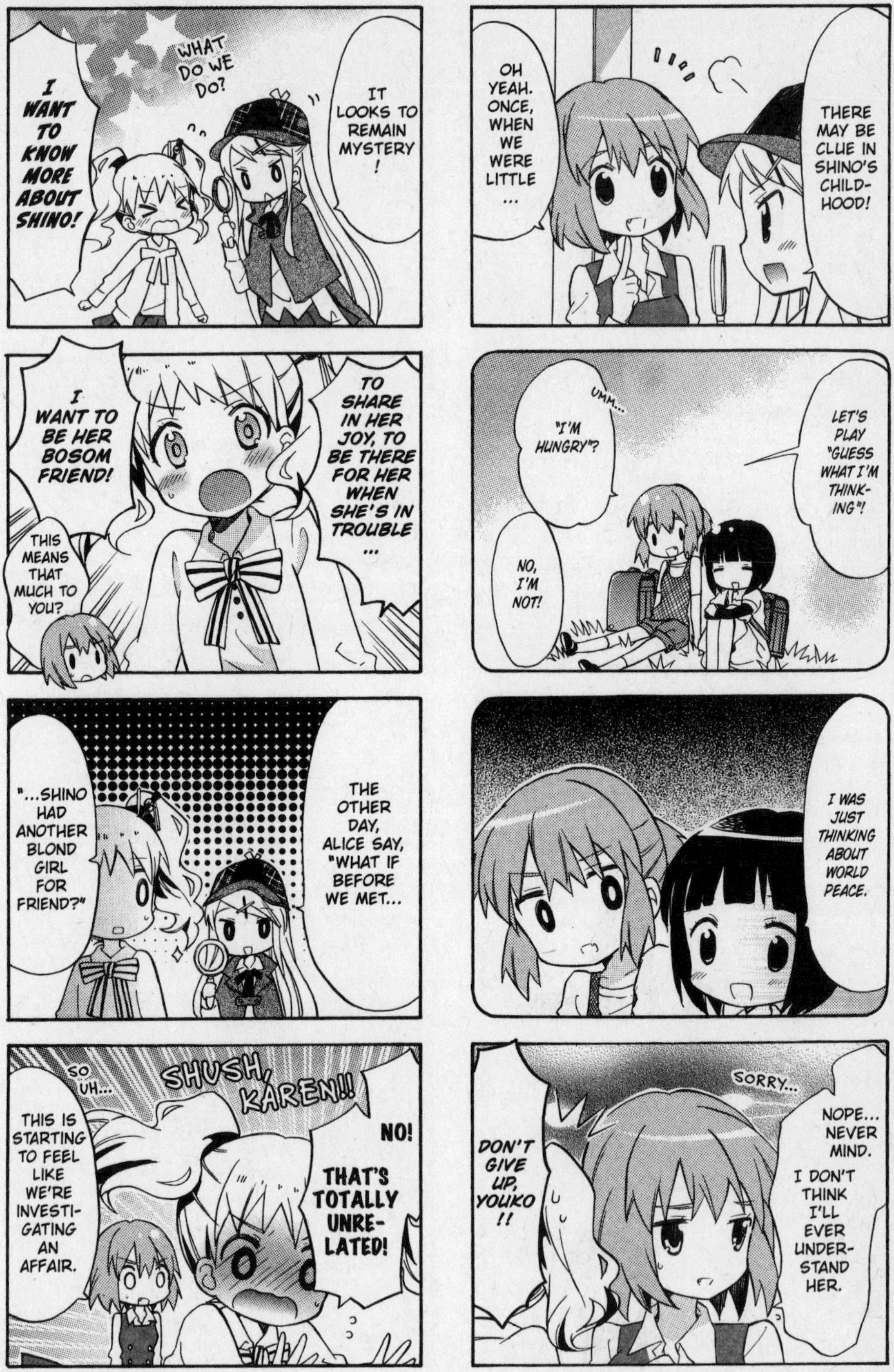
THERE MAY BE CLUE IN SHINO'S CHILDHOOD!
OH YEAH. ONCE, WHEN WE WERE LITTLE ...
LET'S PLAY "GUESS WHAT I'M THINKING"!
UMM...
"I'M HUNGRY"?
NO, I'M NOT!
I WAS JUST THINKING ABOUT WORLD PEACE.
SORRY...
NOPE... NEVER MIND.
I DON'T THINK I'LL EVER UNDERSTAND HER.
DON'T GIVE UP, YOUKO!!
IT LOOKS TO REMAIN MYSTERY!
WHAT DO WE DO?
I WANT TO KNOW MORE ABOUT SHINO!
TO SHARE IN HER JOY, TO BE THERE FOR HER WHEN SHE'S IN TROUBLE ...
I WANT TO BE HER BOSOM FRIEND!
THIS MEANS THAT MUCH TO YOU?
THE OTHER DAY, ALICE SAY, "WHAT IF BEFORE WE MET...
"...SHINO HAD ANOTHER BLOND GIRL FOR FRIEND?"
NO!
THAT'S TOTALLY UNRELATED!
SHUSH, KAREN!!
SO UH...
THIS IS STARTING TO FEEL LIKE WE'RE INVESTIGATING AN AFFAIR.

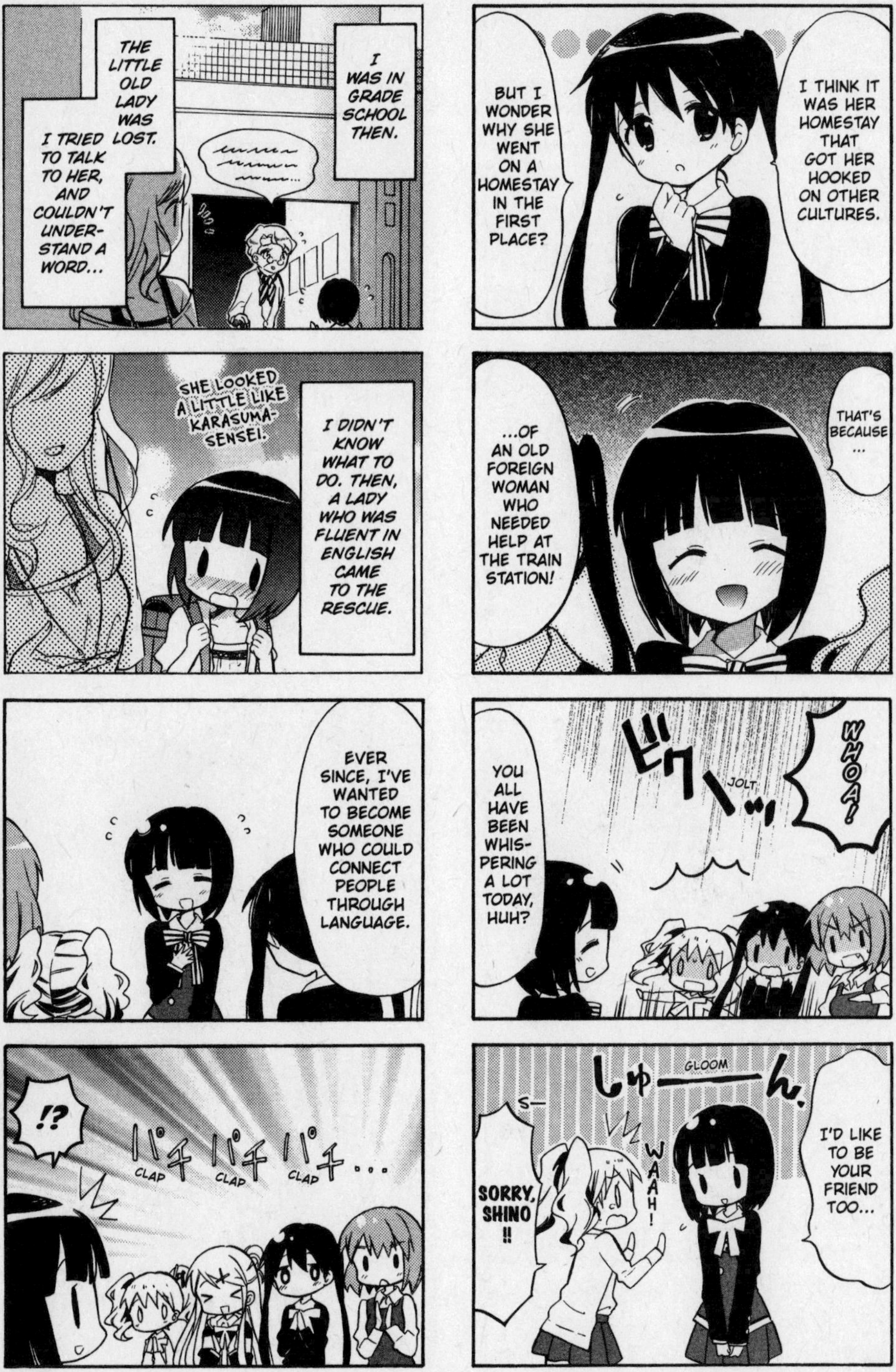
I THINK IT WAS HER HOMESTAY THAT GOT HER HOOKED ON OTHER CULTURES.
BUT I WONDER WHY SHE WENT ON A HOMESTAY IN THE FIRST PLACE?
I WAS IN GRADE SCHOOL THEN.
THE LITTLE OLD LADY WAS LOST.
I TRIED TO TALK TO HER, AND COULDN'T UNDERSTAND A WORD...
THAT'S BECAUSE...
...OF AN OLD FOREIGN WOMAN WHO NEEDED HELP AT THE TRAIN STATION!
I DIDN'T KNOW WHAT TO DO. THEN, A LADY WHO WAS FLUENT IN ENGLISH CAME TO THE RESCUE.
SHE LOOKED A LITTLE LIKE KARASUMA-SENSEI.
WHOA!
ビクッ
JOLT
YOU ALL HAVE BEEN WHISPERING A LOT TODAY, HUH?
EVER SINCE, I'VE WANTED TO BECOME SOMEONE WHO COULD CONNECT PEOPLE THROUGH LANGUAGE.
しゅーーん。
GLOOM
I'D LIKE TO BE YOUR FRIEND TOO...
S—
WAAH!
SORRY, SHINO!!
!?
パチ パチ パチ...
CLAP CLAP CLAP

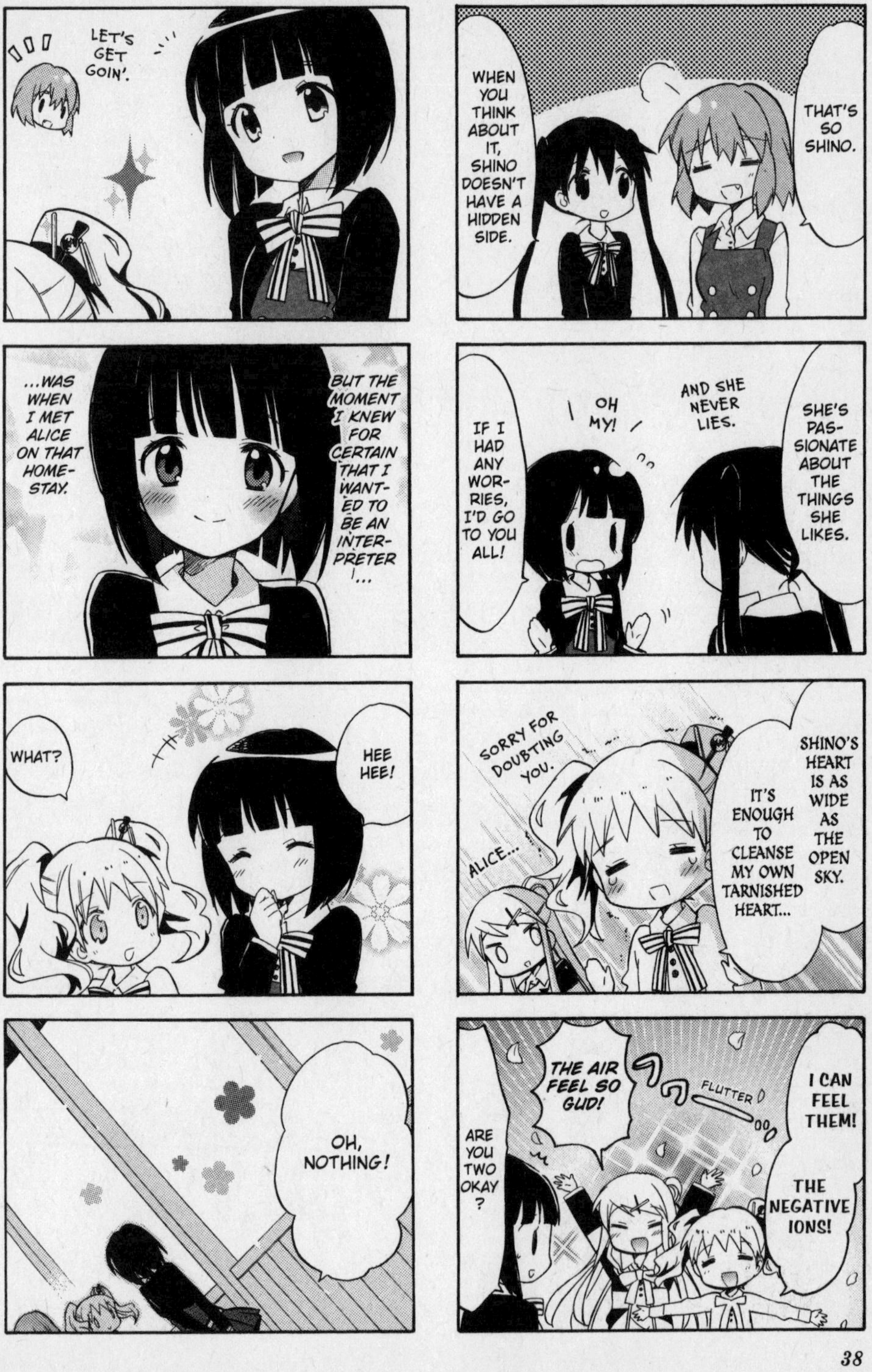
THAT'S SO SHINO.
WHEN YOU THINK ABOUT IT, SHINO DOESN'T HAVE A HIDDEN SIDE.
SHE'S PAS-SIONATE ABOUT THE THINGS SHE LIKES.
AND SHE NEVER LIES.
OH MY!
IF I HAD ANY WOR-RIES, I'D GO TO YOU ALL!
SHINO'S HEART IS AS WIDE AS THE OPEN SKY.
IT'S ENOUGH TO CLEANSE MY OWN TARNISHED HEART...
SORRY FOR DOUBTING YOU.
ALICE...
I CAN FEEL THEM!
THE NEGATIVE IONS!
FLUTTER
THE AIR FEEL SO GUD!
ARE YOU TWO OKAY?
LET'S GET GOIN'.
BUT THE MOMENT I KNEW FOR CERTAIN THAT I WANT-ED TO BE AN INTER-PRETER...
...WAS WHEN I MET ALICE ON THAT HOME-STAY.
HEE HEE!
WHAT?
OH, NOTHING!

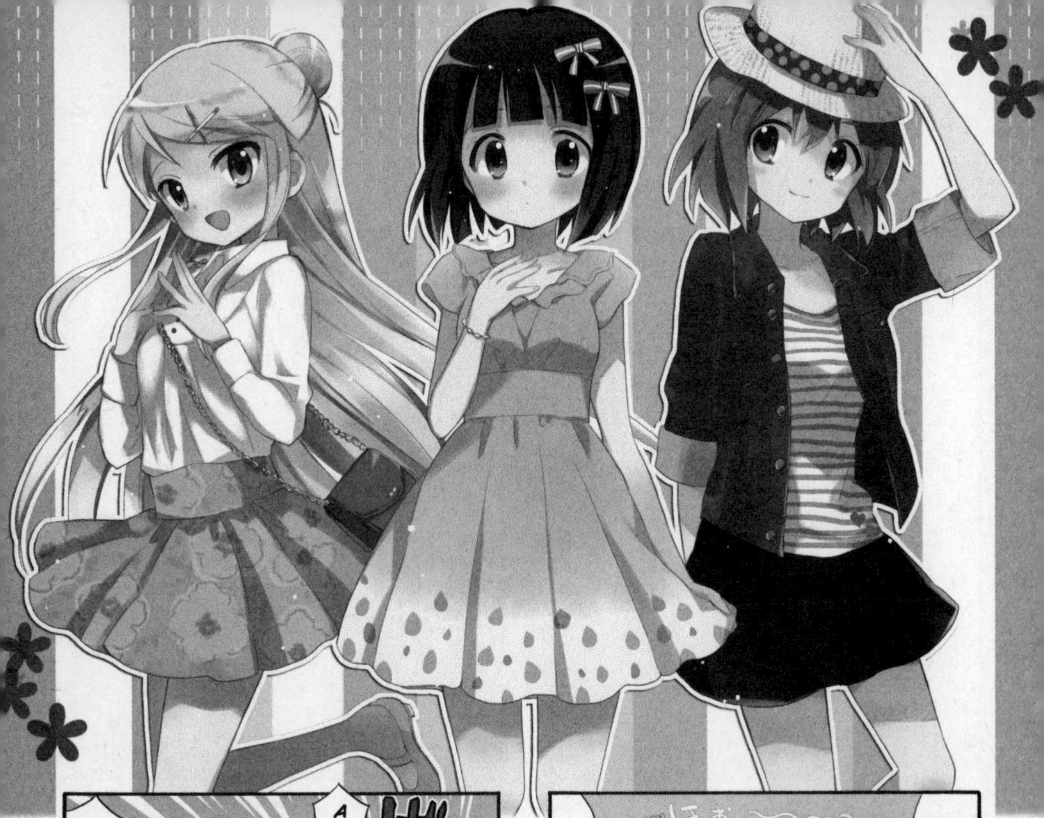

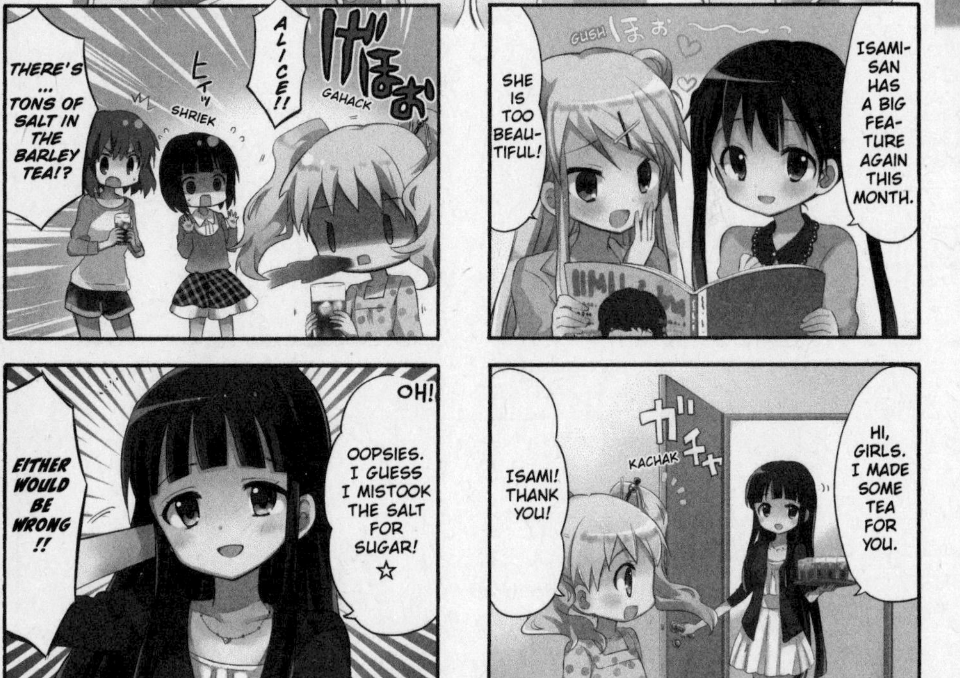

ISAMI-SAN HAS A BIG FEATURE AGAIN THIS MONTH.
GUSH
SHE IS TOO BEAUTIFUL!
ガチャ
KACHAK
HI, GIRLS. I MADE SOME TEA FOR YOU.
ISAMI! THANK YOU!
げほぉ
GAHACK
ALICE!!
SHRIEK
THERE'S ... TONS OF SALT IN THE BARLEY TEA!?
OH!
OOPSIES. I GUESS I MISTOOK THE SALT FOR SUGAR! ☆
EITHER WOULD BE WRONG!!

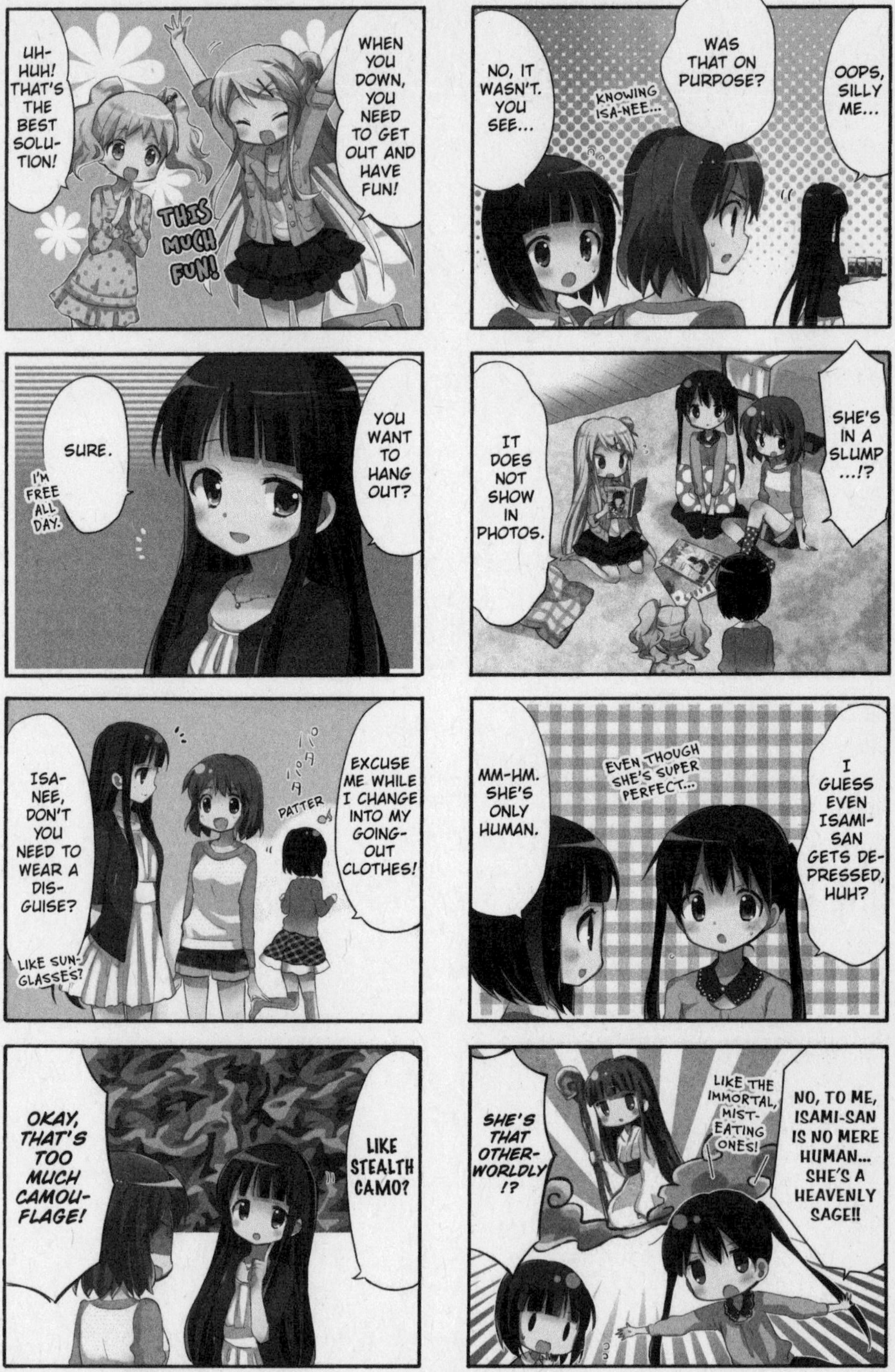
OOPS, SILLY ME...
WAS THAT ON PURPOSE?
KNOWING ISA-NEE...
NO, IT WASN'T. YOU SEE...
SHE'S IN A SLUMP ...!?
IT DOES NOT SHOW IN PHOTOS.
I GUESS EVEN ISAMI-SAN GETS DE-PRESSED, HUH?
EVEN THOUGH SHE'S SUPER PERFECT...
MM-HM. SHE'S ONLY HUMAN.
NO, TO ME, ISAMI-SAN IS NO MERE HUMAN... SHE'S A HEAVENLY SAGE!!
LIKE THE IMMORTAL, MIST-EATING ONES!
SHE'S THAT OTHER-WORLDLY!?
WHEN YOU DOWN, YOU NEED TO GET OUT AND HAVE FUN!
THIS MUCH FUN!
UH-HUH! THAT'S THE BEST SOLU-TION!
YOU WANT TO HANG OUT?
SURE.
I'M FREE ALL DAY.
EXCUSE ME WHILE I CHANGE INTO MY GOING-OUT CLOTHES!
パタ パタ
PATTER
ISA-NEE, DON'T YOU NEED TO WEAR A DIS-GUISE?
LIKE SUN-GLASSES?
LIKE STEALTH CAMO?
OKAY, THAT'S TOO MUCH CAMOU-FLAGE!

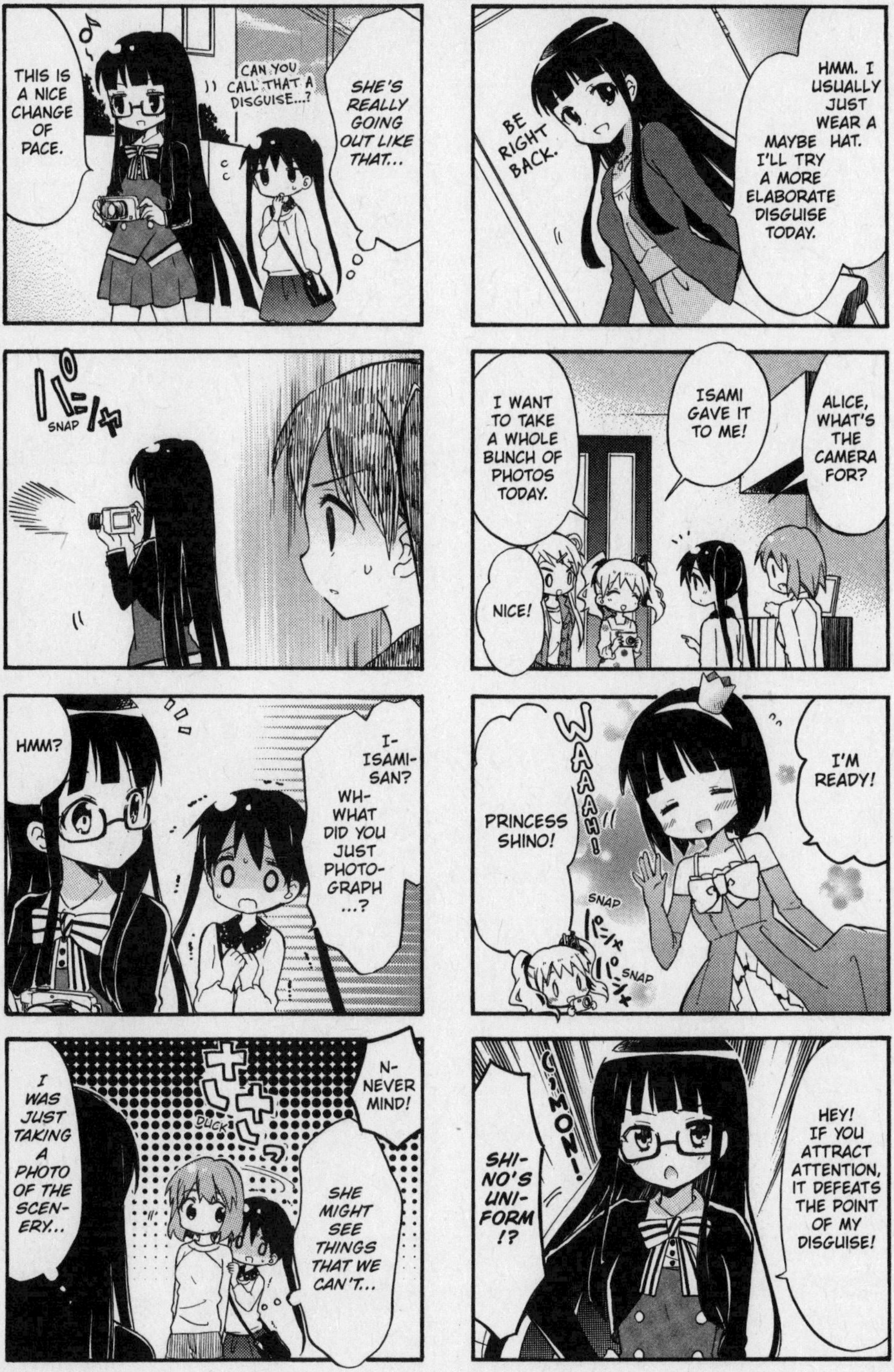
HMM. I USUALLY JUST WEAR A HAT. MAYBE I'LL TRY A MORE ELABORATE DISGUISE TODAY.
BE RIGHT BACK.
SHE'S REALLY GOING OUT LIKE THAT...
CAN YOU CALL THAT A DISGUISE...?
THIS IS A NICE CHANGE OF PACE.
ALICE, WHAT'S THE CAMERA FOR?
ISAMI GAVE IT TO ME!
I WANT TO TAKE A WHOLE BUNCH OF PHOTOS TODAY.
NICE!
SNAP
I'M READY!
WAAAAH!
PRINCESS SHINO!
SNAP
SNAP
I-ISAMI-SAN? WH-WHAT DID YOU JUST PHOTOGRAPH...?
HMM?
HEY! IF YOU ATTRACT ATTENTION, IT DEFEATS THE POINT OF MY DISGUISE!
C'MON!
SHINO'S UNIFORM!?
N-NEVER MIND!
DUCK
SHE MIGHT SEE THINGS THAT WE CAN'T...
I WAS JUST TAKING A PHOTO OF THE SCENERY...

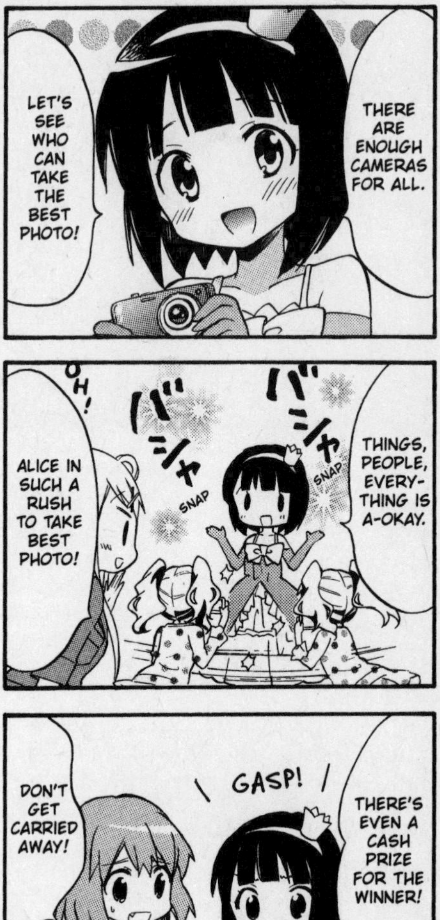
THERE ARE ENOUGH CAMERAS FOR ALL.
LET'S SEE WHO CAN TAKE THE BEST PHOTO!
THINGS, PEOPLE, EVERY-THING IS A-OKAY.
バシャ
SNAP
バシャ
SNAP
ALICE IN SUCH A RUSH TO TAKE BEST PHOTO!
OH!
THERE'S EVEN A CASH PRIZE FOR THE WINNER!
GASP!
DON'T GET CARRIED AWAY!
IT'S OKAY! ALICE AND I HAVE SOME MONEY WE SAVED UP LITTLE BY LITTLE.
WE CAN USE THAT...
SHINO, NO!!
WE DON'T EVEN HAVE THAT MUCH!

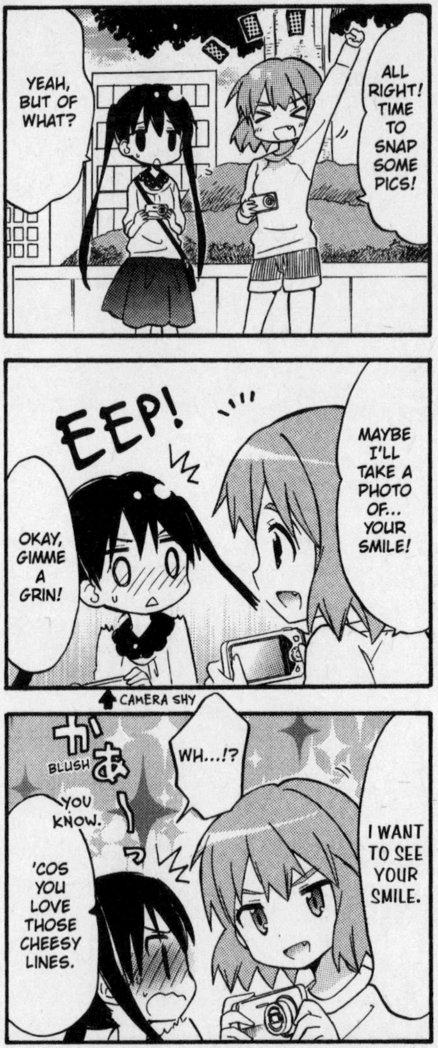
ALL RIGHT! TIME TO SNAP SOME PICS!
YEAH, BUT OF WHAT?
MAYBE I'LL TAKE A PHOTO OF... YOUR SMILE!
EEP!
OKAY, GIMME A GRIN!
CAMERA SHY
I WANT TO SEE YOUR SMILE.
WH...!?
かぁ～っ
BLUSH
YOU KNOW.
'COS YOU LOVE THOSE CHEESY LINES.
I WANT TO PROTECT YOUR SMILE!
NOOOOO!
YOU'RE TOTALLY MAKING FUN OF ME!

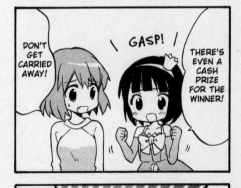

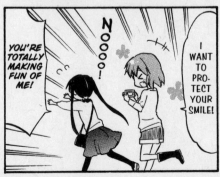

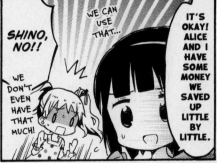

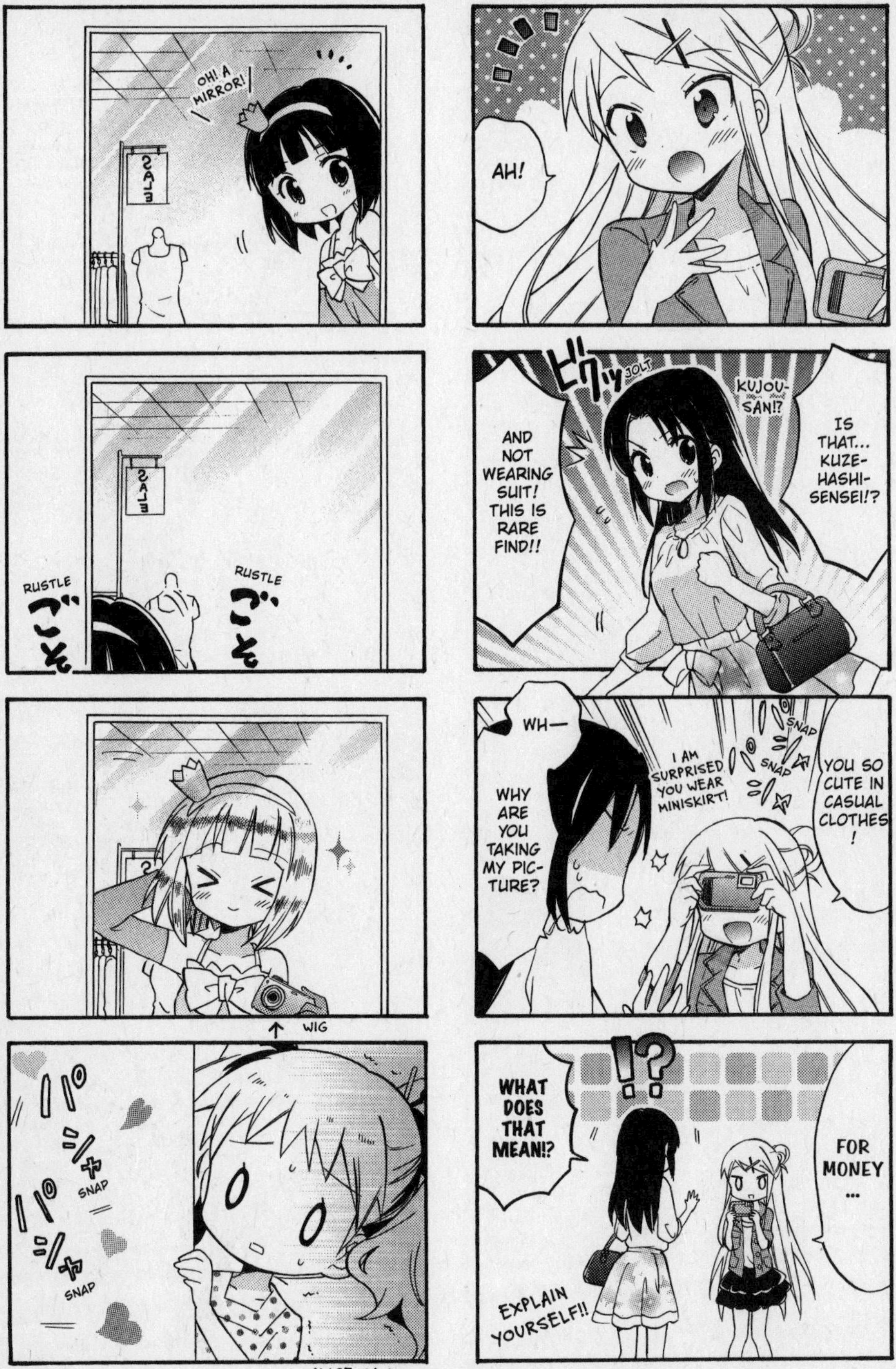
AH!
ビクッ
JOLT
IS THAT... KUZE-HASHI-SENSEI!?
KUJOU-SAN!?
AND NOT WEARING SUIT! THIS IS RARE FIND!!
YOU SO CUTE IN CASUAL CLOTHES!
SNAP
SNAP
I AM SURPRISED YOU WEAR MINISKIRT!
WH—
WHY ARE YOU TAKING MY PICTURE?
FOR MONEY...
!?
WHAT DOES THAT MEAN!?
EXPLAIN YOURSELF!!
OH! A MIRROR!
RUSTLE
ごそ
RUSTLE
ごそ
WIG
SNAP
SNAP
ALICE SAW.

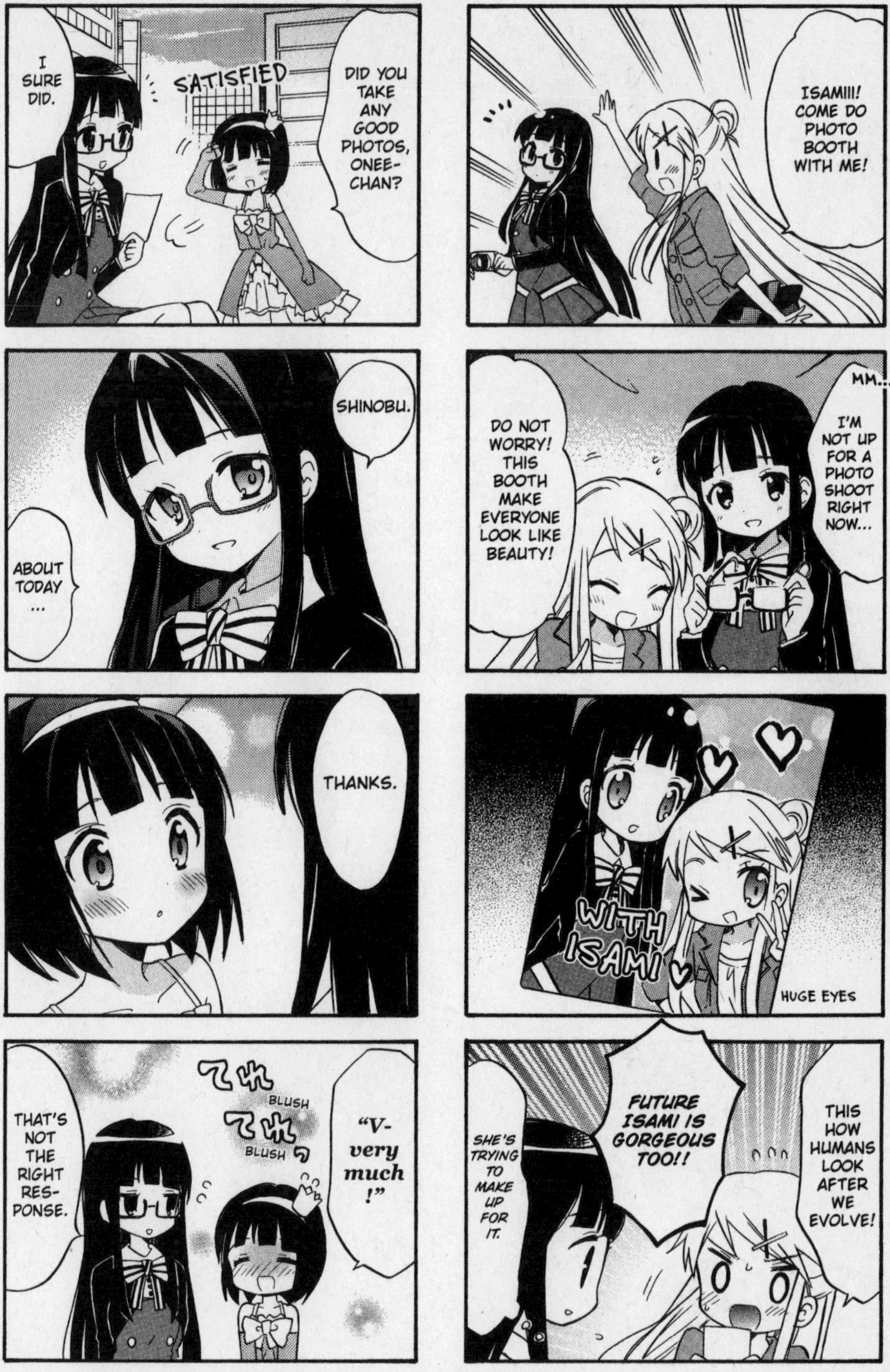
ISAMIII! COME DO PHOTO BOOTH WITH ME!
MM... I'M NOT UP FOR A PHOTO SHOOT RIGHT NOW...
DO NOT WORRY! THIS BOOTH MAKE EVERYONE LOOK LIKE BEAUTY!
WITH ISAMI
HUGE EYES
THIS HOW HUMANS LOOK AFTER WE EVOLVE!
FUTURE ISAMI IS GORGEOUS TOO!!
SHE'S TRYING TO MAKE UP FOR IT.
DID YOU TAKE ANY GOOD PHOTOS, ONEE-CHAN?
SATISFIED
I SURE DID.
SHINOBU.
ABOUT TODAY ...
THANKS.
"V-very much!"
てれ BLUSH
てれ BLUSH
THAT'S NOT THE RIGHT RES-PONSE.

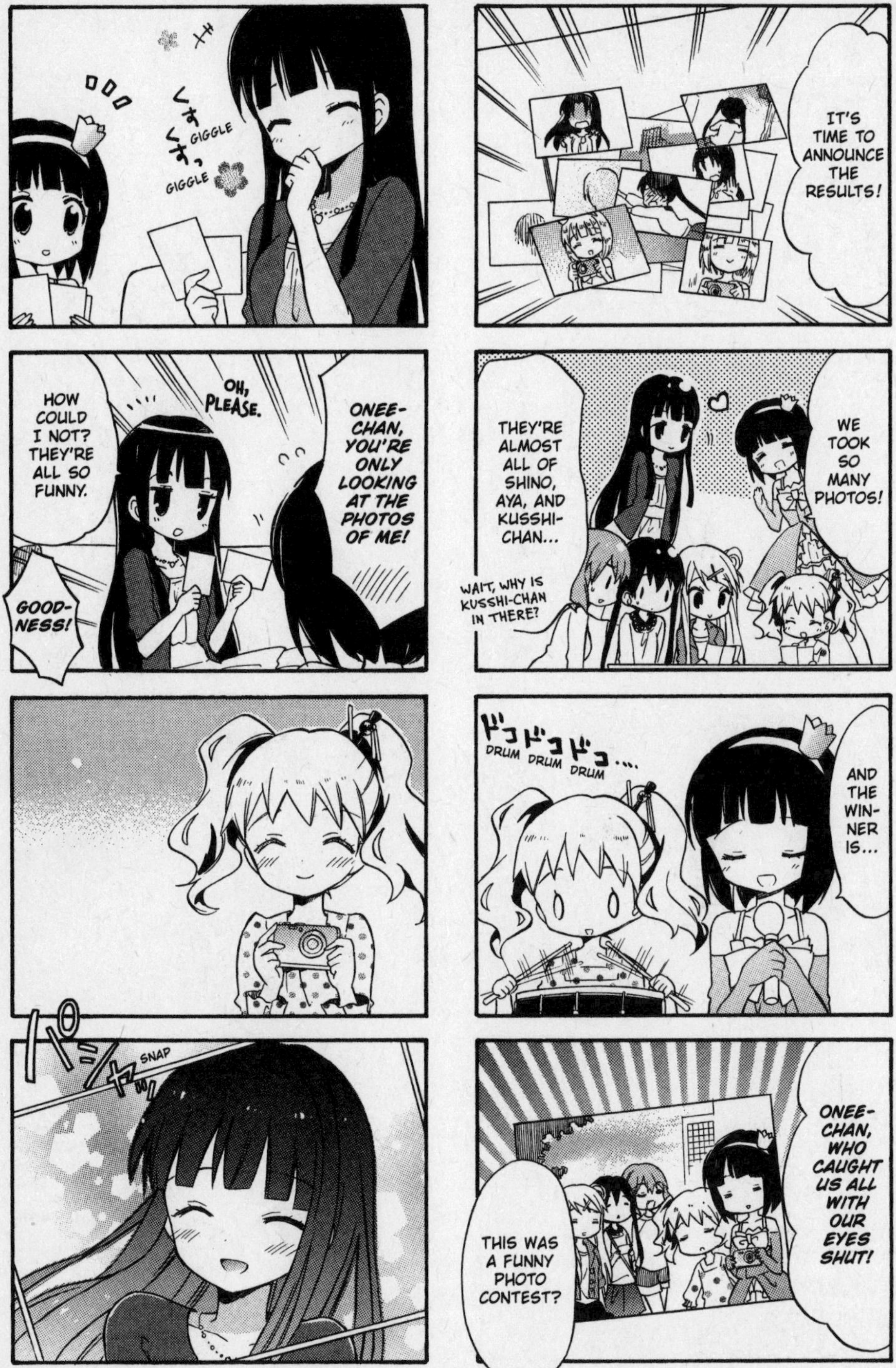
IT'S TIME TO ANNOUNCE THE RESULTS!
WE TOOK SO MANY PHOTOS!
THEY'RE ALMOST ALL OF SHINO, AYA, AND KUSSHI-CHAN...
WAIT, WHY IS KUSSHI-CHAN IN THERE?
AND THE WINNER IS...
DRUM DRUM DRUM
ONEE-CHAN, WHO CAUGHT US ALL WITH OUR EYES SHUT!
THIS WAS A FUNNY PHOTO CONTEST?
くすくすっ
GIGGLE GIGGLE
ONEE-CHAN, YOU'RE ONLY LOOKING AT THE PHOTOS OF ME!
OH, PLEASE.
HOW COULD I NOT? THEY'RE ALL SO FUNNY.
GOODNESS!
SNAP

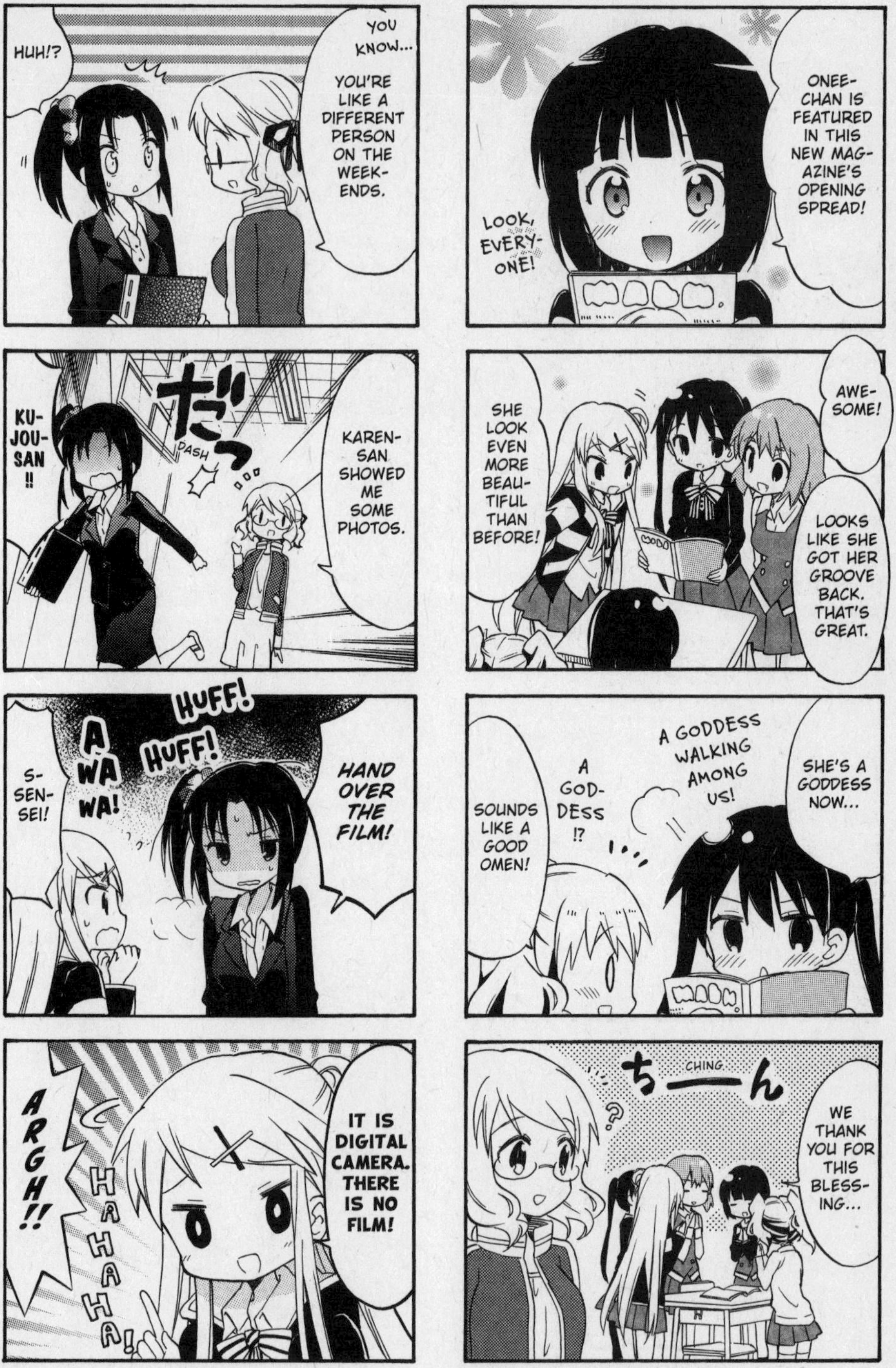
ONEE-CHAN IS FEATURED IN THIS NEW MAGAZINE'S OPENING SPREAD!
LOOK, EVERYONE!
AWESOME!
LOOKS LIKE SHE GOT HER GROOVE BACK. THAT'S GREAT.
SHE LOOK EVEN MORE BEAUTIFUL THAN BEFORE!
SHE'S A GODDESS NOW...
A GODDESS WALKING AMONG US!
A GODDESS!?
SOUNDS LIKE A GOOD OMEN!
ちーん
CHING
WE THANK YOU FOR THIS BLESSING...
YOU KNOW... YOU'RE LIKE A DIFFERENT PERSON ON THE WEEKENDS.
HUH!?
KAREN-SAN SHOWED ME SOME PHOTOS.
だっ
DASH
KUJOU-SAN!!
HAND OVER THE FILM!
HUFF! HUFF!
AWAWA!
S-SENSEI!
IT IS DIGITAL CAMERA. THERE IS NO FILM!
HAHAHAHA!
ARGH!!

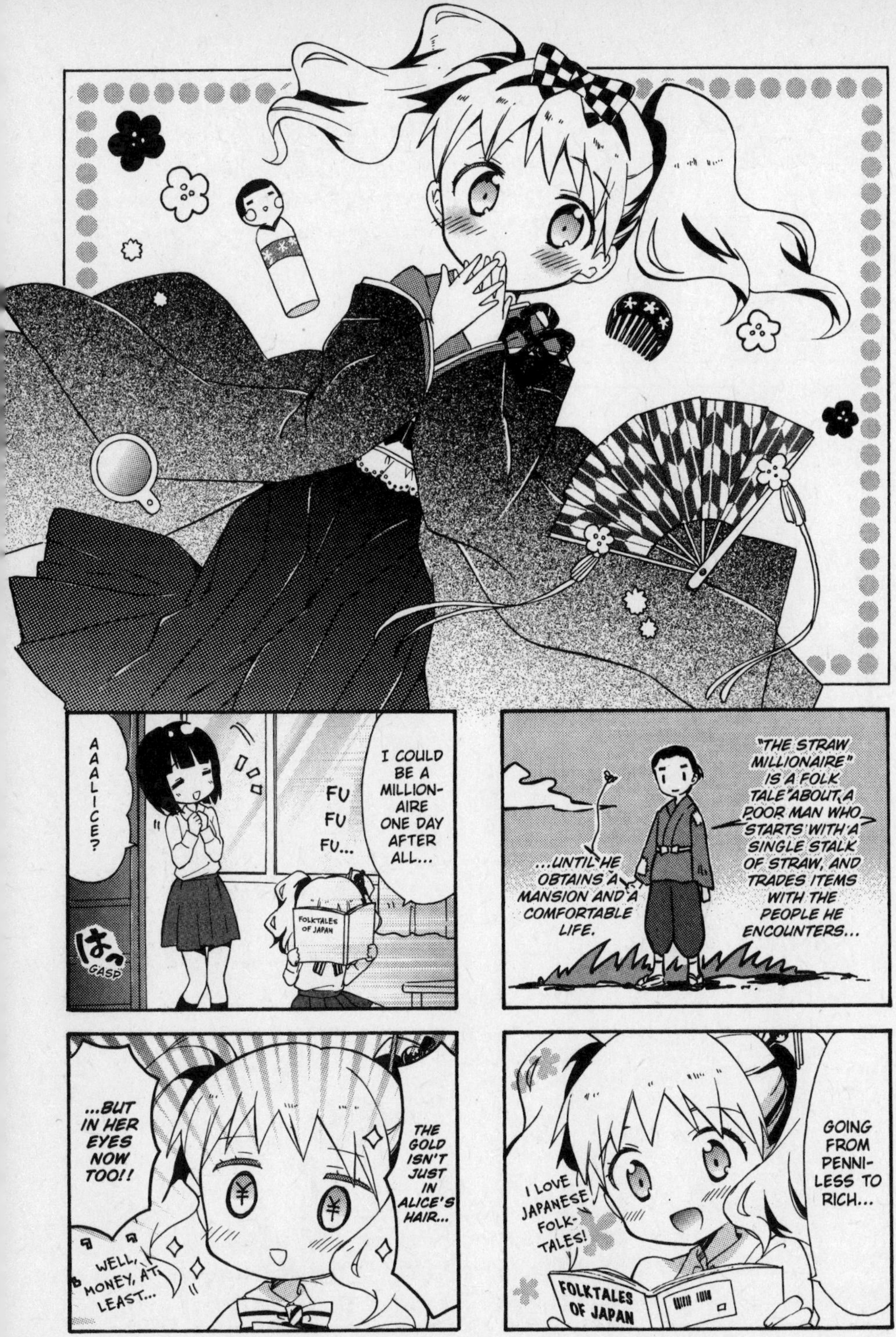
"THE STRAW MILLIONAIRE" IS A FOLK TALE ABOUT A POOR MAN WHO STARTS WITH A SINGLE STALK OF STRAW, AND TRADES ITEMS WITH THE PEOPLE HE ENCOUNTERS...
...UNTIL HE OBTAINS A MANSION AND A COMFORTABLE LIFE.
I COULD BE A MILLION-AIRE ONE DAY AFTER ALL...
FU FU FU...
FOLKTALES OF JAPAN
AAALICE?
はっ
GASP
GOING FROM PENNI-LESS TO RICH...
I LOVE JAPANESE FOLK-TALES!
FOLKTALES OF JAPAN
THE GOLD ISN'T JUST IN ALICE'S HAIR...
...BUT IN HER EYES NOW TOO!!
WELL, MONEY, AT LEAST...

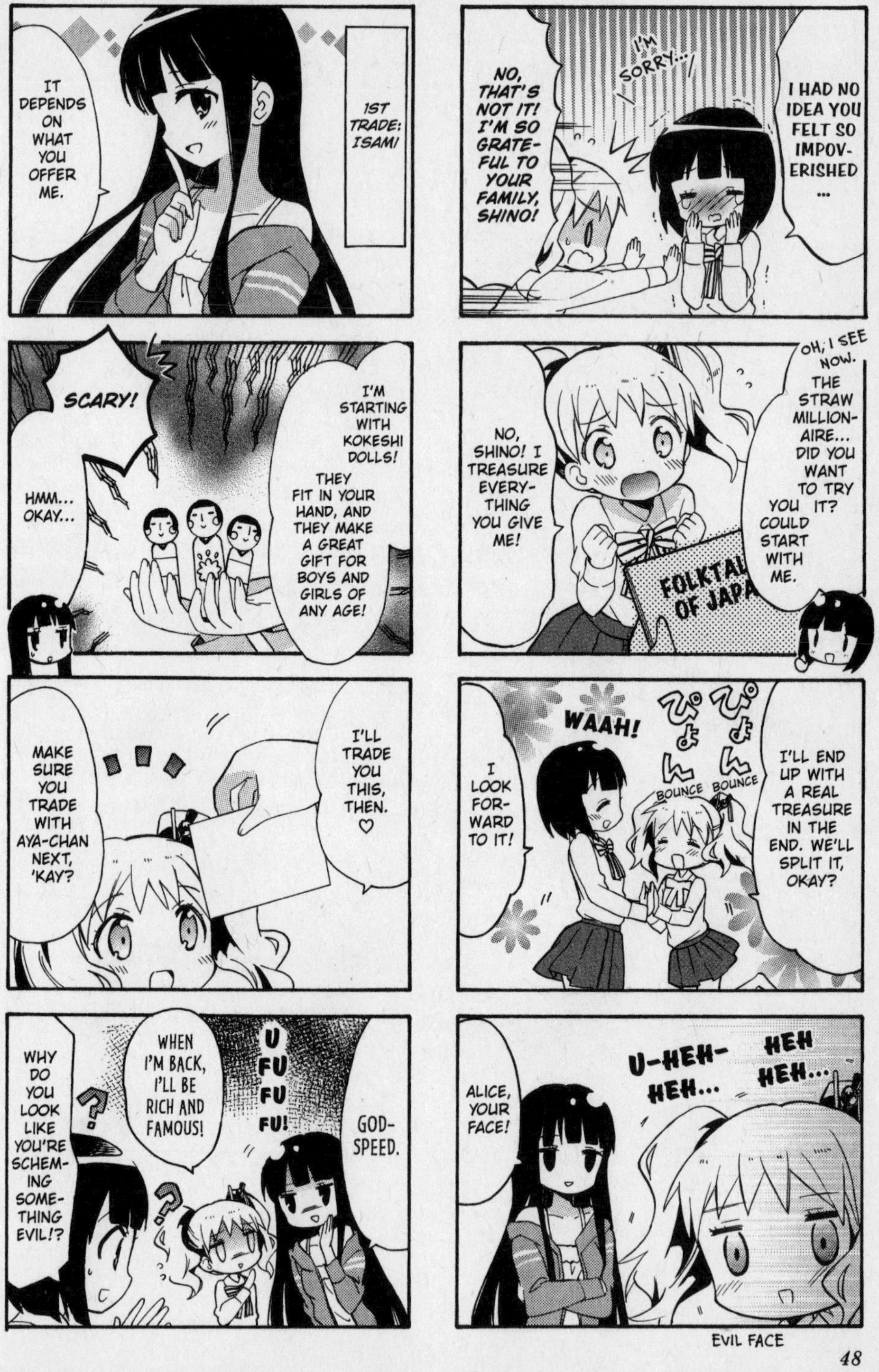
I HAD NO IDEA YOU FELT SO IMPOVERISHED...
I'M SORRY...
NO, THAT'S NOT IT! I'M SO GRATEFUL TO YOUR FAMILY, SHINO!
OH, I SEE NOW. THE STRAW MILLIONAIRE... DID YOU WANT TO TRY IT? YOU COULD START WITH ME.
NO, SHINO! I TREASURE EVERYTHING YOU GIVE ME!
FOLKTAL OF JAPA
I'LL END UP WITH A REAL TREASURE IN THE END. WE'LL SPLIT IT, OKAY?
ぴょん BOUNCE
ぴょん BOUNCE
WAAH!
I LOOK FORWARD TO IT!
HEH HEH...
U-HEH-HEH...
ALICE, YOUR FACE!
1ST TRADE: ISAMI
IT DEPENDS ON WHAT YOU OFFER ME.
I'M STARTING WITH KOKESHI DOLLS! THEY FIT IN YOUR HAND, AND THEY MAKE A GREAT GIFT FOR BOYS AND GIRLS OF ANY AGE!
SCARY!
HMM... OKAY...
I'LL TRADE YOU THIS, THEN. ♡
MAKE SURE YOU TRADE WITH AYA-CHAN NEXT, 'KAY?
GOD-SPEED.
UFUFUFU!
WHEN I'M BACK, I'LL BE RICH AND FAMOUS!
WHY DO YOU LOOK LIKE YOU'RE SCHEMING SOMETHING EVIL!?

EVIL FACE

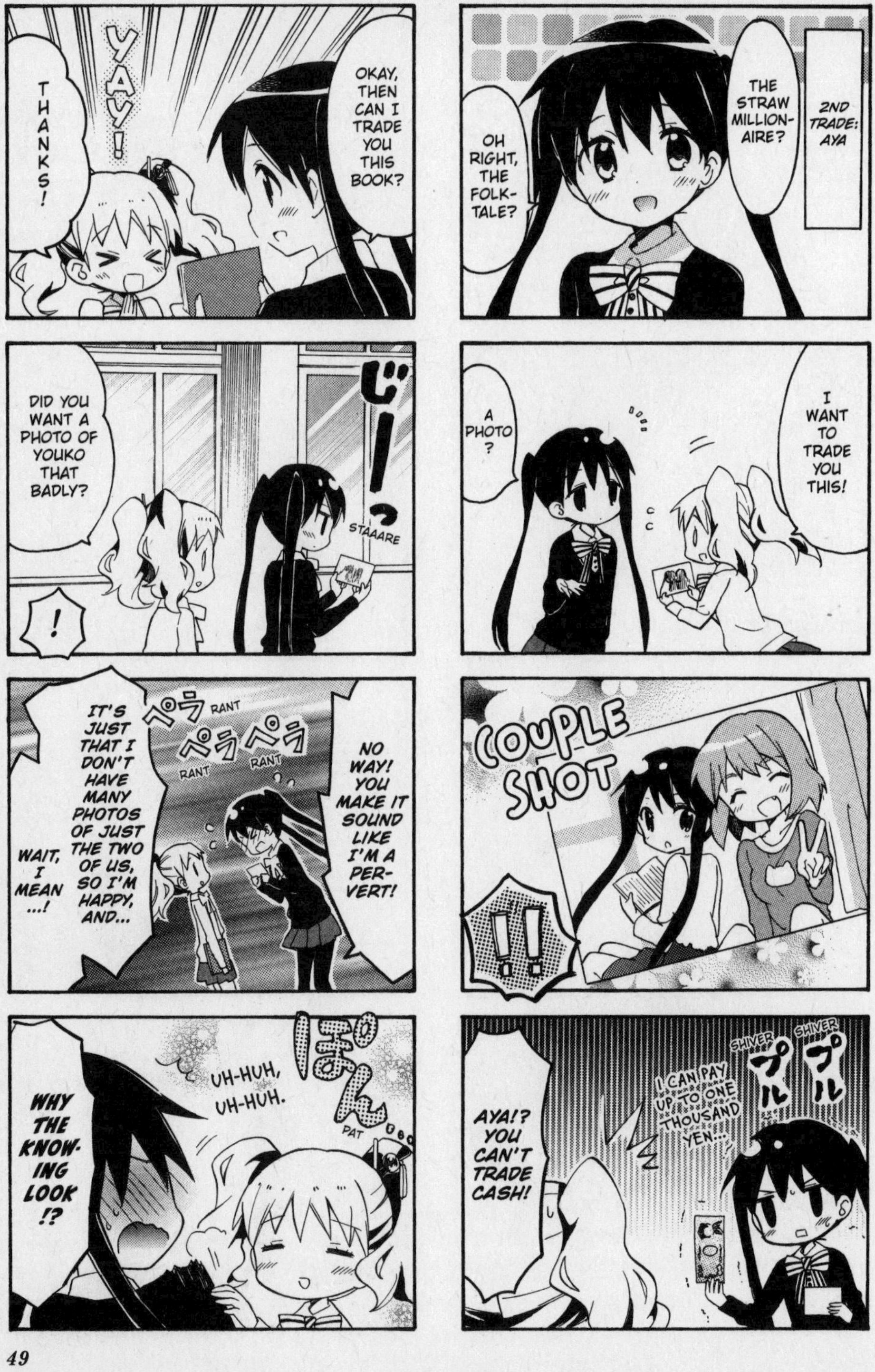
2ND TRADE: AYA
THE STRAW MILLION-AIRE?
OH RIGHT, THE FOLK-TALE?
OKAY, THEN CAN I TRADE YOU THIS BOOK?
YAY!
THANKS!
I WANT TO TRADE YOU THIS!
A PHOTO?
じーっ
STAAARE
DID YOU WANT A PHOTO OF YOUKO THAT BADLY?
!
COUPLE SHOT
!!
NO WAY! YOU MAKE IT SOUND LIKE I'M A PER-VERT!
ペラ RANT
ペラペラ RANT RANT
IT'S JUST THAT I DON'T HAVE MANY PHOTOS OF JUST THE TWO OF US, SO I'M HAPPY, AND...
WAIT, I MEAN ...!
プル SHIVER
プル SHIVER
I CAN PAY UP TO ONE THOUSAND YEN...
AYA!? YOU CAN'T TRADE CASH!
ぽん
PAT
UH-HUH, UH-HUH.
WHY THE KNOWING LOOK!?

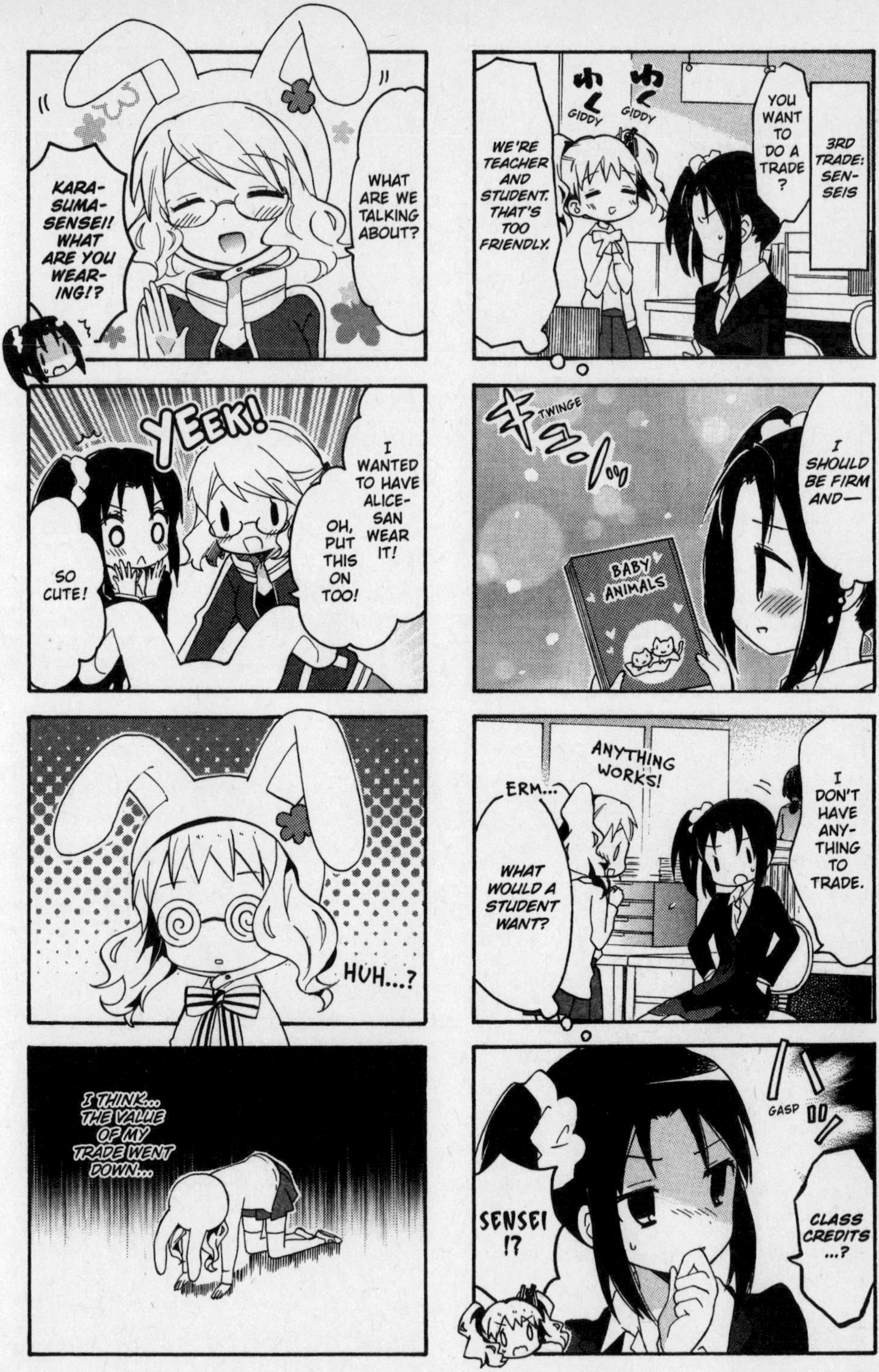
GIDDY
GIDDY
3RD TRADE: SEN-SEIS
YOU WANT TO DO A TRADE?
WE'RE TEACHER AND STUDENT. THAT'S TOO FRIENDLY.
TWINGE
I SHOULD BE FIRM AND—
BABY ANIMALS
I DON'T HAVE ANYTHING TO TRADE.
ANYTHING WORKS!
ERM...
WHAT WOULD A STUDENT WANT?
GASP
CLASS CREDITS ...?
SENSEI !?
WHAT ARE WE TALKING ABOUT?
KARA-SUMA-SENSEI!! WHAT ARE YOU WEAR-ING!?
YEEK!
I WANTED TO HAVE ALICE-SAN WEAR IT!
OH, PUT THIS ON TOO!
SO CUTE!
HUH...?
I THINK... THE VALUE OF MY TRADE WENT DOWN...

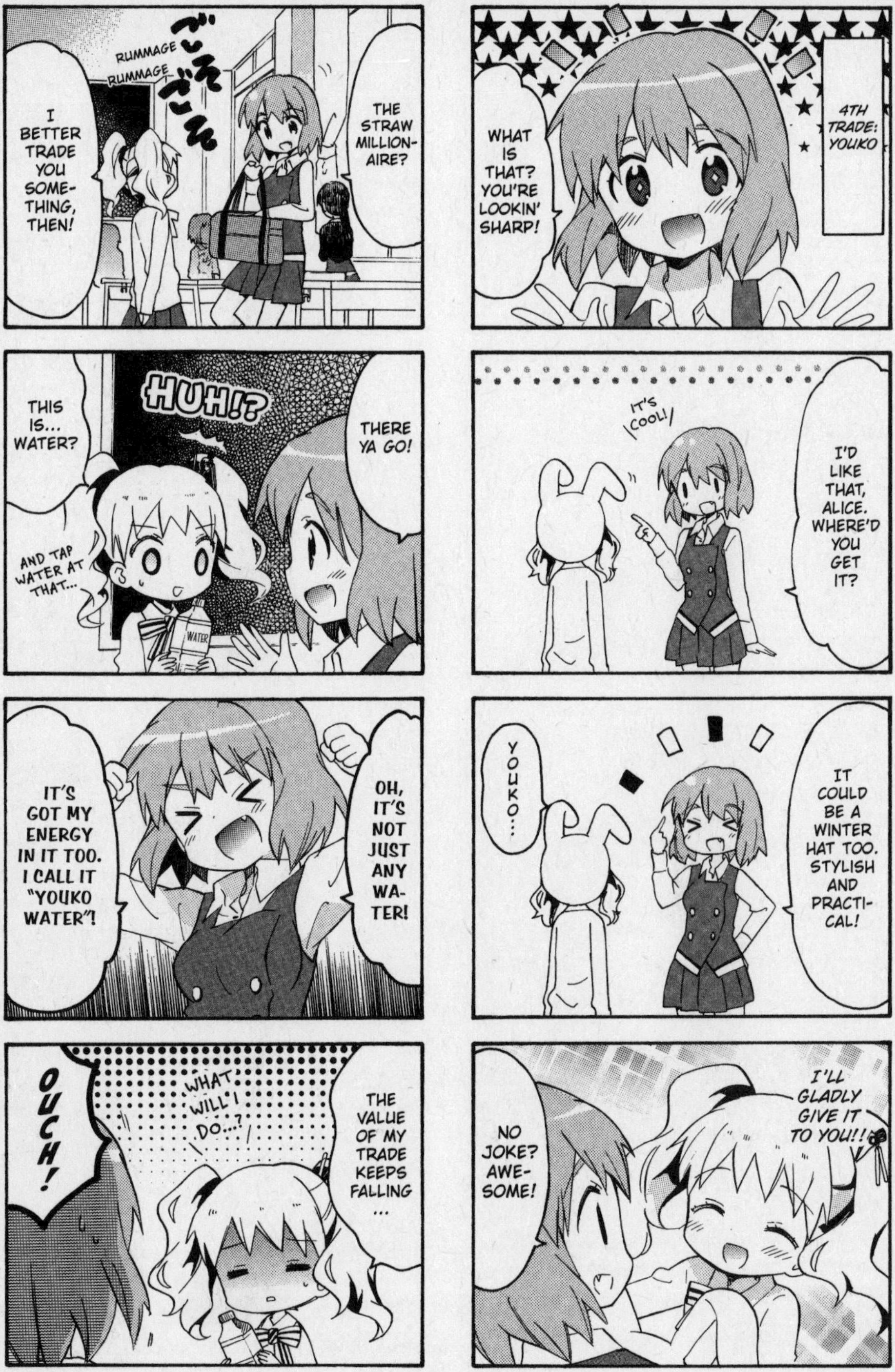
4TH TRADE: YOUKO
WHAT IS THAT? YOU'RE LOOKIN' SHARP!
I'D LIKE THAT, ALICE. WHERE'D YOU GET IT?
IT'S COOL!
IT COULD BE A WINTER HAT TOO. STYLISH AND PRACTICAL!
YOUKO...
I'LL GLADLY GIVE IT TO YOU!!
NO JOKE? AWESOME!
THE STRAW MILLIONAIRE?
ごそごそ
RUMMAGE RUMMAGE
I BETTER TRADE YOU SOMETHING, THEN!
THERE YA GO!
HUH!?
THIS IS... WATER?
WATER
AND TAP WATER AT THAT...
OH, IT'S NOT JUST ANY WATER!
IT'S GOT MY ENERGY IN IT TOO. I CALL IT "YOUKO WATER"!
THE VALUE OF MY TRADE KEEPS FALLING...
WHAT WILL I DO...?
OUCH!

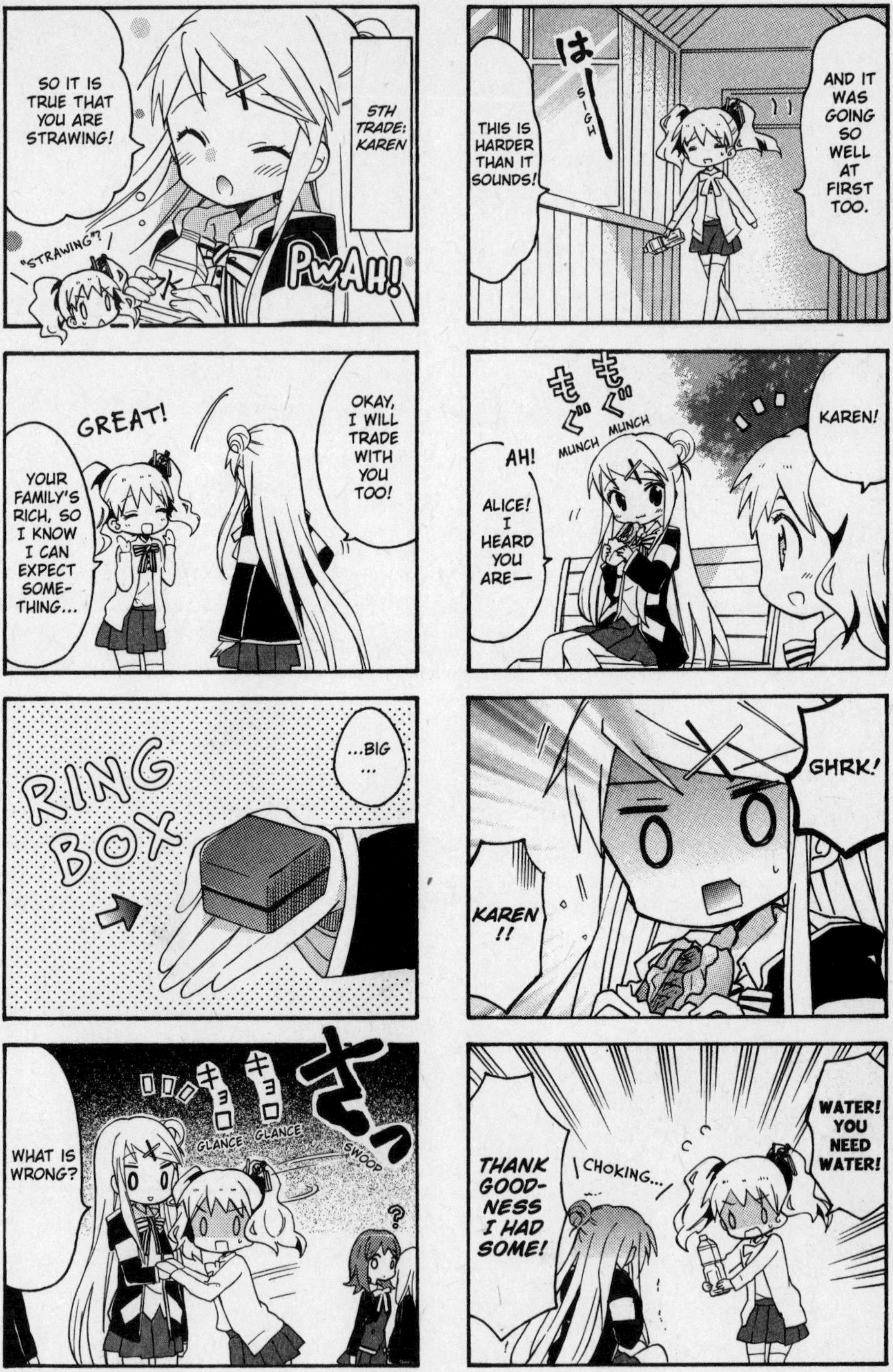
AND IT WAS GOING SO WELL AT FIRST TOO.
はー
SIGH
THIS IS HARDER THAN IT SOUNDS!
5TH TRADE: KAREN
SO IT IS TRUE THAT YOU ARE STRAWING!
PWAH!
"STRAWING"?
KAREN!
AH!
もぐ もぐ
MUNCH MUNCH
ALICE! I HEARD YOU ARE—
OKAY, I WILL TRADE WITH YOU TOO!
GREAT!
YOUR FAMILY'S RICH, SO I KNOW I CAN EXPECT SOMETHING...
GHRK!
KAREN!!
...BIG ...
RING BOX
WATER! YOU NEED WATER!
CHOKING...
THANK GOODNESS I HAD SOME!
さっ
SWOOP
キョロ キョロ
GLANCE GLANCE
WHAT IS WRONG?
?

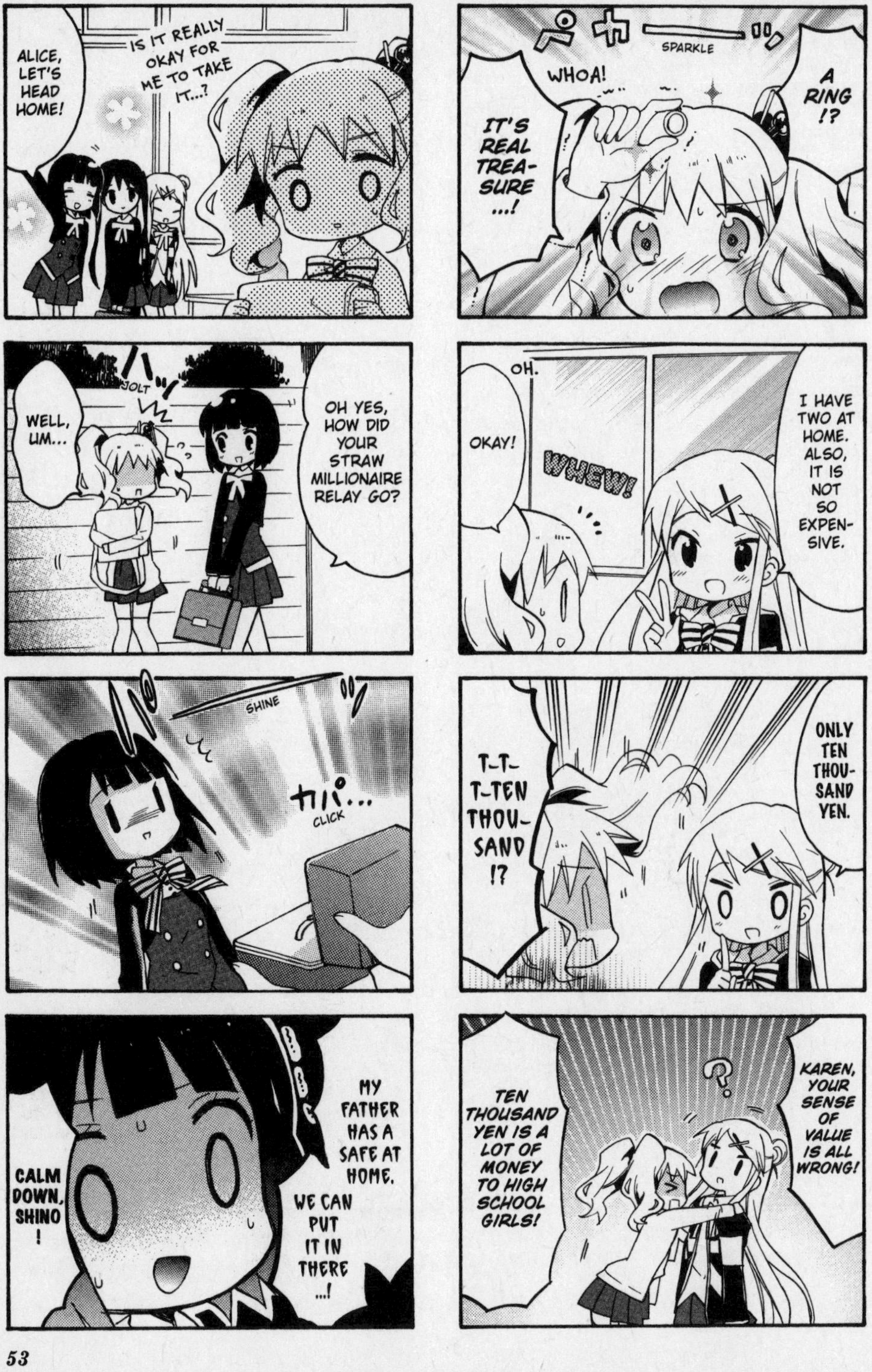
パカ――
A RING!?
SPARKLE
WHOA!
IT'S REAL TREASURE...!
I HAVE TWO AT HOME. ALSO, IT IS NOT SO EXPENSIVE.
WHEW!
OH.
OKAY!
ONLY TEN THOUSAND YEN.
T-T-T-TEN THOUSAND!?
KAREN, YOUR SENSE OF VALUE IS ALL WRONG!
TEN THOUSAND YEN IS A LOT OF MONEY TO HIGH SCHOOL GIRLS!
IS IT REALLY OKAY FOR ME TO TAKE IT...?
ALICE, LET'S HEAD HOME!
OH YES, HOW DID YOUR STRAW MILLIONAIRE RELAY GO?
JOLT
WELL, UM...
SHINE
カパ...
CLICK
MY FATHER HAS A SAFE AT HOME.
WE CAN PUT IT IN THERE...!
CALM DOWN, SHINO!

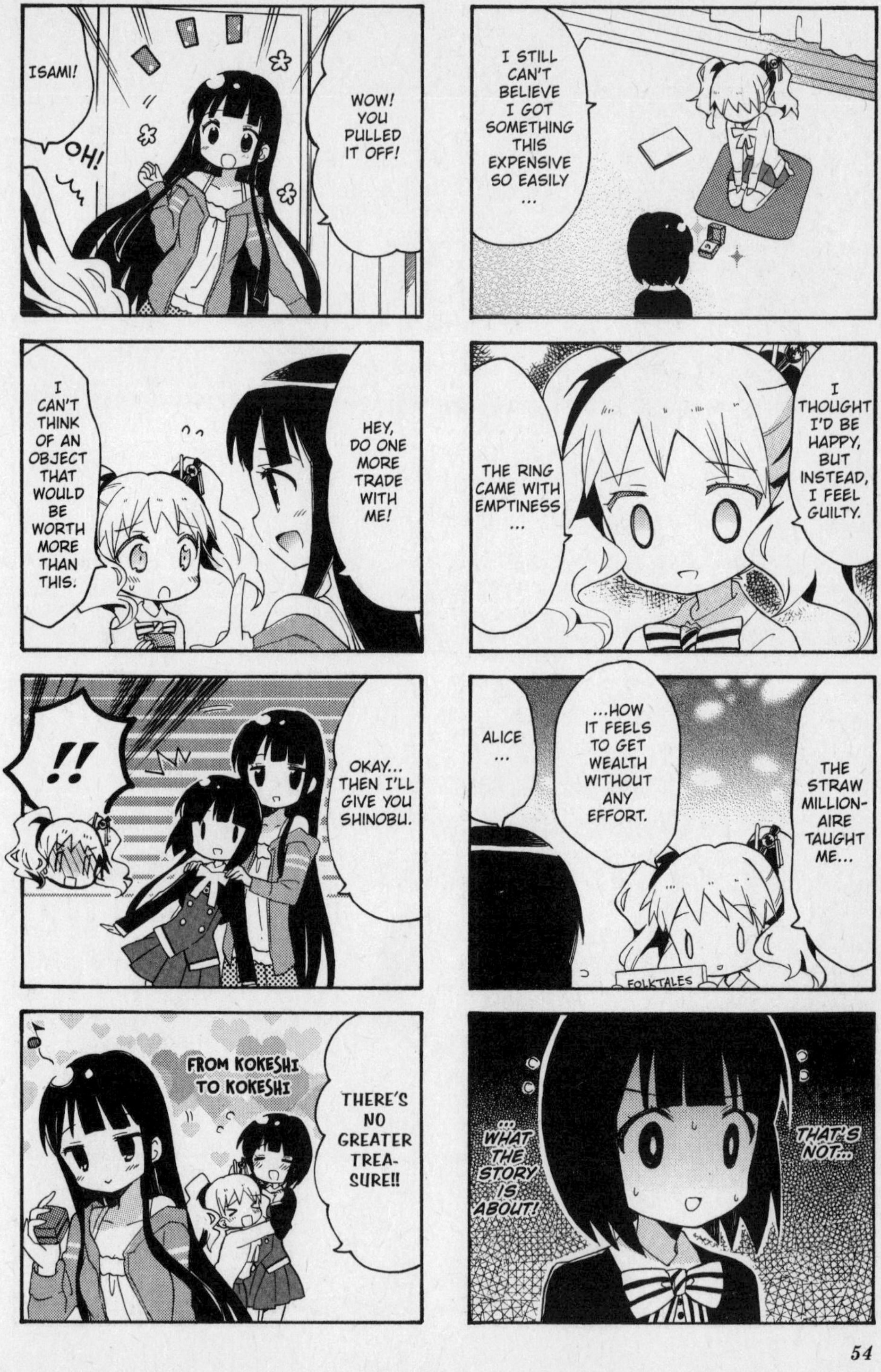
I STILL CAN'T BELIEVE I GOT SOMETHING THIS EXPENSIVE SO EASILY ...
WOW! YOU PULLED IT OFF!
ISAMI!
OH!
I THOUGHT I'D BE HAPPY, BUT INSTEAD, I FEEL GUILTY.
THE RING CAME WITH EMPTINESS ...
HEY, DO ONE MORE TRADE WITH ME!
I CAN'T THINK OF AN OBJECT THAT WOULD BE WORTH MORE THAN THIS.
THE STRAW MILLION-AIRE TAUGHT ME...
...HOW IT FEELS TO GET WEALTH WITHOUT ANY EFFORT.
ALICE ...
FOLKTALES
OKAY... THEN I'LL GIVE YOU SHINOBU.
!!
THAT'S NOT...
...WHAT THE STORY IS ABOUT!
THERE'S NO GREATER TREA-SURE!!
FROM KOKESHI TO KOKESHI

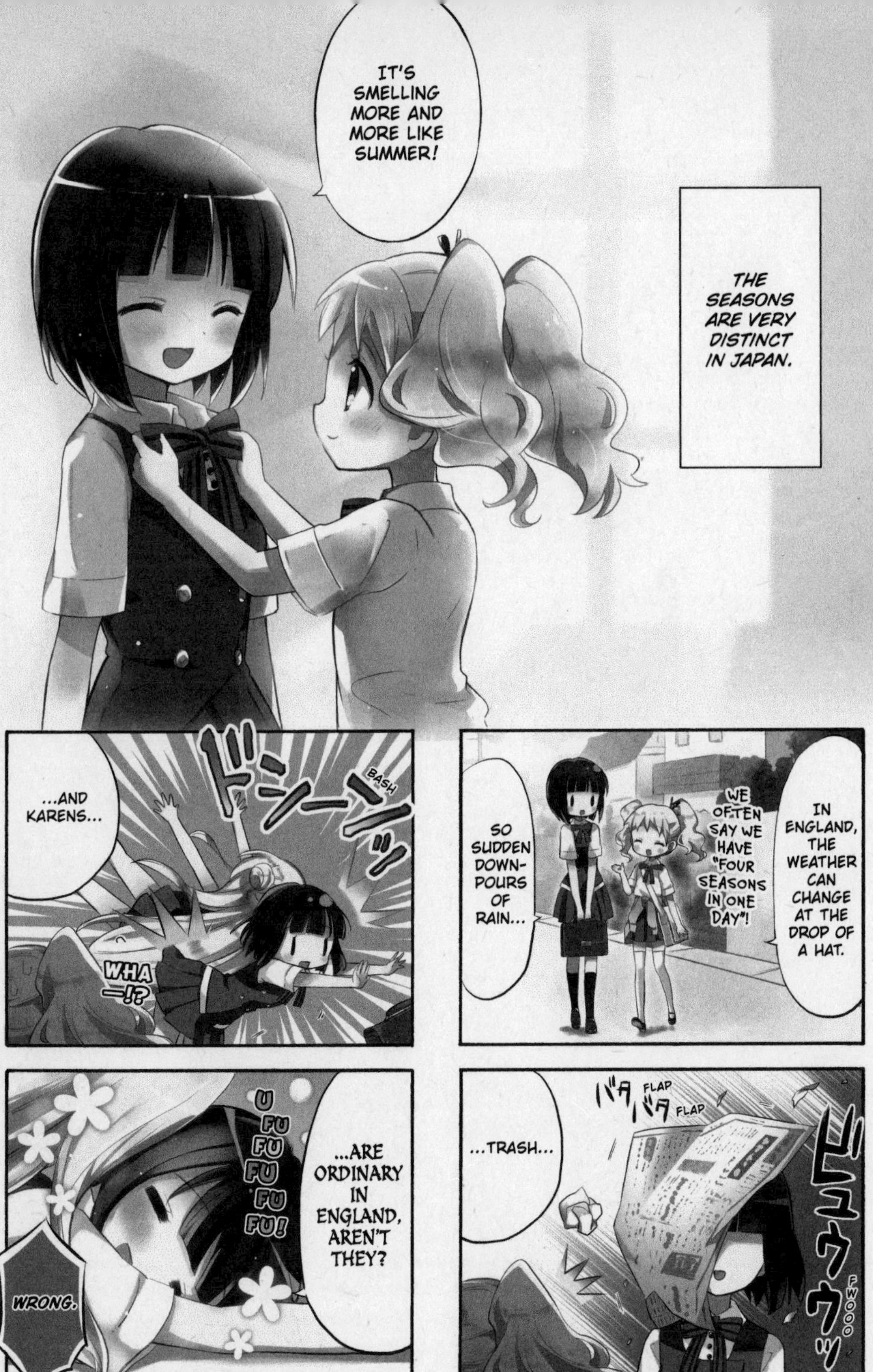
IT'S SMELLING MORE AND MORE LIKE SUMMER!
THE SEASONS ARE VERY DISTINCT IN JAPAN.
IN ENGLAND, THE WEATHER CAN CHANGE AT THE DROP OF A HAT.
WE OFTEN SAY WE HAVE "FOUR SEASONS IN ONE DAY"!
SO SUDDEN DOWN-POURS OF RAIN...
...AND KARENS...
ドーン
BASH
WHA—!?
...TRASH...
バタバタ
FLAP FLAP
ビュウウッ
FWOOO
...ARE ORDINARY IN ENGLAND, AREN'T THEY?
UFUFUFUFUFUFU!
WRONG.

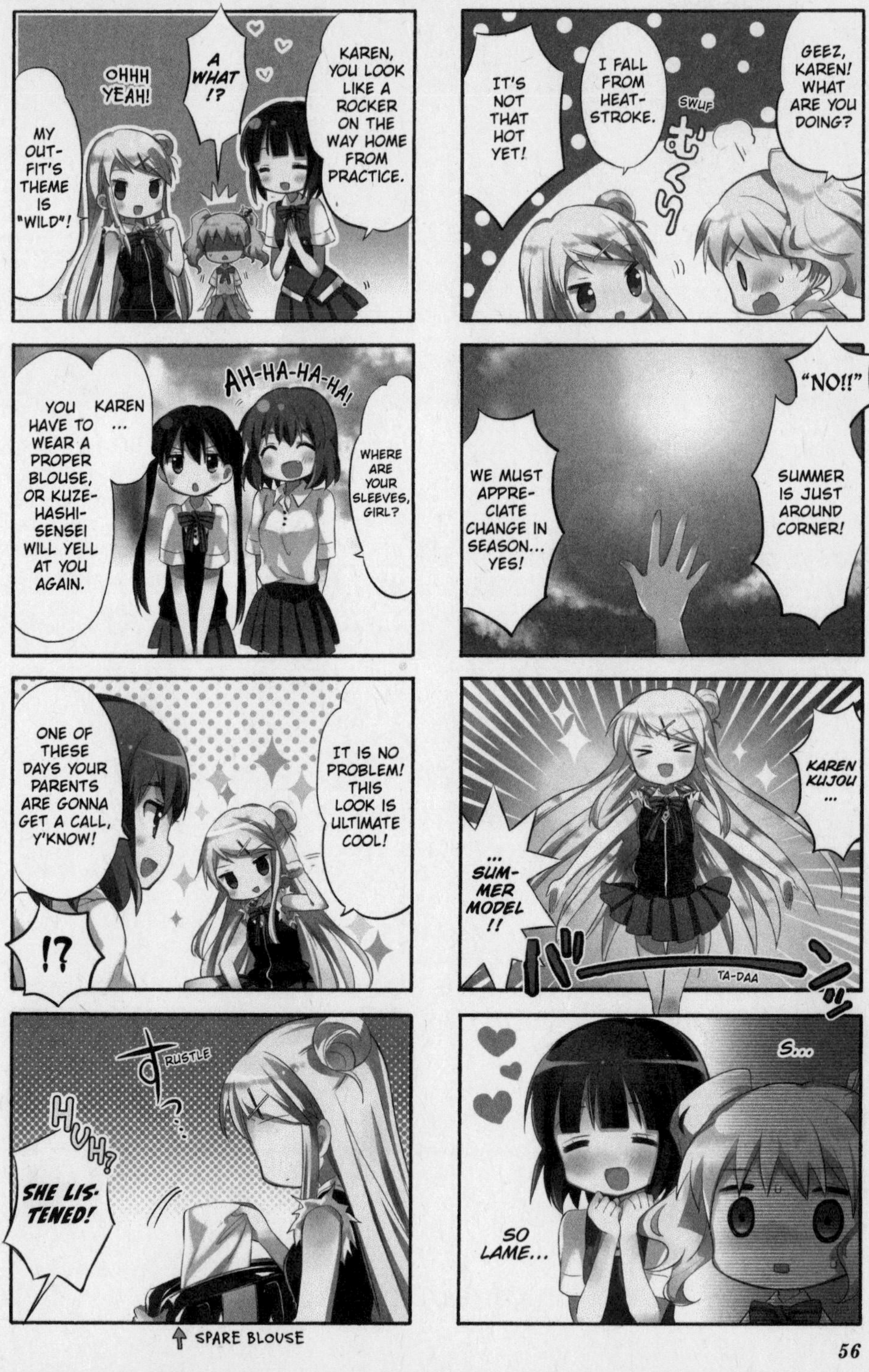
GEEZ, KAREN! WHAT ARE YOU DOING?
SWUF
I FALL FROM HEAT-STROKE.
IT'S NOT THAT HOT YET!
"NO!!"
SUMMER IS JUST AROUND CORNER!
WE MUST APPRE-CIATE CHANGE IN SEASON... YES!
KAREN KUJOU ...
... SUM-MER MODEL !!
TA-DAA
S...
SO LAME...
KAREN, YOU LOOK LIKE A ROCKER ON THE WAY HOME FROM PRACTICE.
A WHAT !?
OHHH YEAH!
MY OUT-FIT'S THEME IS "WILD"!
AH-HA-HA-HA!
WHERE ARE YOUR SLEEVES, GIRL?
KAREN ...
YOU HAVE TO WEAR A PROPER BLOUSE, OR KUZE-HASHI-SENSEI WILL YELL AT YOU AGAIN.
IT IS NO PROBLEM! THIS LOOK IS ULTIMATE COOL!
ONE OF THESE DAYS YOUR PARENTS ARE GONNA GET A CALL, Y'KNOW!
!?
RUSTLE
HUH?
SHE LIS-TENED!
↑ SPARE BLOUSE

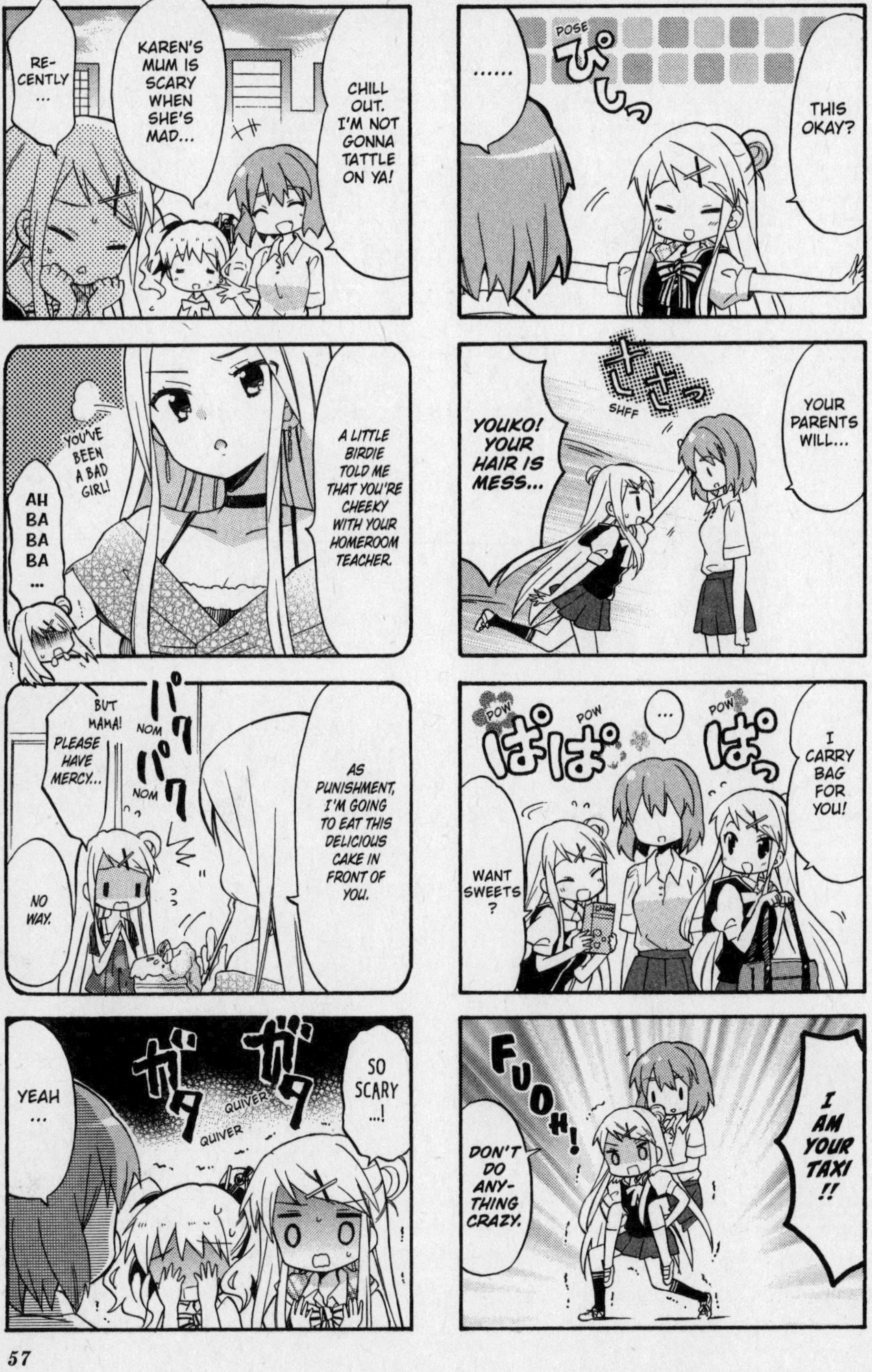
THIS OKAY?
ぴしっ
POSE
......
YOUR PARENTS WILL...
さささっ
SHFF
YOUKO! YOUR HAIR IS MESS...
I CARRY BAG FOR YOU!
ぱっ
POW
...
ぱぱ
POW
POW
WANT SWEETS?
I AM YOUR TAXI!!
FUOH!
DON'T DO ANY-THING CRAZY.
CHILL OUT. I'M NOT GONNA TATTLE ON YA!
KAREN'S MUM IS SCARY WHEN SHE'S MAD...
RE-CENTLY...
A LITTLE BIRDIE TOLD ME THAT YOU'RE CHEEKY WITH YOUR HOMEROOM TEACHER.
YOU'VE BEEN A BAD GIRL!
AH BA BA BA...
AS PUNISHMENT, I'M GOING TO EAT THIS DELICIOUS CAKE IN FRONT OF YOU.
パクパク
NOM
NOM
BUT MAMA! PLEASE HAVE MERCY...
NO WAY.
SO SCARY...!
ガタガタ
QUIVER
QUIVER
YEAH...

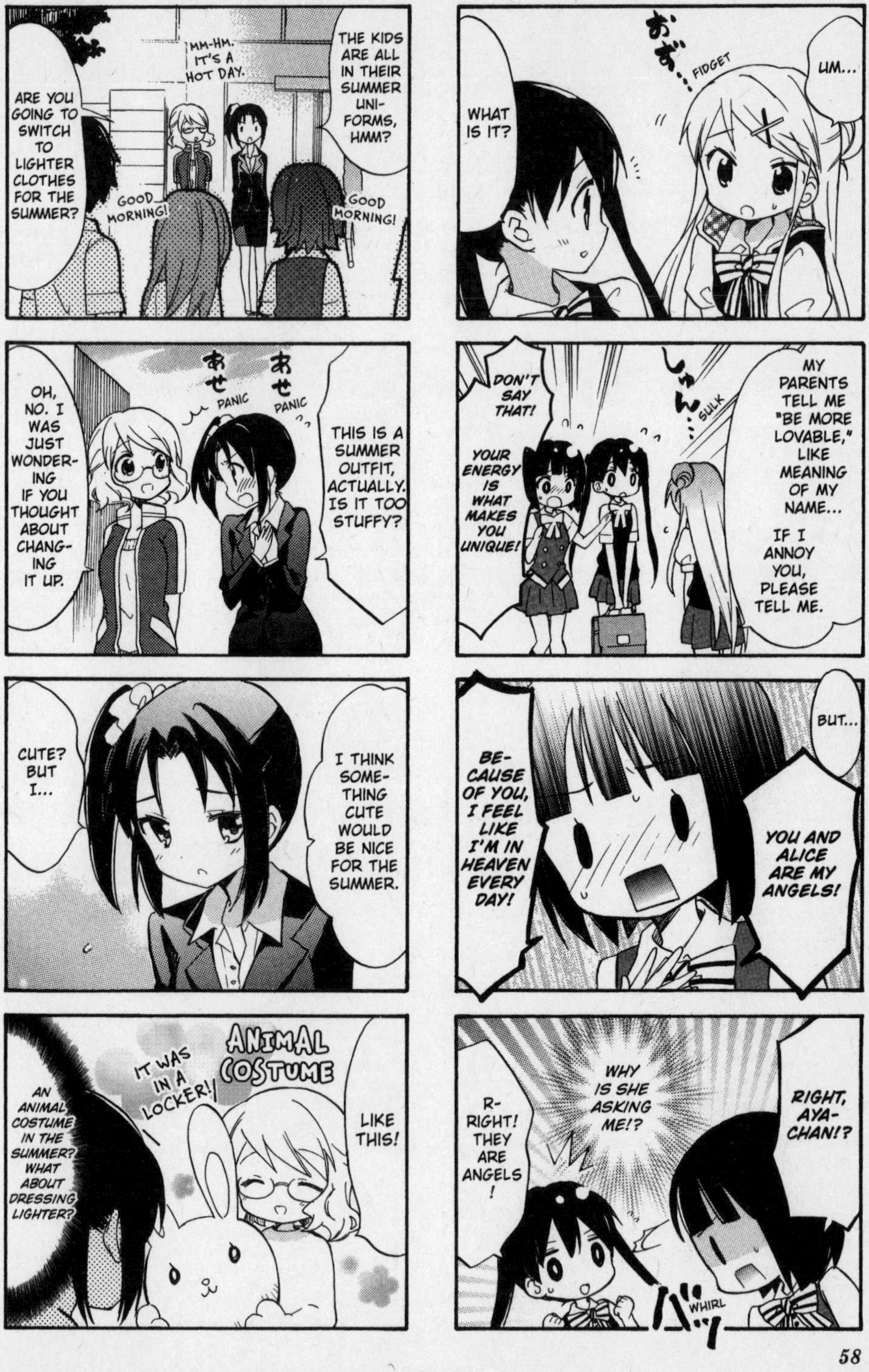
UM...
おず...
FIDGET
WHAT IS IT?
MY PARENTS TELL ME "BE MORE LOVABLE," LIKE MEANING OF MY NAME...
IF I ANNOY YOU, PLEASE TELL ME.
しゅん...
SULK
DON'T SAY THAT!
YOUR ENERGY IS WHAT MAKES YOU UNIQUE!
BUT...
YOU AND ALICE ARE MY ANGELS!
BE-CAUSE OF YOU, I FEEL LIKE I'M IN HEAVEN EVERY DAY!
RIGHT, AYA-CHAN!?
WHY IS SHE ASKING ME!?
R-RIGHT! THEY ARE ANGELS!
バッ
WHIRL
THE KIDS ARE ALL IN THEIR SUMMER UNI-FORMS, HMM?
MM-HM. IT'S A HOT DAY.
ARE YOU GOING TO SWITCH TO LIGHTER CLOTHES FOR THE SUMMER?
GOOD MORNING!
GOOD MORNING!
THIS IS A SUMMER OUTFIT, ACTUALLY. IS IT TOO STUFFY?
あせ
PANIC
あせ
PANIC
OH, NO. I WAS JUST WONDER-ING IF YOU THOUGHT ABOUT CHANG-ING IT UP.
I THINK SOME-THING CUTE WOULD BE NICE FOR THE SUMMER.
CUTE? BUT I...
LIKE THIS!
ANIMAL COSTUME
IT WAS IN A LOCKER!
AN ANIMAL COSTUME IN THE SUMMER? WHAT ABOUT DRESSING LIGHTER?

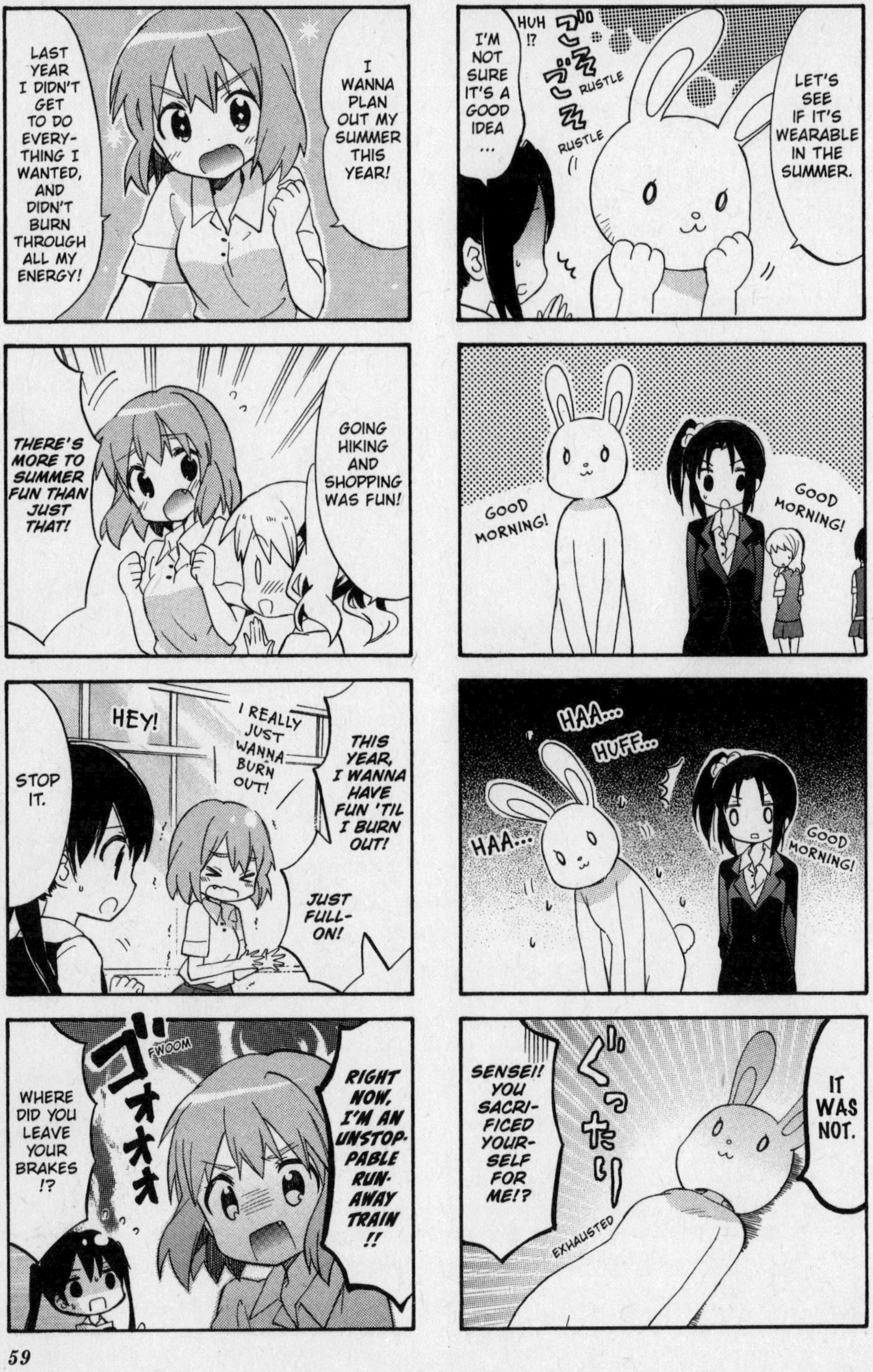
LET'S SEE IF IT'S WEARABLE IN THE SUMMER.
ごそごそ
RUSTLE
RUSTLE
HUH !?
I'M NOT SURE IT'S A GOOD IDEA ...
GOOD MORNING!
GOOD MORNING!
GOOD MORNING!
HUFF...
HAA...
HAA...
IT WAS NOT.
ぐったり
EXHAUSTED
SENSEI! YOU SACRI-FICED YOUR-SELF FOR ME!?
I WANNA PLAN OUT MY SUMMER THIS YEAR!
LAST YEAR I DIDN'T GET TO DO EVERY-THING I WANTED, AND DIDN'T BURN THROUGH ALL MY ENERGY!
GOING HIKING AND SHOPPING WAS FUN!
THERE'S MORE TO SUMMER FUN THAN JUST THAT!
THIS YEAR, I WANNA HAVE FUN 'TIL I BURN OUT!
JUST FULL-ON!
I REALLY JUST WANNA BURN OUT!
HEY!
STOP IT.
RIGHT NOW, I'M AN UNSTOP-PABLE RUN-AWAY TRAIN !!
ゴォォォ
FWOOM
WHERE DID YOU LEAVE YOUR BRAKES !?

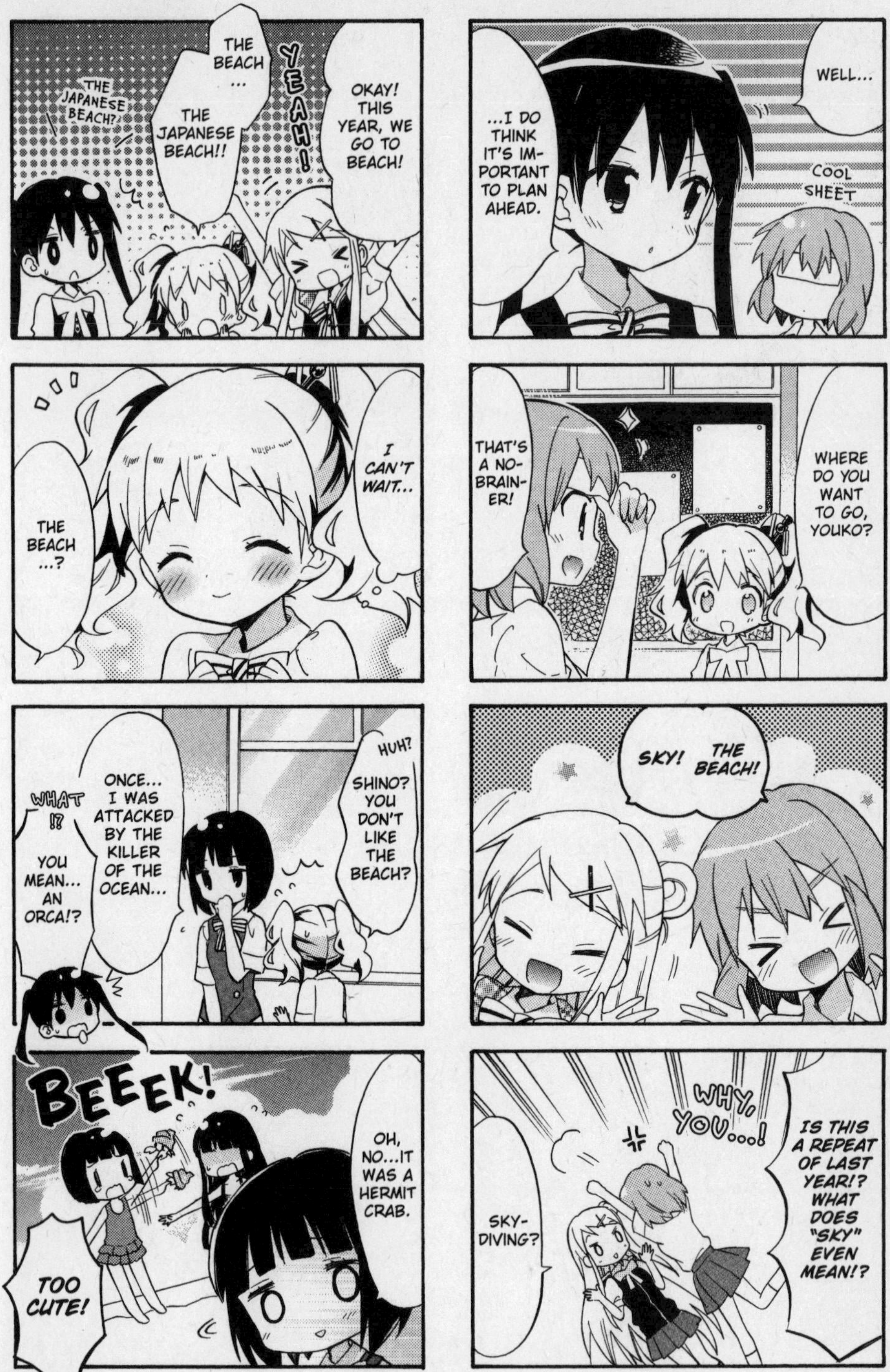
WELL...
COOL SHEET
...I DO THINK IT'S IMPORTANT TO PLAN AHEAD.
OKAY! THIS YEAR, WE GO TO BEACH!
YEAH!
THE BEACH... THE JAPANESE BEACH!!
THE JAPANESE BEACH?
WHERE DO YOU WANT TO GO, YOUKO?
THAT'S A NO-BRAINER!
I CAN'T WAIT...
THE BEACH...?
THE BEACH!
SKY!
HUH?
SHINO? YOU DON'T LIKE THE BEACH?
ONCE... I WAS ATTACKED BY THE KILLER OF THE OCEAN...
WHAT!?
YOU MEAN... AN ORCA!?
IS THIS A REPEAT OF LAST YEAR!? WHAT DOES "SKY" EVEN MEAN!?
WHY, YOU...!
SKY-DIVING?
OH, NO...IT WAS A HERMIT CRAB.
BEEEK!
TOO CUTE!

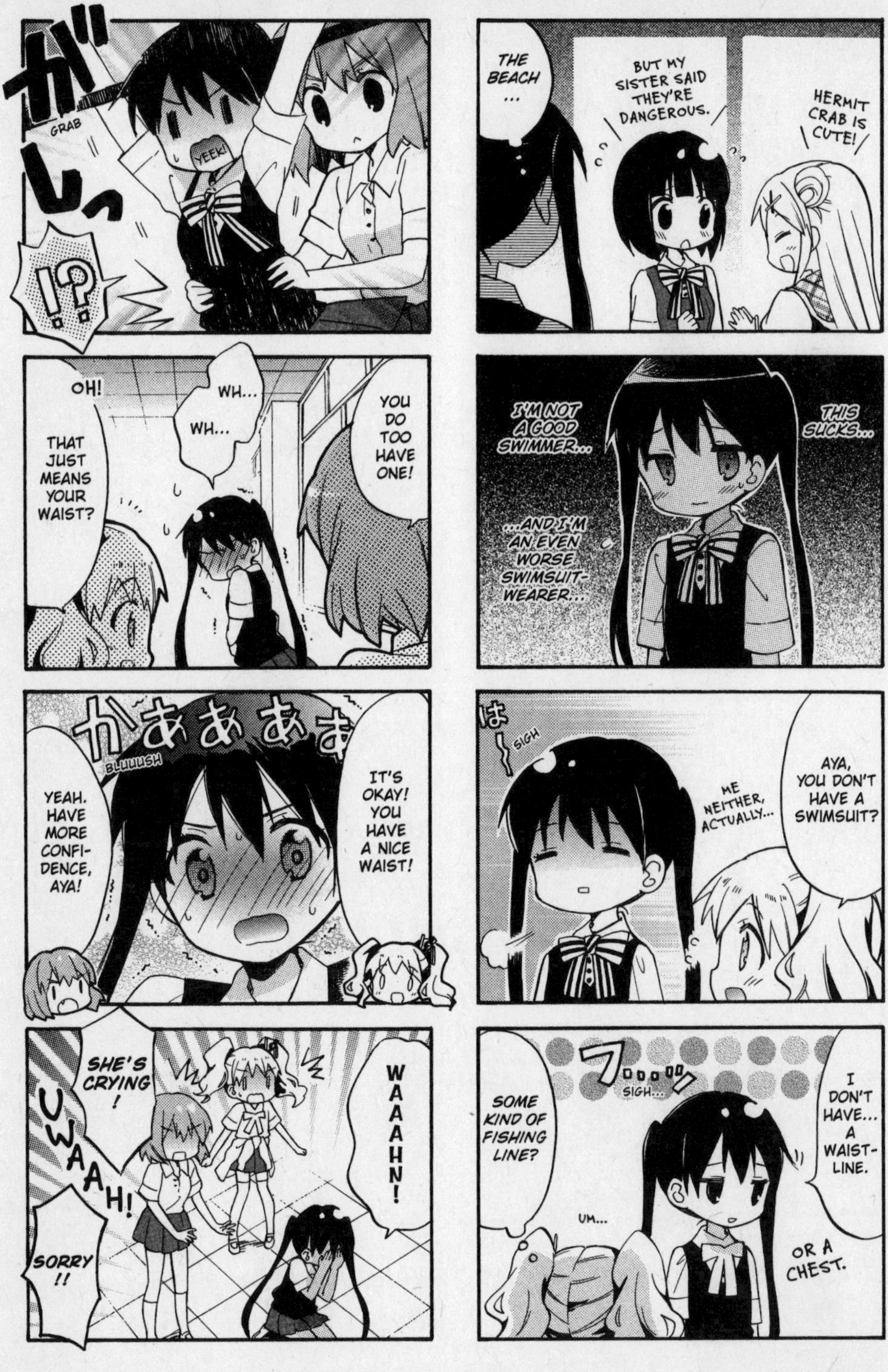
HERMIT CRAB IS CUTE!
BUT MY SISTER SAID THEY'RE DANGEROUS.
THE BEACH ...
THIS SUCKS...
I'M NOT A GOOD SWIMMER...
...AND I'M AN EVEN WORSE SWIMSUIT-WEARER...
AYA, YOU DON'T HAVE A SWIMSUIT?
ME NEITHER, ACTUALLY...
は～
SIGH
I DON'T HAVE... A WAIST-LINE.
SIGH...
SOME KIND OF FISHING LINE?
UM...
OR A CHEST.
がしっ
GRAB
YEEK!
!?
YOU DO TOO HAVE ONE!
WH...
WH...
OH!
THAT JUST MEANS YOUR WAIST?
IT'S OKAY! YOU HAVE A NICE WAIST!
かあああああ
BLUUUSH
YEAH. HAVE MORE CONFI-DENCE, AYA!
WAAAAHN!
SHE'S CRYING!
UWAAAH!
SORRY!!

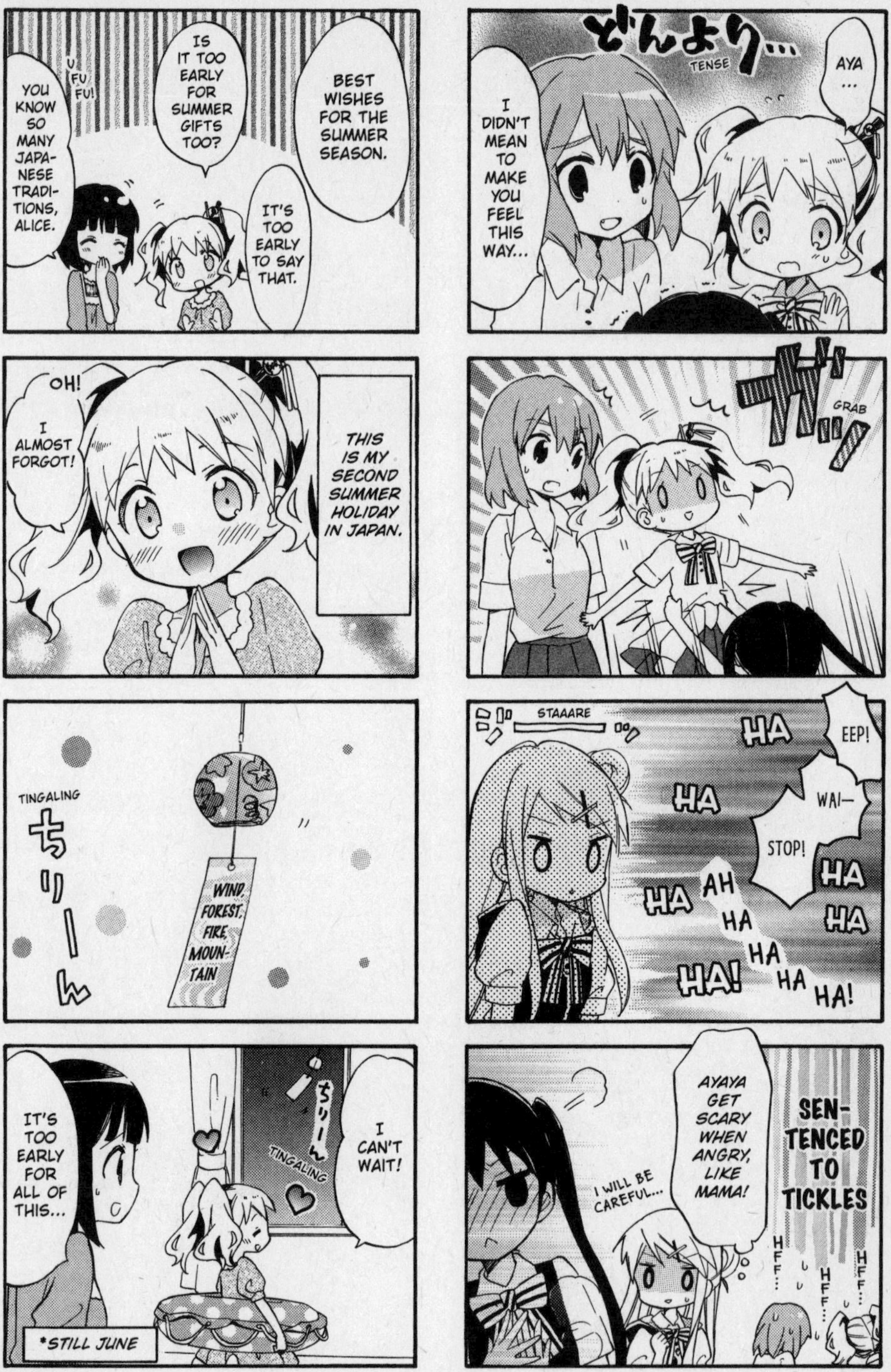

どんより…
TENSE
AYA…
I DIDN'T MEAN TO MAKE YOU FEEL THIS WAY…
GRAB
STAAARE
EEP!
HA
WAI— STOP!
HA
HA
HA
HA
AH HA HA HA HA HA!
HA
HA!
AYAYA GET SCARY WHEN ANGRY, LIKE MAMA!
SENTENCED TO TICKLES
I WILL BE CAREFUL…
HFF…
HFF…
HFF…
BEST WISHES FOR THE SUMMER SEASON.
IS IT TOO EARLY FOR SUMMER GIFTS TOO?
IT'S TOO EARLY TO SAY THAT.
UFUFU!
YOU KNOW SO MANY JAPANESE TRADITIONS, ALICE.
THIS IS MY SECOND SUMMER HOLIDAY IN JAPAN.
OH! I ALMOST FORGOT!
TINGALING
ちりーん
WIND, FOREST, FIRE, MOUNTAIN
I CAN'T WAIT!
ちりーん
TINGALING
IT'S TOO EARLY FOR ALL OF THIS…
*STILL JUNE

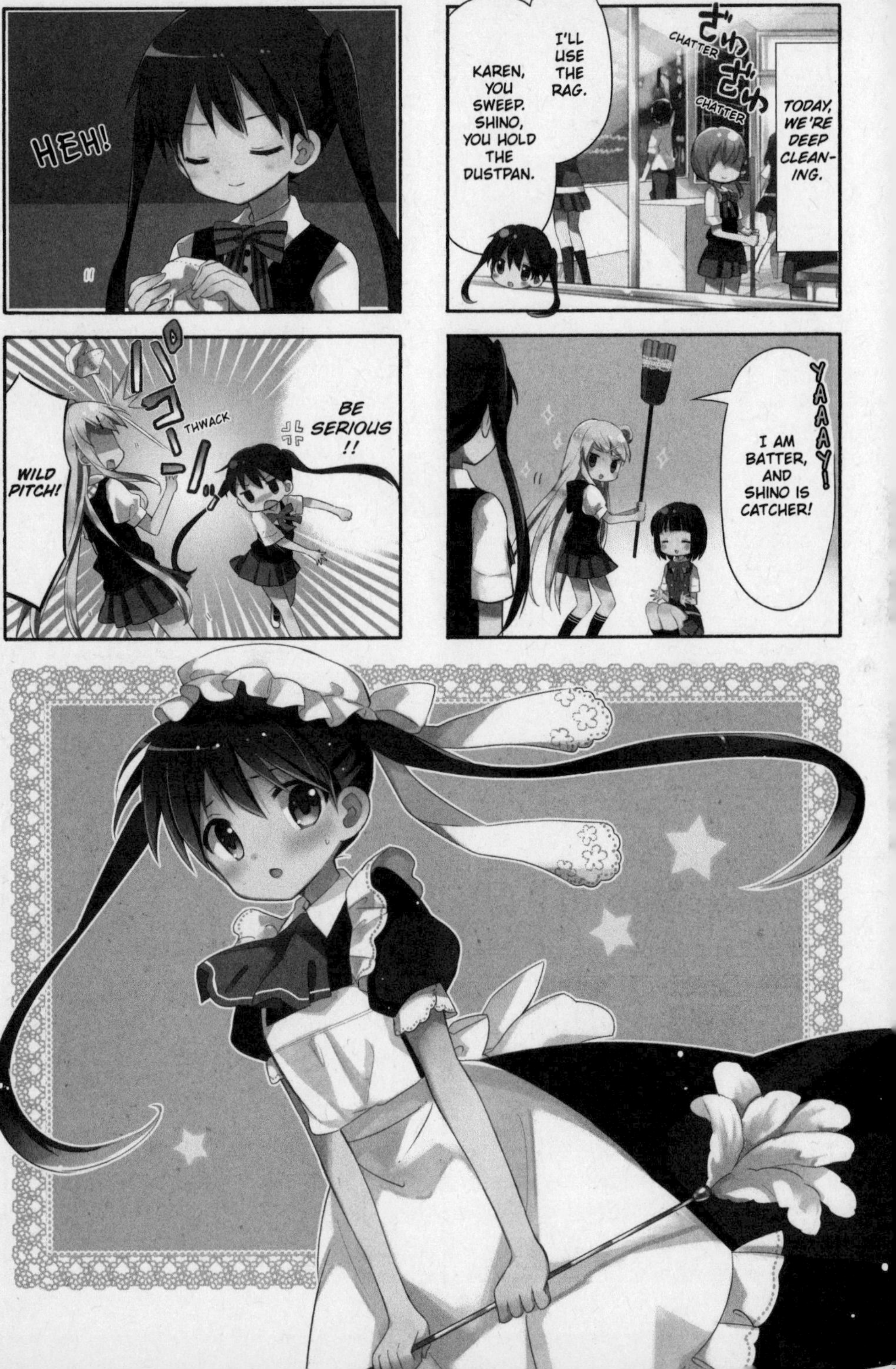
TODAY, WE'RE DEEP CLEANING.
CHATTER CHATTER
KAREN, YOU SWEEP. SHINO, YOU HOLD THE DUSTPAN. I'LL USE THE RAG.
HEH!
YAAAAY!
I AM BATTER, AND SHINO IS CATCHER!
BE SERIOUS!!
THWACK
WILD PITCH!

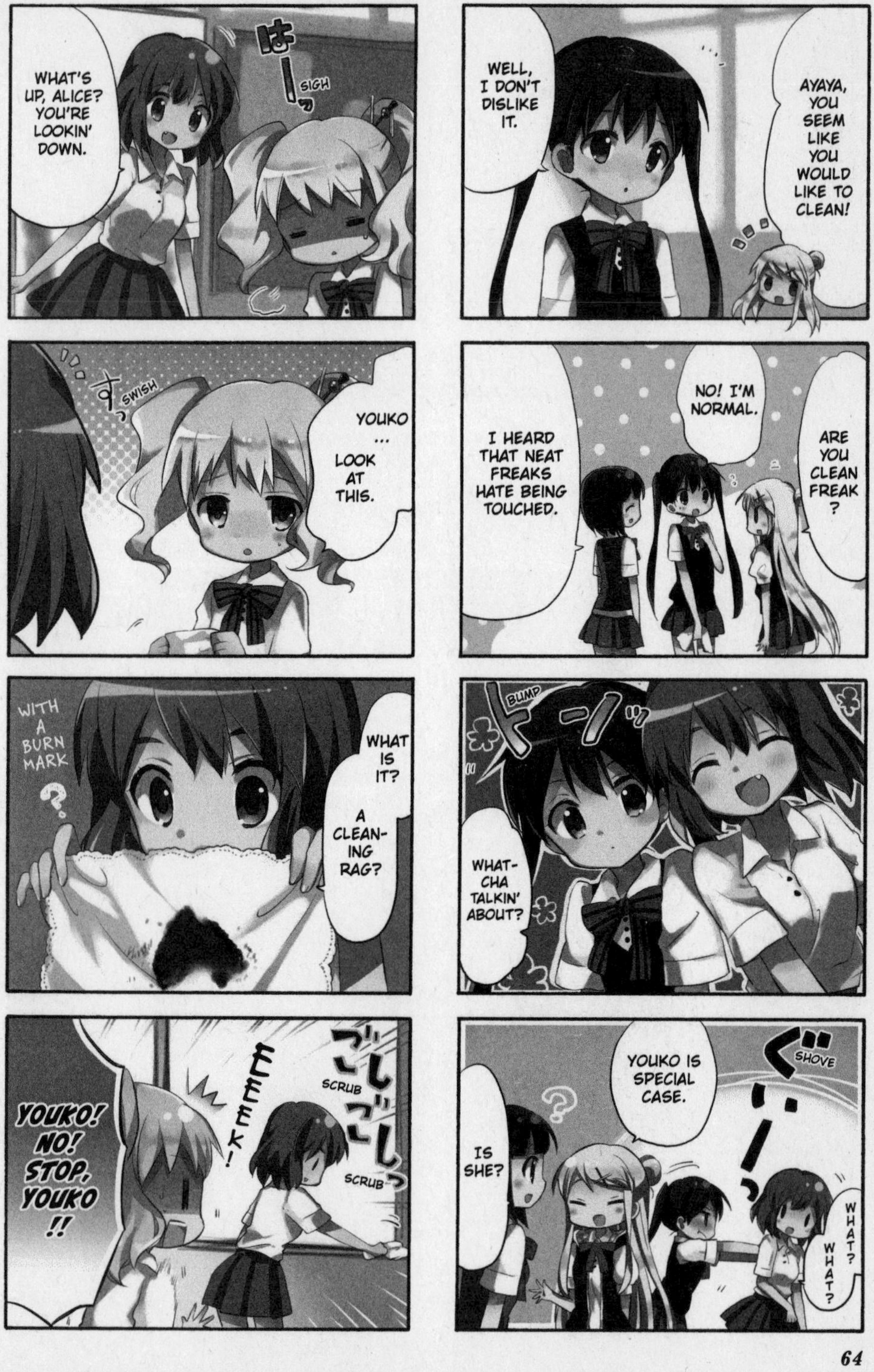
AYAYA, YOU SEEM LIKE YOU WOULD LIKE TO CLEAN!
WELL, I DON'T DISLIKE IT.
ARE YOU CLEAN FREAK?
NO! I'M NORMAL.
I HEARD THAT NEAT FREAKS HATE BEING TOUCHED.
BUMP
WHAT-CHA TALKIN' ABOUT?
SHOVE
YOUKO IS SPECIAL CASE.
WHAT? WHAT?
IS SHE?
SIGH
WHAT'S UP, ALICE? YOU'RE LOOKIN' DOWN.
YOUKO ... LOOK AT THIS.
SWISH
WHAT IS IT? A CLEAN-ING RAG?
WITH A BURN MARK
SCRUB
SCRUB
EEEEK!
YOUKO! NO! STOP, YOUKO!!

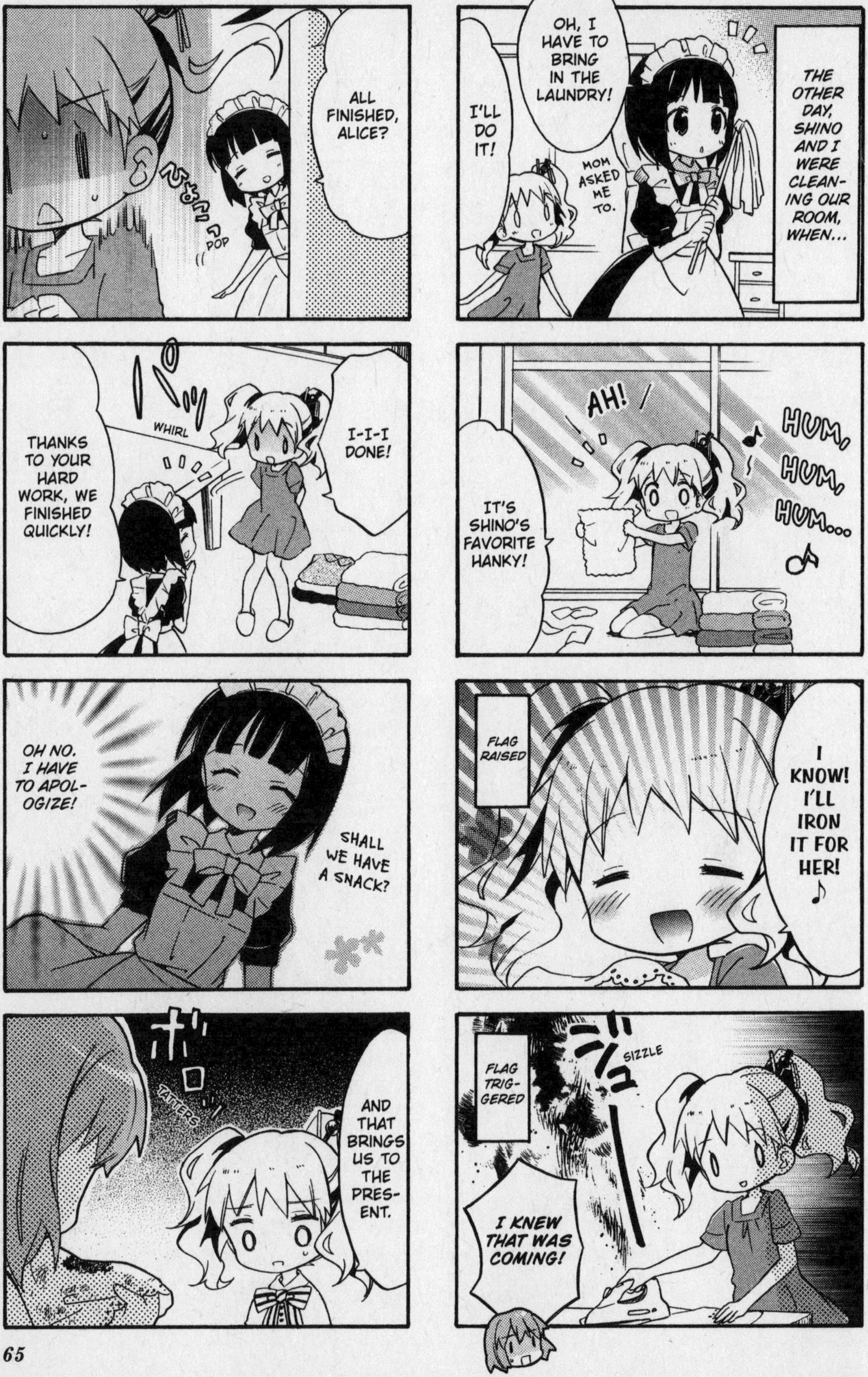
THE OTHER DAY, SHINO AND I WERE CLEANING OUR ROOM, WHEN...
OH, I HAVE TO BRING IN THE LAUNDRY!
MOM ASKED ME TO.
I'LL DO IT!
HUM, HUM, HUM...
AH!
IT'S SHINO'S FAVORITE HANKY!
I KNOW! I'LL IRON IT FOR HER! ♪
FLAG RAISED
SIZZLE
FLAG TRIGGERED
I KNEW THAT WAS COMING!
ALL FINISHED, ALICE?
POP
I-I-I DONE!
WHIRL
THANKS TO YOUR HARD WORK, WE FINISHED QUICKLY!
SHALL WE HAVE A SNACK?
OH NO. I HAVE TO APOLOGIZE!
AND THAT BRINGS US TO THE PRESENT.
TATTERS

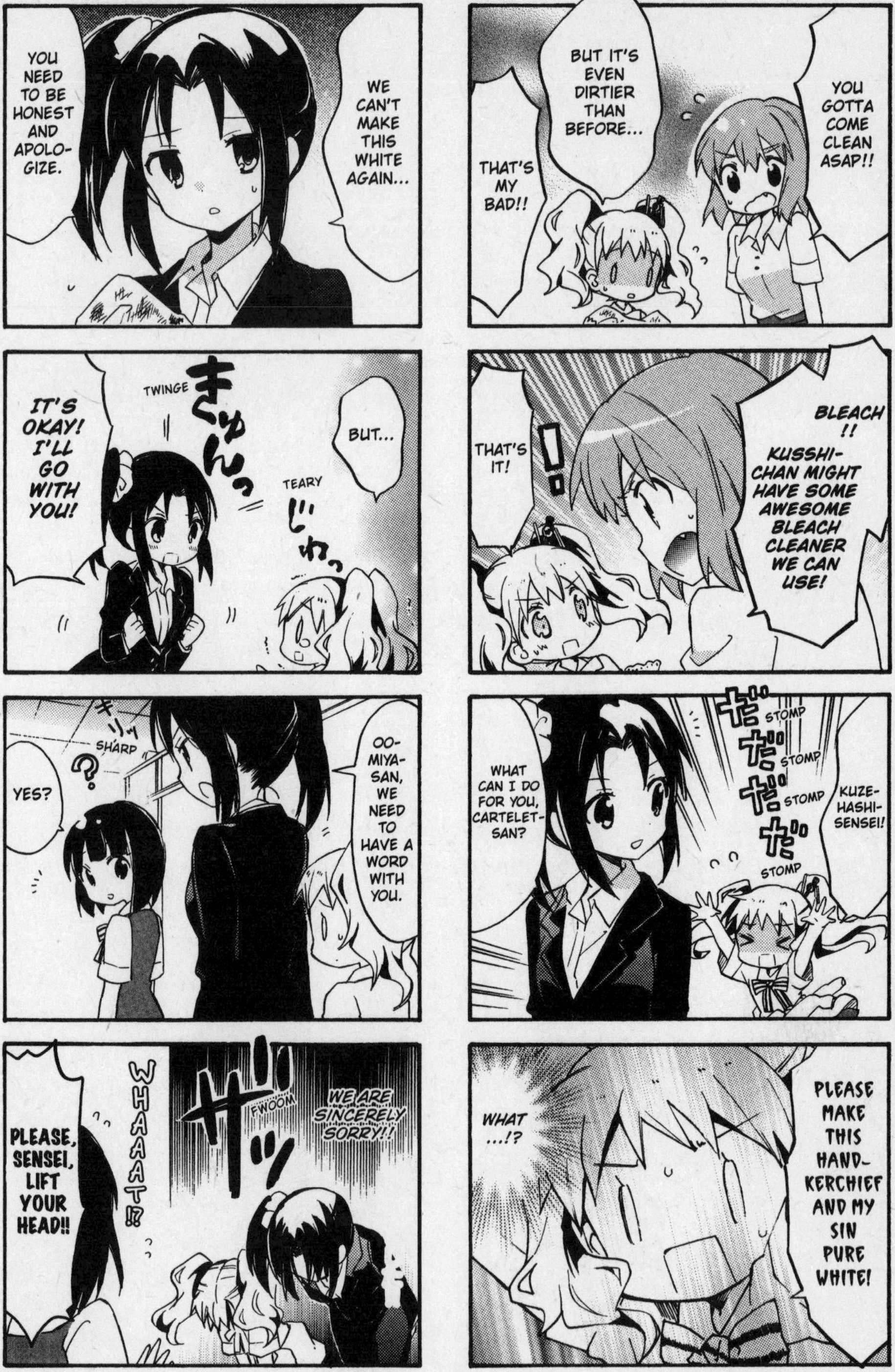
YOU GOTTA COME CLEAN ASAP!!
BUT IT'S EVEN DIRTIER THAN BEFORE...
THAT'S MY BAD!!
WE CAN'T MAKE THIS WHITE AGAIN...
YOU NEED TO BE HONEST AND APOLOGIZE.
BLEACH!! KUSSHI-CHAN MIGHT HAVE SOME AWESOME BLEACH CLEANER WE CAN USE!
!
THAT'S IT!
BUT...
TEARY じわっ
TWINGE きゅんっ
IT'S OKAY! I'LL GO WITH YOU!
KUZE-HASHI-SENSEI!
ダッ STOMP
ダッ STOMP
ダッ STOMP
ダッ STOMP
WHAT CAN I DO FOR YOU, CARTELET-SAN?
OO-MIYA-SAN, WE NEED TO HAVE A WORD WITH YOU.
キリッ SHARP
?
YES?
PLEASE MAKE THIS HAND-KERCHIEF AND MY SIN PURE WHITE!
WHAT ...!?
WE ARE SINCERELY SORRY!!
ザッ FWOOM
WHAAAAT!?
PLEASE, SENSEI, LIFT YOUR HEAD!!

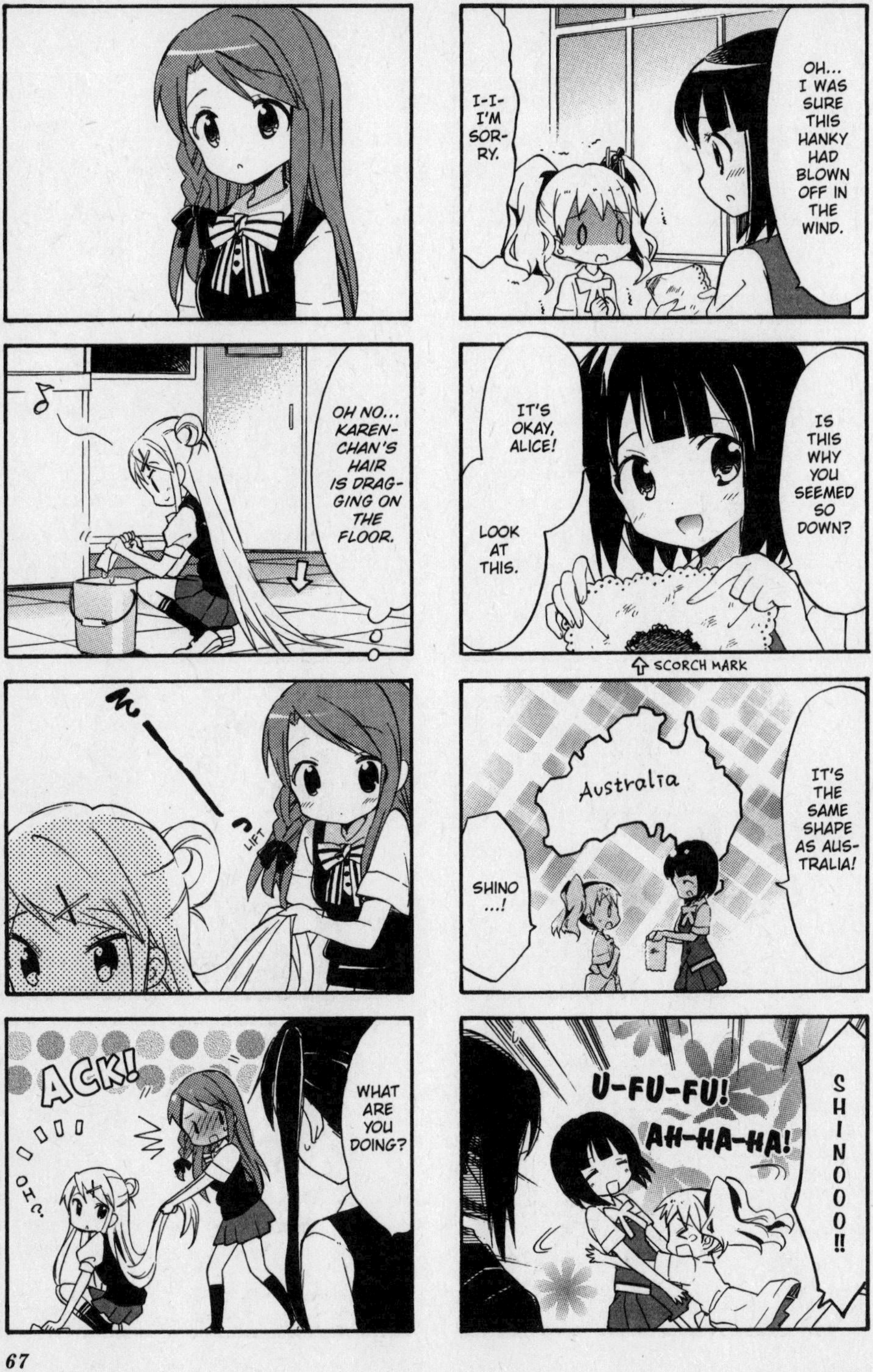
OH... I WAS SURE THIS HANKY HAD BLOWN OFF IN THE WIND.
I-I- I'M SORRY.
IS THIS WHY YOU SEEMED SO DOWN?
IT'S OKAY, ALICE!
LOOK AT THIS.
SCORCH MARK
IT'S THE SAME SHAPE AS AUSTRALIA!
Australia
SHINO ...!
SHINOOOO!!
U-FU-FU!
AH-HA-HA!
OH NO... KAREN-CHAN'S HAIR IS DRAGGING ON THE FLOOR.
LIFT
WHAT ARE YOU DOING?
ACK!
OH?

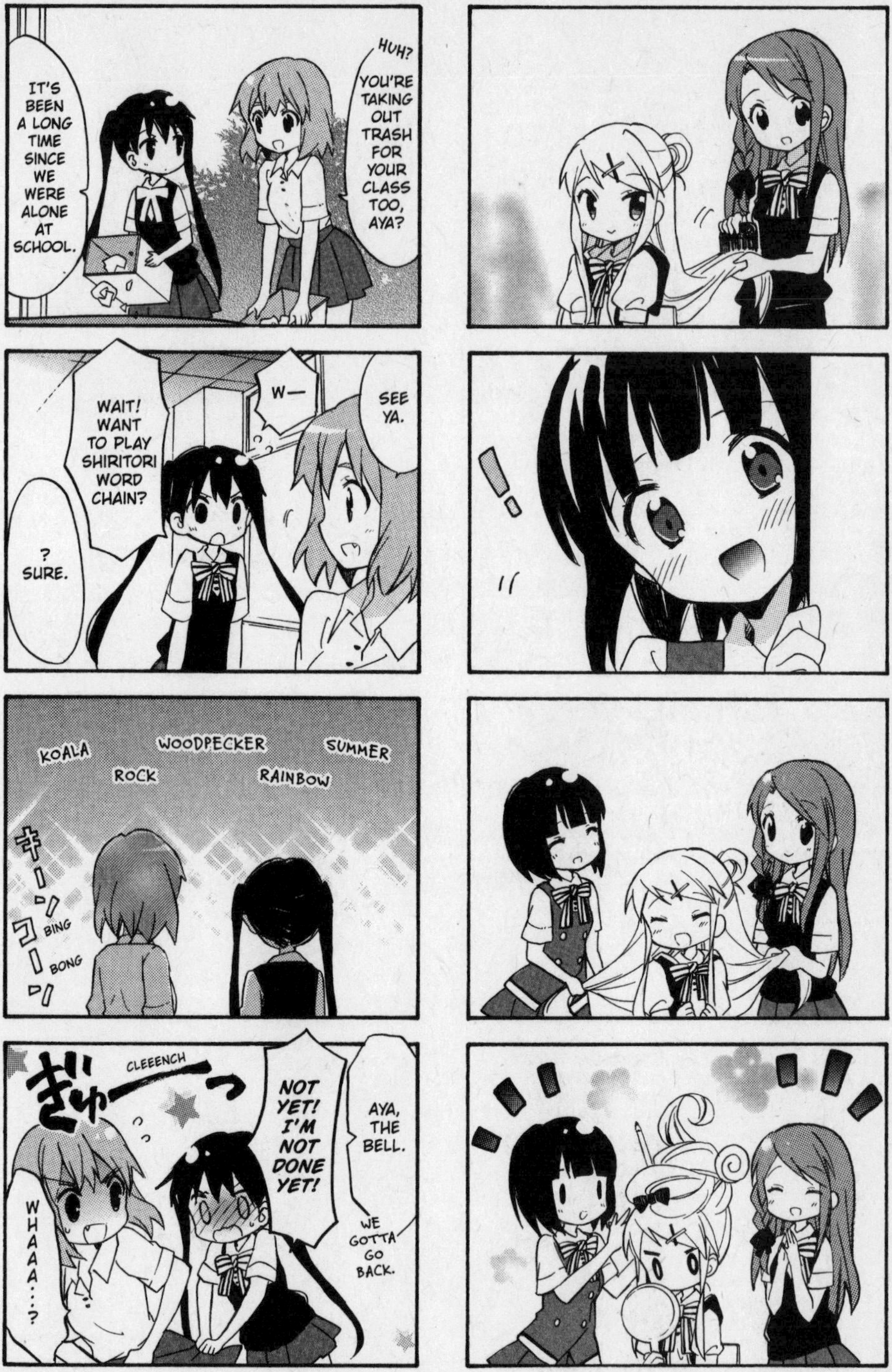
HUH? YOU'RE TAKING OUT TRASH FOR YOUR CLASS TOO, AYA?
IT'S BEEN A LONG TIME SINCE WE WERE ALONE AT SCHOOL.
SEE YA.
W—
WAIT! WANT TO PLAY SHIRITORI WORD CHAIN?
? SURE.
SUMMER
RAINBOW
WOODPECKER
ROCK
KOALA
キーンコーン
BING
BONG
AYA, THE BELL.
WE GOTTA GO BACK.
NOT YET! I'M NOT DONE YET!
ぎゅーっ
CLEEENCH
WHAAAA...?

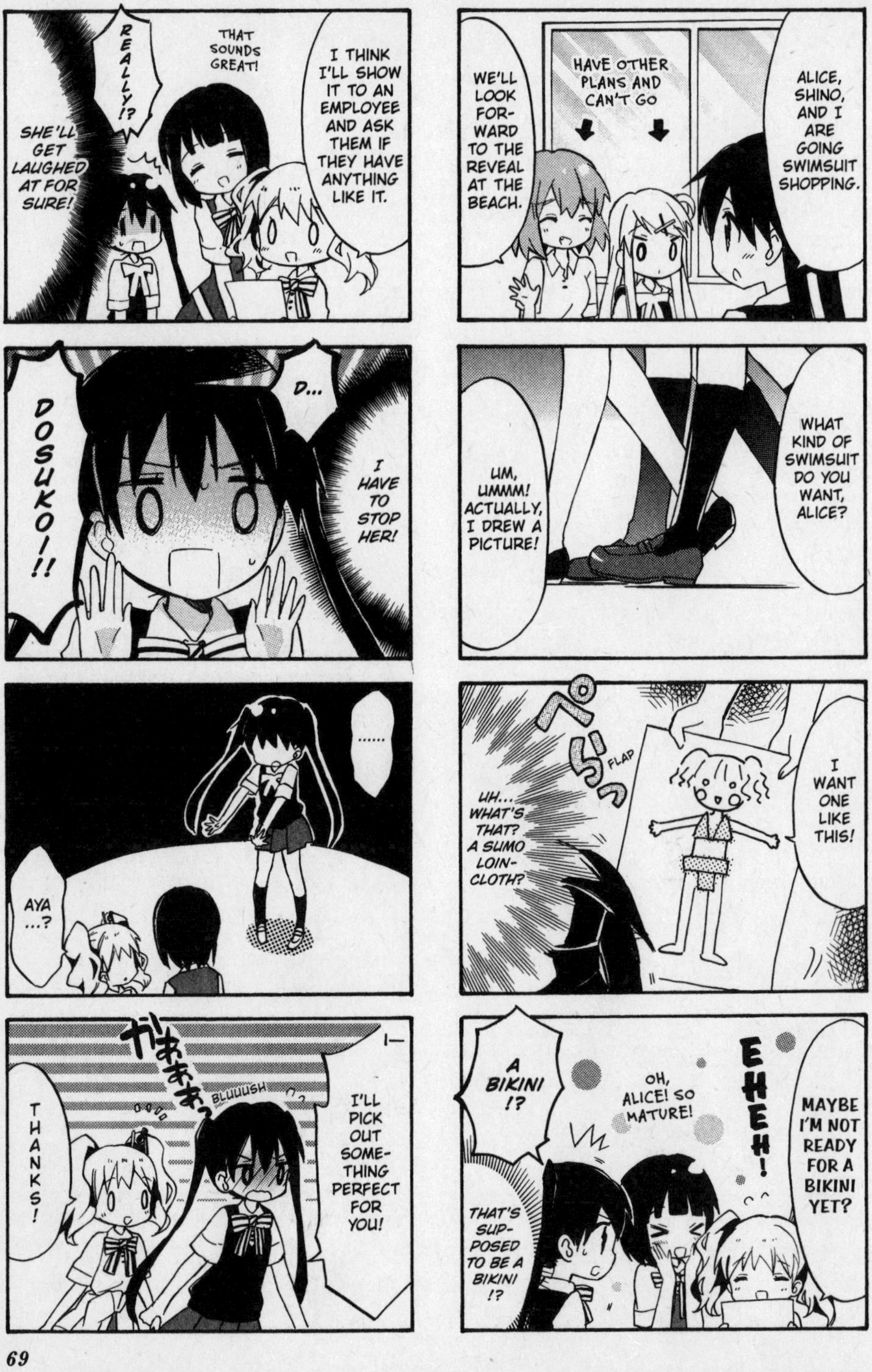
ALICE, SHINO, AND I ARE GOING SWIMSUIT SHOPPING.
HAVE OTHER PLANS AND CAN'T GO
WE'LL LOOK FOR-WARD TO THE REVEAL AT THE BEACH.
WHAT KIND OF SWIMSUIT DO YOU WANT, ALICE?
UM, UMMM! ACTUALLY, I DREW A PICTURE!
ぺらっ
FLAP
I WANT ONE LIKE THIS!
UH... WHAT'S THAT? A SUMO LOIN-CLOTH?
MAYBE I'M NOT READY FOR A BIKINI YET?
EHEH!
OH, ALICE! SO MATURE!
A BIKINI !?
THAT'S SUP-POSED TO BE A BIKINI !?
I THINK I'LL SHOW IT TO AN EMPLOYEE AND ASK THEM IF THEY HAVE ANYTHING LIKE IT.
THAT SOUNDS GREAT!
REALLY!?
SHE'LL GET LAUGHED AT FOR SURE!
D...
I HAVE TO STOP HER!
DOSUKO!!!
......
AYA ...?
I—
がああああっ
BLUUUSH
I'LL PICK OUT SOME-THING PERFECT FOR YOU!
THANKS!

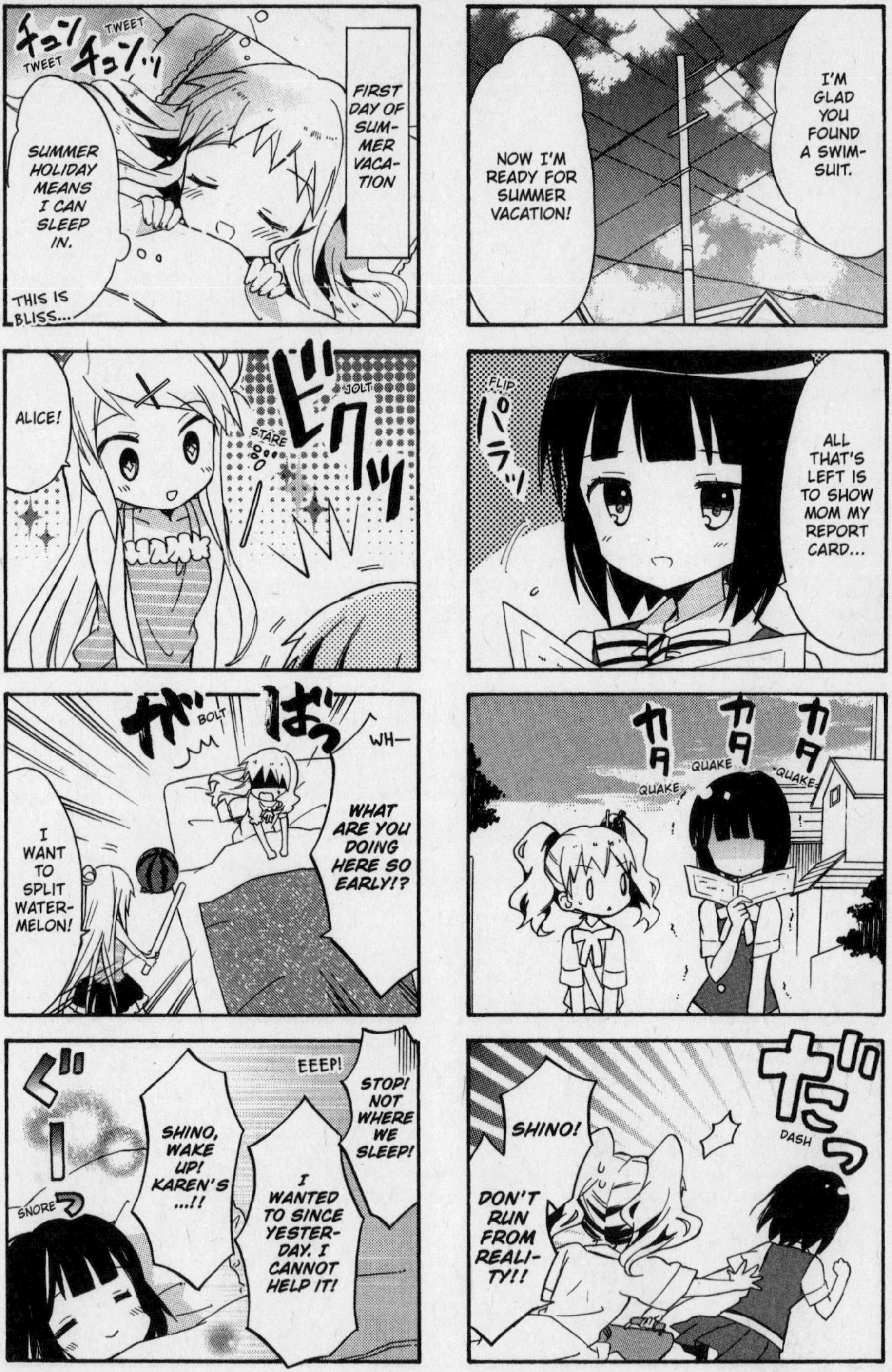
I'M GLAD YOU FOUND A SWIM-SUIT.
NOW I'M READY FOR SUMMER VACATION!
FLIP
ALL THAT'S LEFT IS TO SHOW MOM MY REPORT CARD...
QUAKE
QUAKE
QUAKE
DASH
SHINO!
DON'T RUN FROM REALI-TY!!
FIRST DAY OF SUMMER VACATION
TWEET
TWEET
SUMMER HOLIDAY MEANS I CAN SLEEP IN.
THIS IS BLISS...
JOLT
STARE
ALICE!
WH—
BOLT
WHAT ARE YOU DOING HERE SO EARLY!?
I WANT TO SPLIT WATER-MELON!
EEEP!
STOP! NOT WHERE WE SLEEP!
I WANTED TO SINCE YESTER-DAY. I CANNOT HELP IT!
SHINO, WAKE UP! KAREN'S ...!!
SNORE

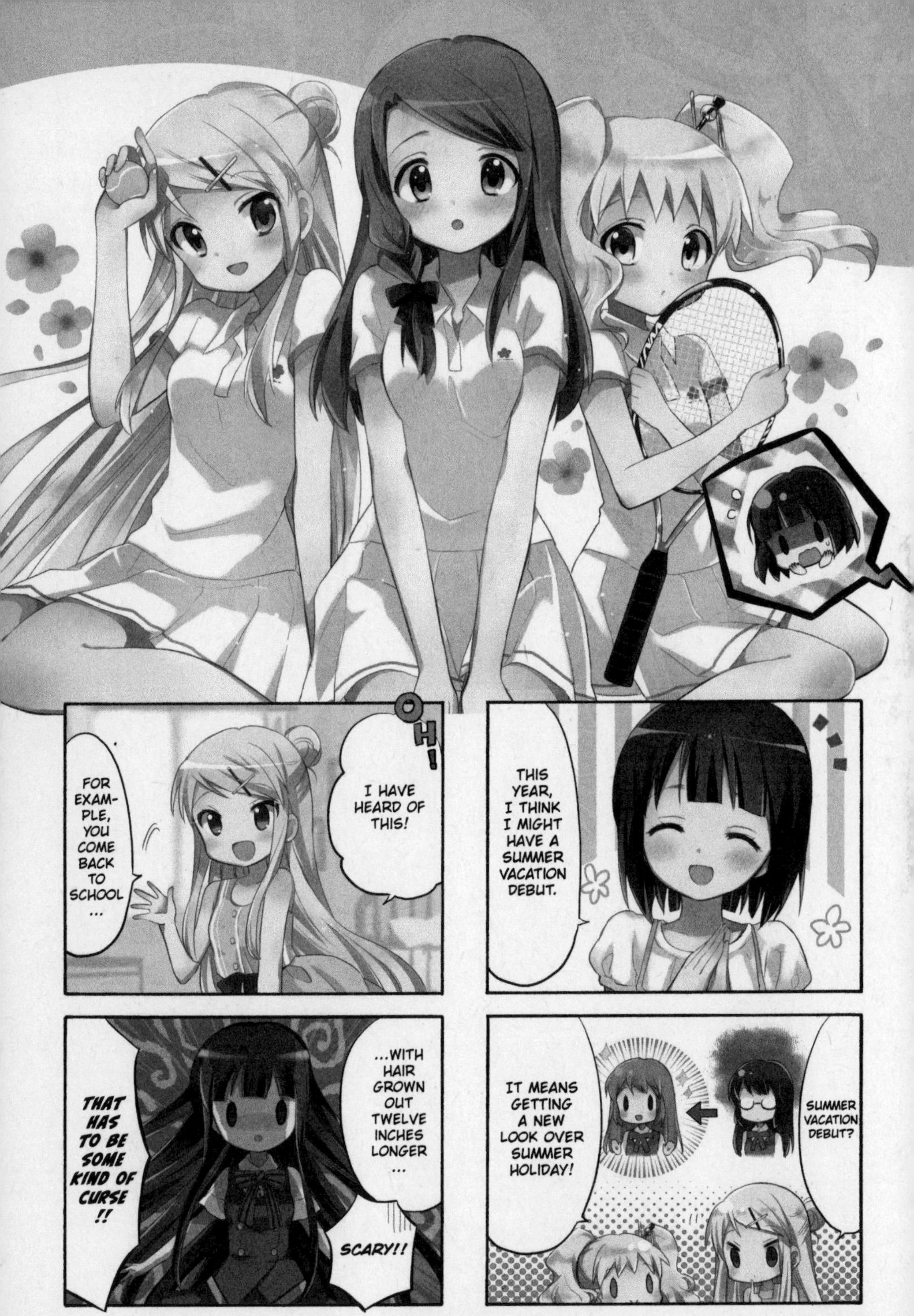
THIS YEAR, I THINK I MIGHT HAVE A SUMMER VACATION DEBUT.
OH!
I HAVE HEARD OF THIS!
FOR EXAMPLE, YOU COME BACK TO SCHOOL...
SUMMER VACATION DEBUT?
IT MEANS GETTING A NEW LOOK OVER SUMMER HOLIDAY!
...WITH HAIR GROWN OUT TWELVE INCHES LONGER...
SCARY!!
THAT HAS TO BE SOME KIND OF CURSE!!

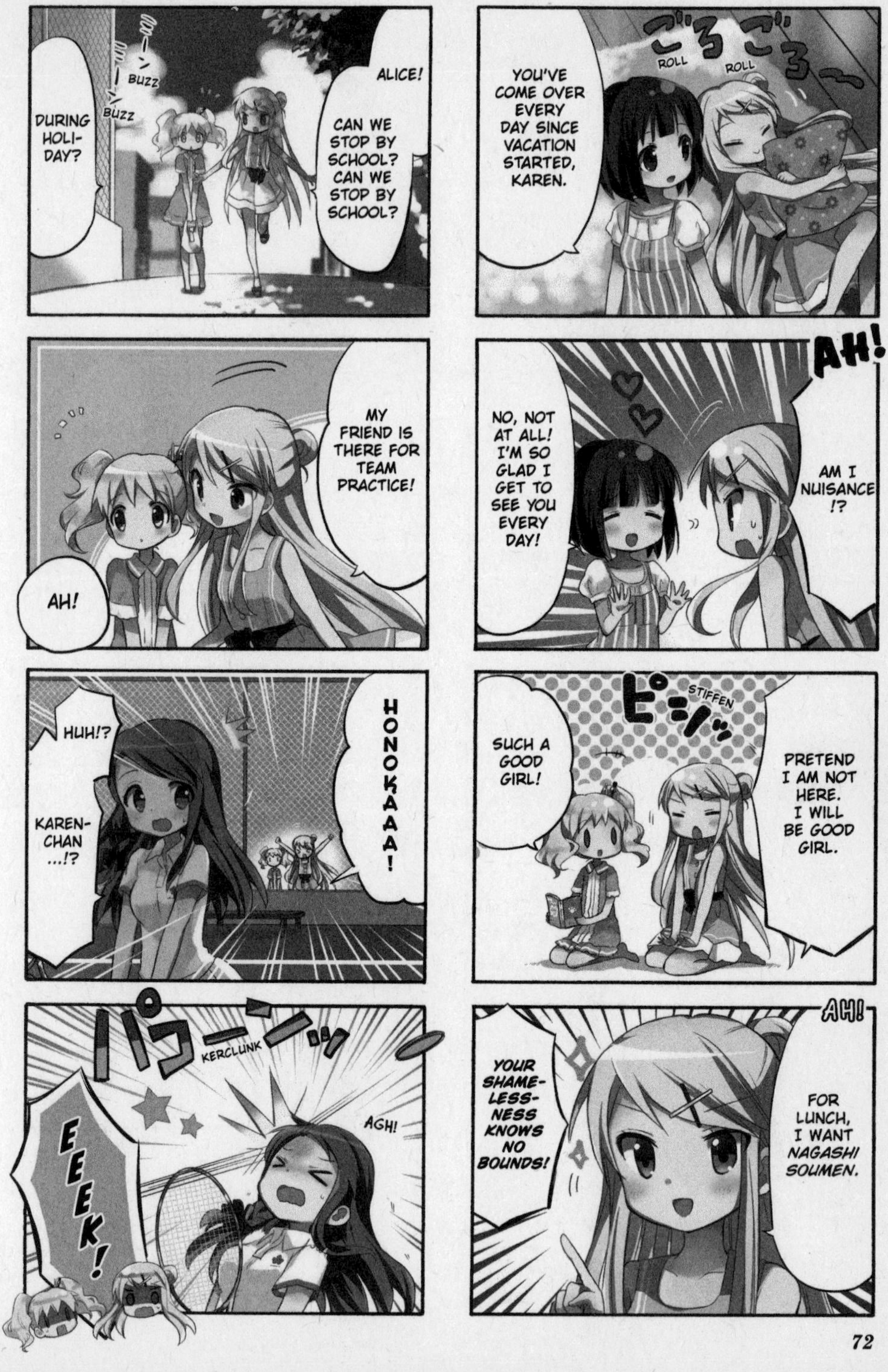
ROLL ROLL
YOU'VE COME OVER EVERY DAY SINCE VACATION STARTED, KAREN.
AH!
AM I NUISANCE !?
NO, NOT AT ALL! I'M SO GLAD I GET TO SEE YOU EVERY DAY!
STIFFEN
PRETEND I AM NOT HERE. I WILL BE GOOD GIRL.
SUCH A GOOD GIRL!
AH!
FOR LUNCH, I WANT NAGASHI SOUMEN.
YOUR SHAMELESSNESS KNOWS NO BOUNDS!
ALICE!
CAN WE STOP BY SCHOOL? CAN WE STOP BY SCHOOL?
BUZZ
BUZZ
DURING HOLIDAY?
MY FRIEND IS THERE FOR TEAM PRACTICE!
AH!
HONOKAAAA!
HUH!?
KAREN-CHAN ...!?
KERCLUNK
AGH!
EEEK!

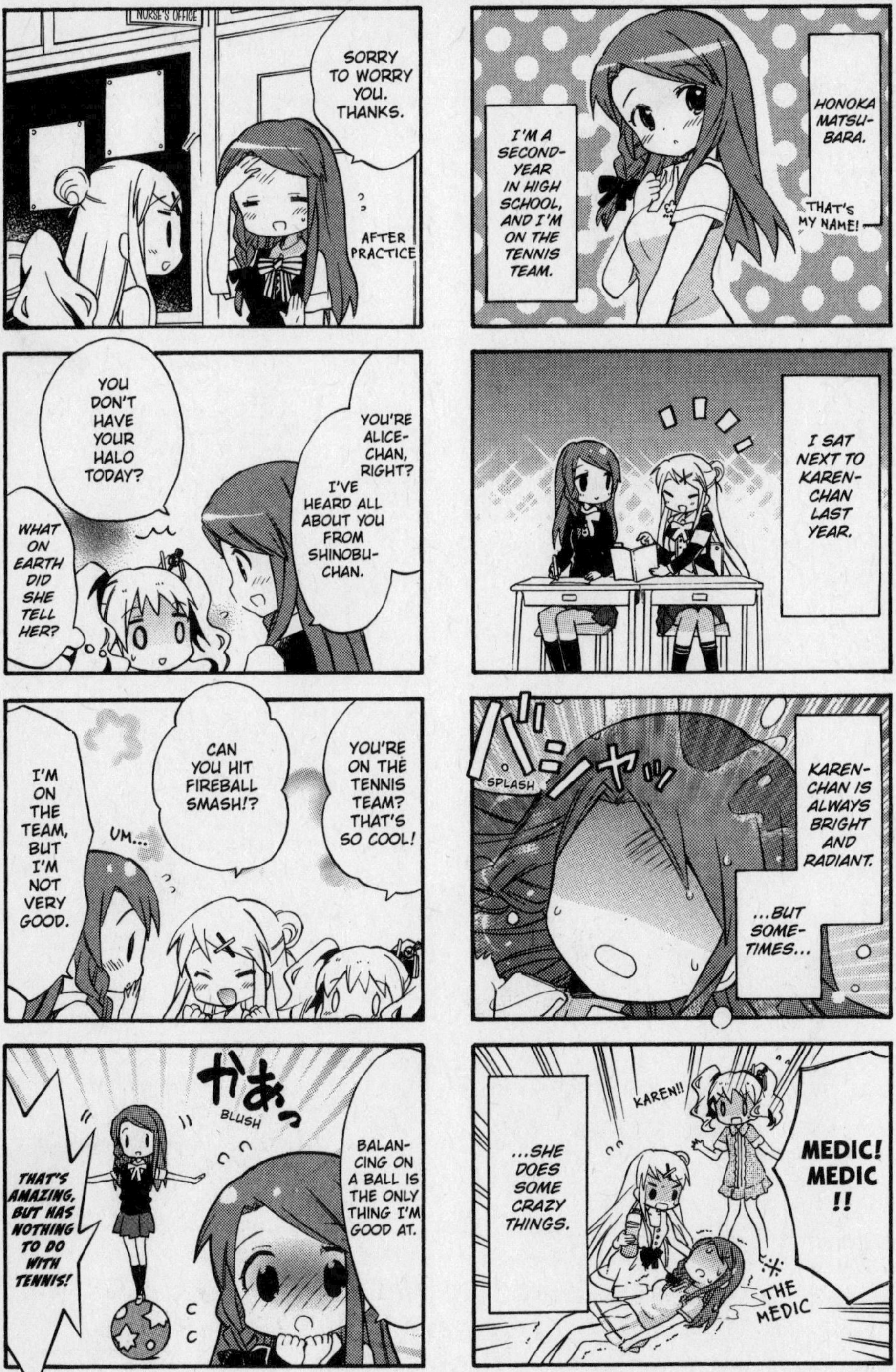
HONOKA MATSUBARA.
THAT'S MY NAME!
I'M A SECOND-YEAR IN HIGH SCHOOL, AND I'M ON THE TENNIS TEAM.
I SAT NEXT TO KAREN-CHAN LAST YEAR.
KAREN-CHAN IS ALWAYS BRIGHT AND RADIANT.
...BUT SOMETIMES...
バシャッ
SPLASH
MEDIC! MEDIC !!
KAREN!!
...SHE DOES SOME CRAZY THINGS.
THE MEDIC
NURSE'S OFFICE
SORRY TO WORRY YOU. THANKS.
AFTER PRACTICE
YOU'RE ALICE-CHAN, RIGHT?
I'VE HEARD ALL ABOUT YOU FROM SHINOBU-CHAN.
YOU DON'T HAVE YOUR HALO TODAY?
WHAT ON EARTH DID SHE TELL HER?
YOU'RE ON THE TENNIS TEAM? THAT'S SO COOL!
CAN YOU HIT FIREBALL SMASH!?
UM...
I'M ON THE TEAM, BUT I'M NOT VERY GOOD.
BALANCING ON A BALL IS THE ONLY THING I'M GOOD AT.
かあっ
BLUSH
THAT'S AMAZING, BUT HAS NOTHING TO DO WITH TENNIS!

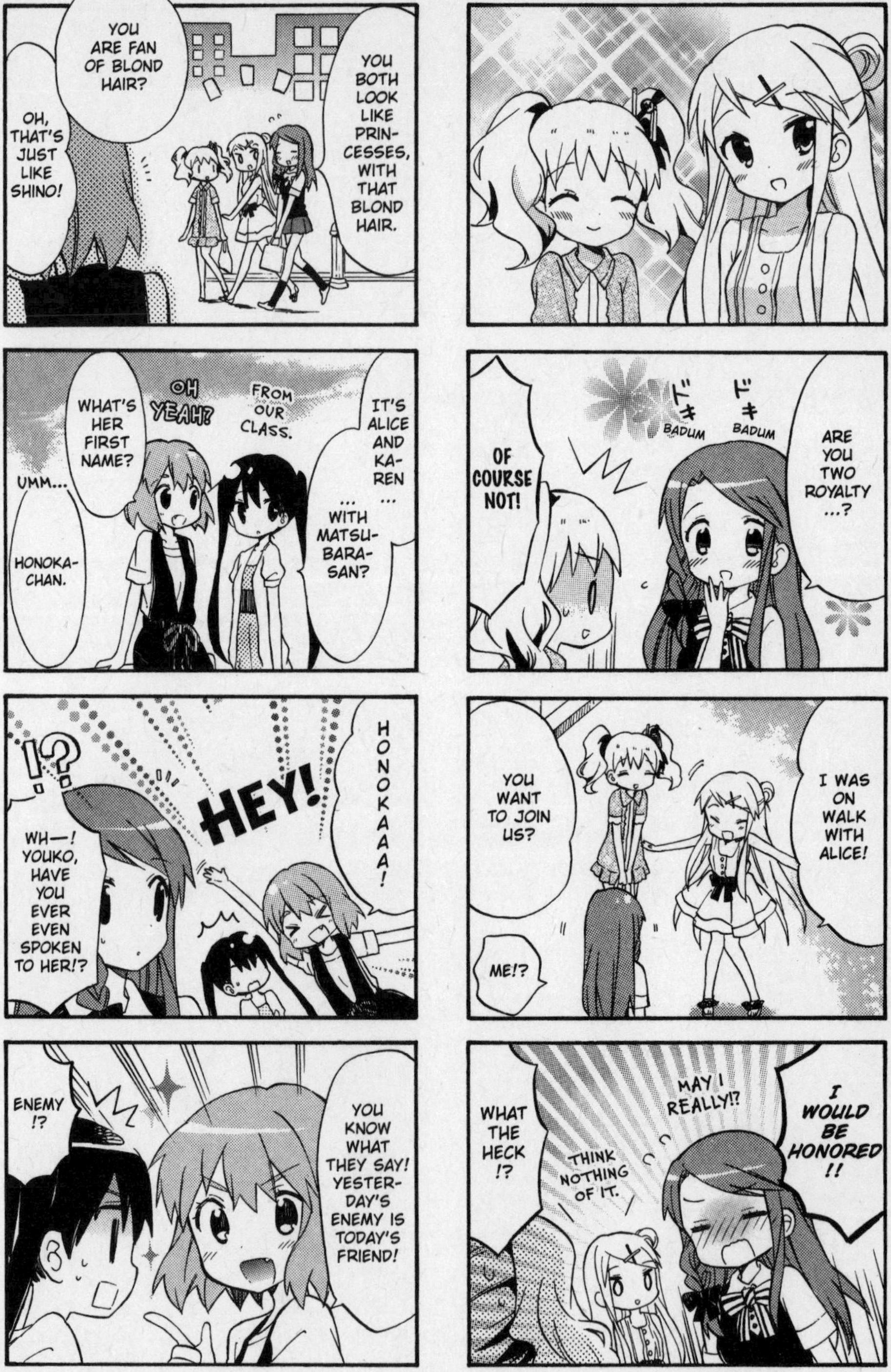
ARE YOU TWO ROYALTY …?
ドキ BADUM
ドキ BADUM
OF COURSE NOT!
I WAS ON WALK WITH ALICE!
YOU WANT TO JOIN US?
ME!?
I WOULD BE HONORED!!
MAY I REALLY!?
THINK NOTHING OF IT.
WHAT THE HECK !?
YOU BOTH LOOK LIKE PRINCESSES, WITH THAT BLOND HAIR.
YOU ARE FAN OF BLOND HAIR?
OH, THAT'S JUST LIKE SHINO!
IT'S ALICE AND KAREN … WITH MATSUBARA-SAN?
FROM OUR CLASS.
OH YEAH?
WHAT'S HER FIRST NAME?
UMM…
HONOKA-CHAN.
HONOKAAAA!
HEY!
!?
WH—! YOUKO, HAVE YOU EVER EVEN SPOKEN TO HER!?
YOU KNOW WHAT THEY SAY! YESTERDAY'S ENEMY IS TODAY'S FRIEND!
ENEMY !?

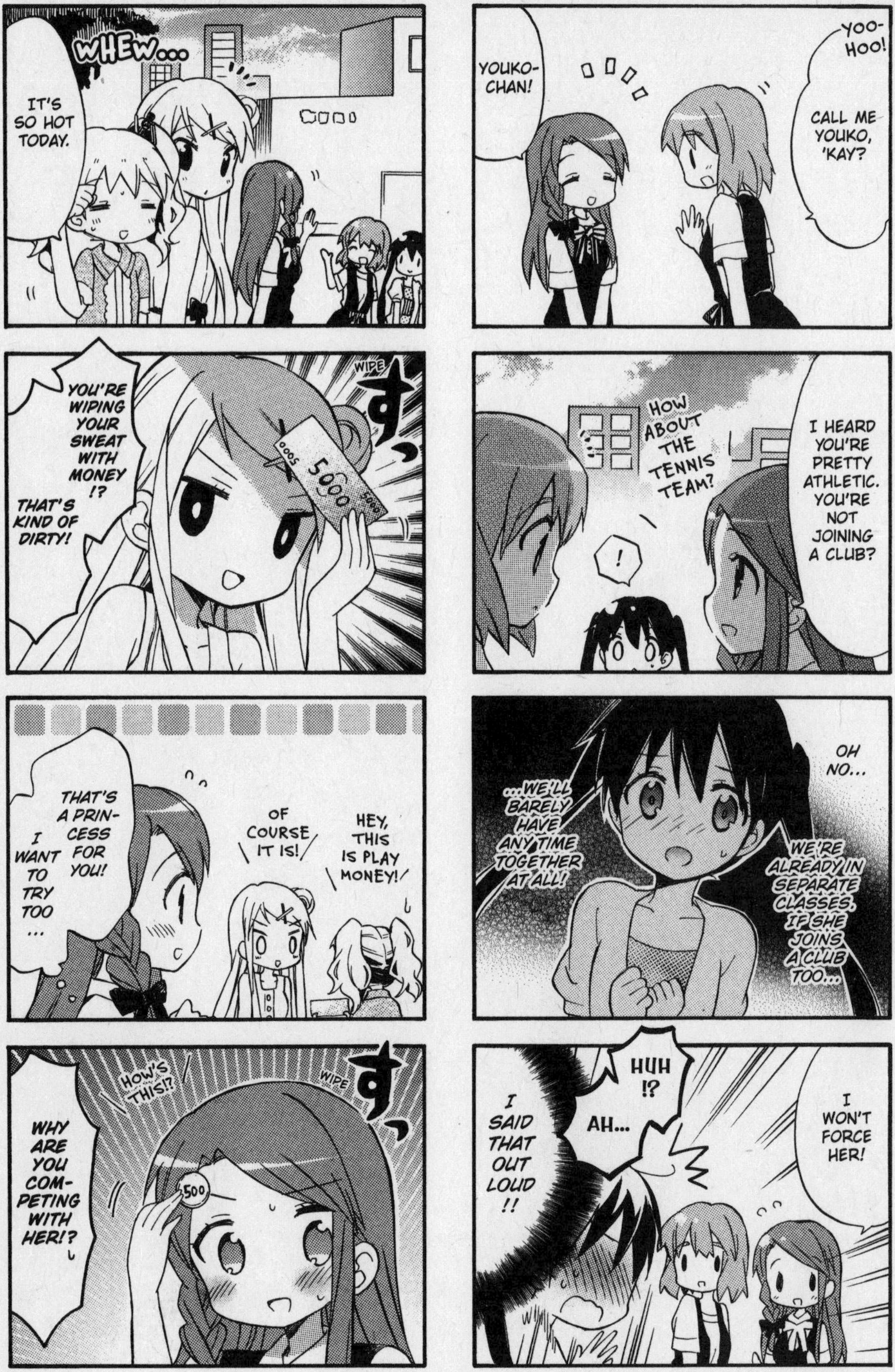
YOO-HOO!
YOUKO-CHAN!
CALL ME YOUKO, 'KAY?
I HEARD YOU'RE PRETTY ATHLETIC. YOU'RE NOT JOINING A CLUB?
HOW ABOUT THE TENNIS TEAM?
!
OH NO...
WE'RE ALREADY IN SEPARATE CLASSES. IF SHE JOINS A CLUB TOO...
...WE'LL BARELY HAVE ANY TIME TOGETHER AT ALL!
I WON'T FORCE HER!
HUH !?
AH...
I SAID THAT OUT LOUD !!
WHEW...
IT'S SO HOT TODAY.
WIPE
5000
YOU'RE WIPING YOUR SWEAT WITH MONEY !?
THAT'S KIND OF DIRTY!
HEY, THIS IS PLAY MONEY!
OF COURSE IT IS!
THAT'S A PRINCESS FOR YOU!
I WANT TO TRY TOO ...
WIPE
HOW'S THIS!?
500
WHY ARE YOU COMPETING WITH HER!?

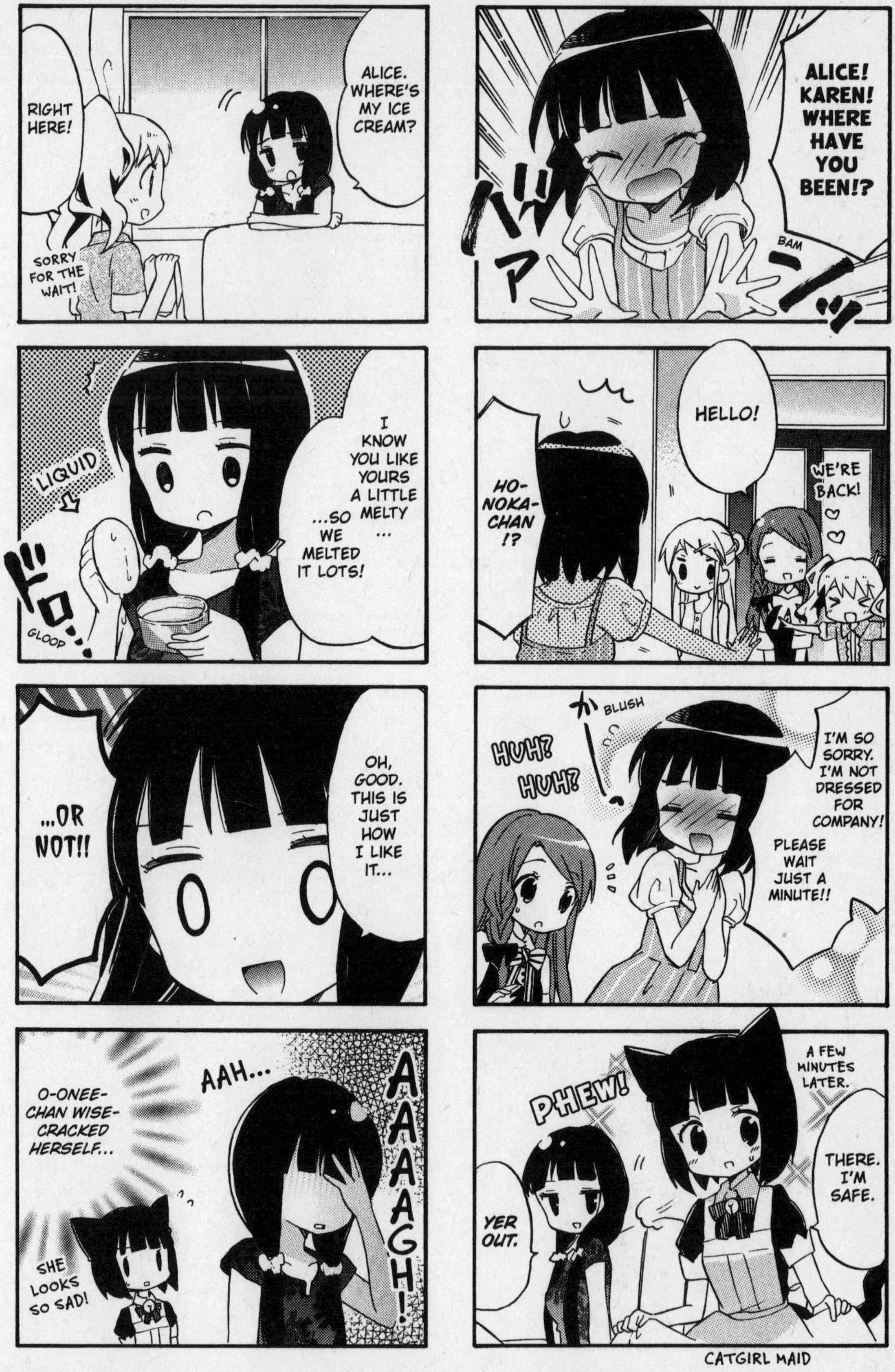
ALICE! KAREN! WHERE HAVE YOU BEEN!?
BAM
HELLO!
WE'RE BACK!
HO-NOKA-CHAN!?
I'M SO SORRY. I'M NOT DRESSED FOR COMPANY!
PLEASE WAIT JUST A MINUTE!!
BLUSH
HUH? HUH?
A FEW MINUTES LATER.
PHEW!
THERE. I'M SAFE.
YER OUT.
ALICE. WHERE'S MY ICE CREAM?
RIGHT HERE!
SORRY FOR THE WAIT!
I KNOW YOU LIKE YOURS A LITTLE MELTY ...
...SO WE MELTED IT LOTS!
LIQUID
GLOOP
OH, GOOD. THIS IS JUST HOW I LIKE IT...
...OR NOT!!
AAH...
AAAAAGH!
O-ONEE-CHAN WISE-CRACKED HERSELF...
SHE LOOKS SO SAD!
CATGIRL MAID

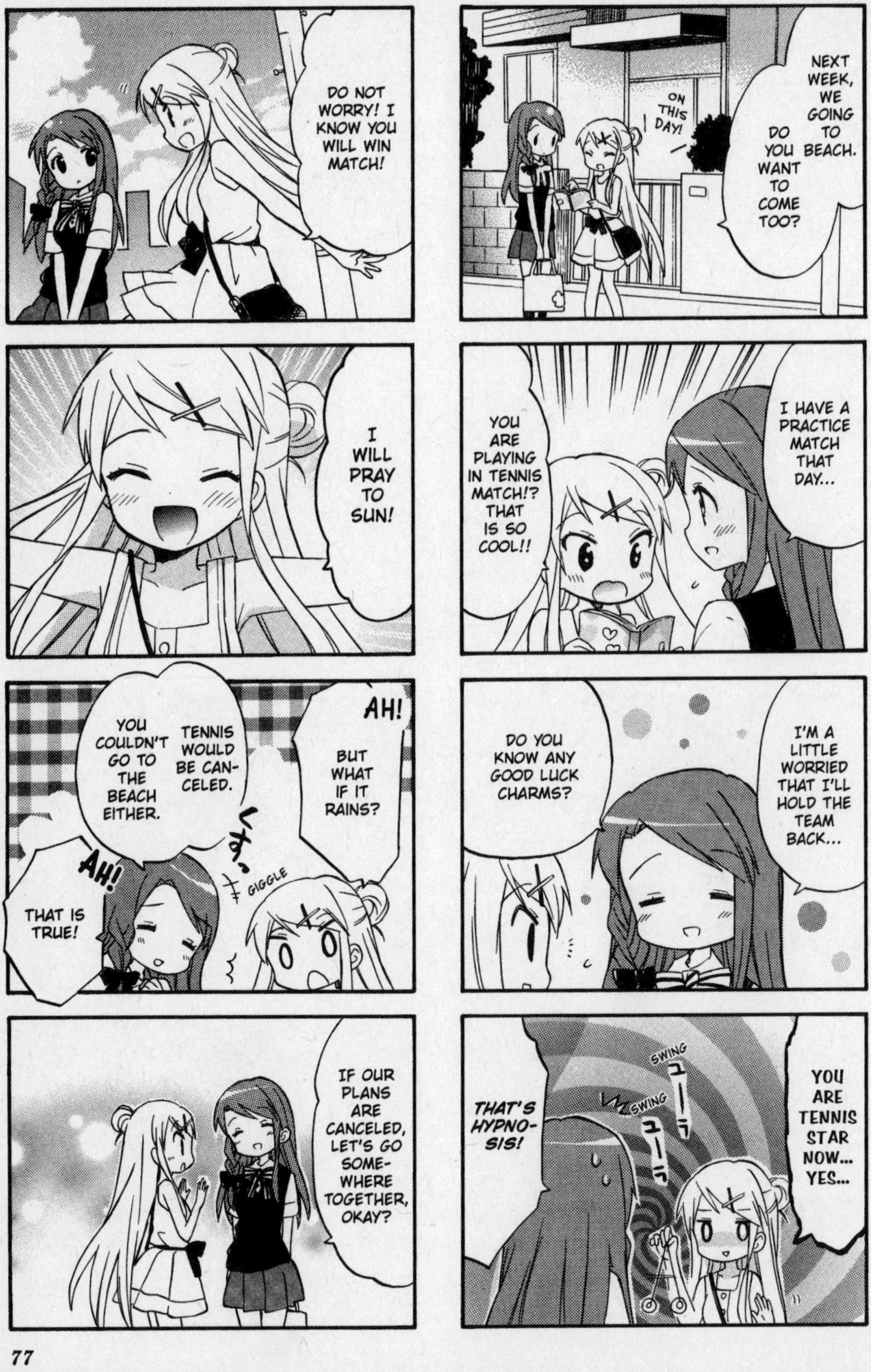
NEXT WEEK, WE GOING TO BEACH.
DO YOU WANT TO COME TOO?
ON THIS DAY!
I HAVE A PRACTICE MATCH THAT DAY...
YOU ARE PLAYING IN TENNIS MATCH!? THAT IS SO COOL!!
I'M A LITTLE WORRIED THAT I'LL HOLD THE TEAM BACK...
DO YOU KNOW ANY GOOD LUCK CHARMS?
YOU ARE TENNIS STAR NOW... YES...
SWING
SWING
THAT'S HYPNOSIS!
DO NOT WORRY! I KNOW YOU WILL WIN MATCH!
I WILL PRAY TO SUN!
AH!
BUT WHAT IF IT RAINS?
TENNIS WOULD BE CANCELED.
YOU COULDN'T GO TO THE BEACH EITHER.
GIGGLE
AH!
THAT IS TRUE!
IF OUR PLANS ARE CANCELED, LET'S GO SOMEWHERE TOGETHER, OKAY?

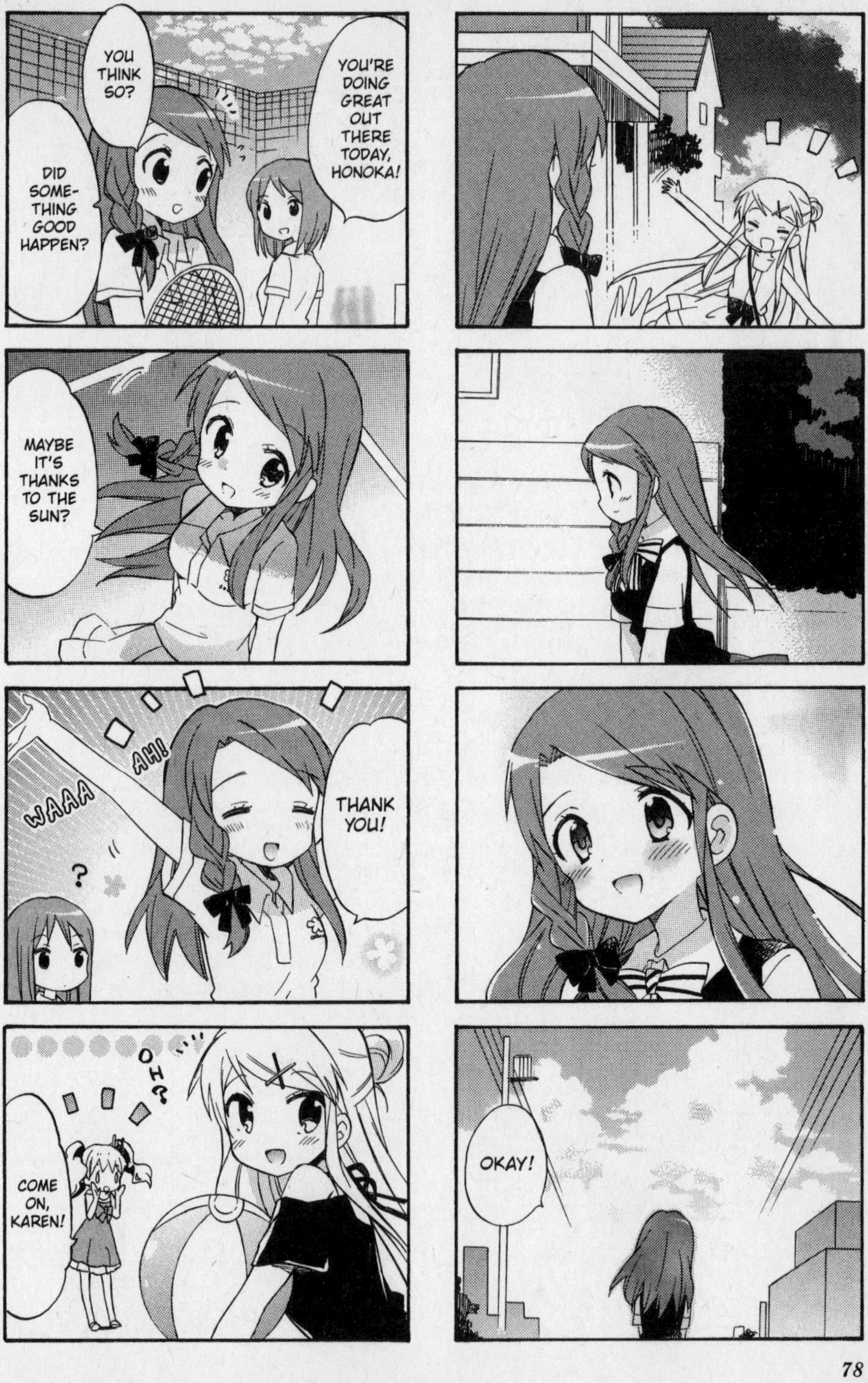
YOU'RE DOING GREAT OUT THERE TODAY, HONOKA!
YOU THINK SO?
DID SOME-THING GOOD HAPPEN?
MAYBE IT'S THANKS TO THE SUN?
THANK YOU!
AH!
WAAAA
OKAY!
OH?
COME ON, KAREN!

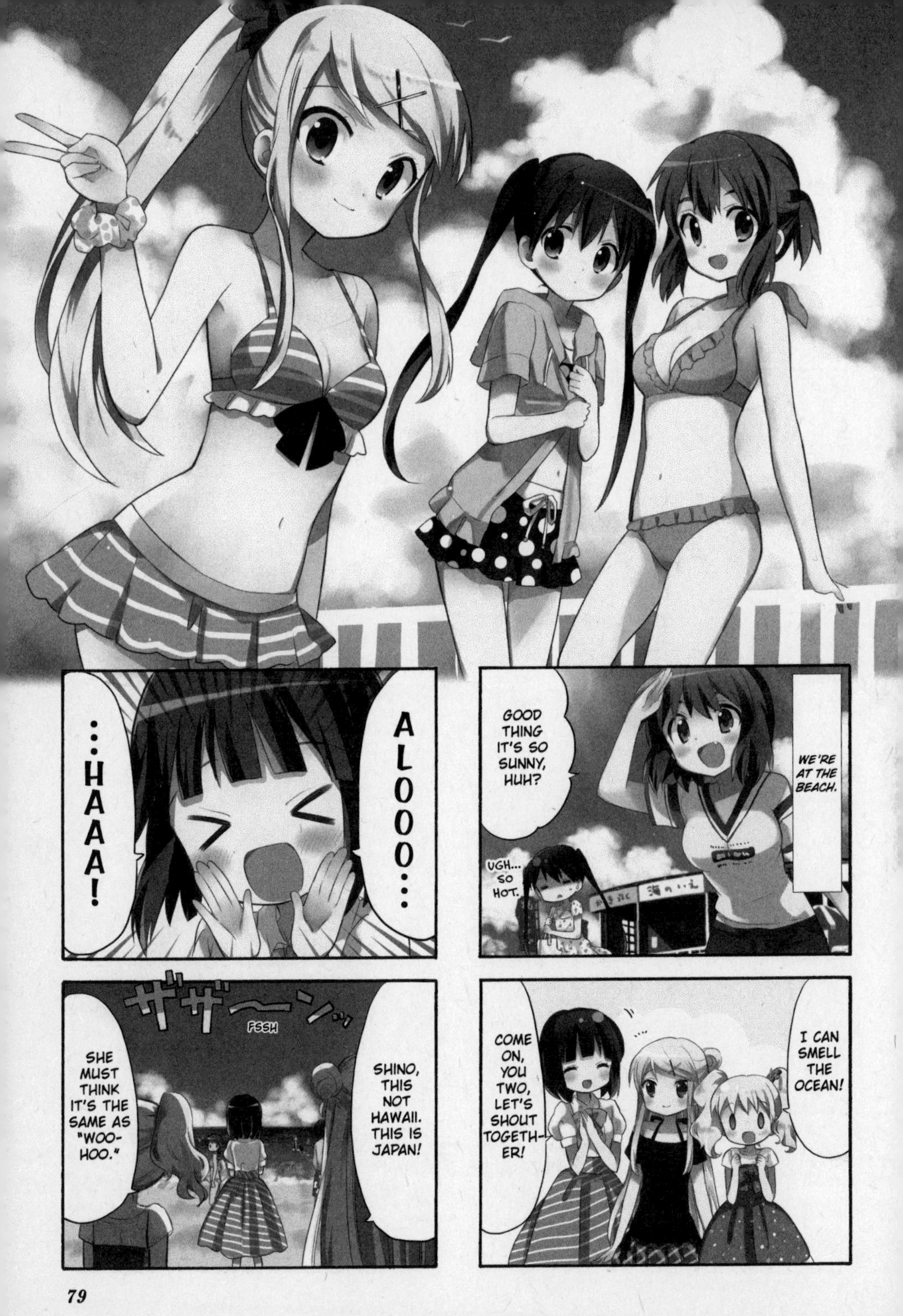

WE'RE AT THE BEACH.
GOOD THING IT'S SO SUNNY, HUH?
UGH... SO HOT.
ALOOOO...
...HAAAA!
I CAN SMELL THE OCEAN!
COME ON, YOU TWO, LET'S SHOUT TOGETHER!
FSSH
SHINO, THIS NOT HAWAII. THIS IS JAPAN!
SHE MUST THINK IT'S THE SAME AS "WOO-HOO."

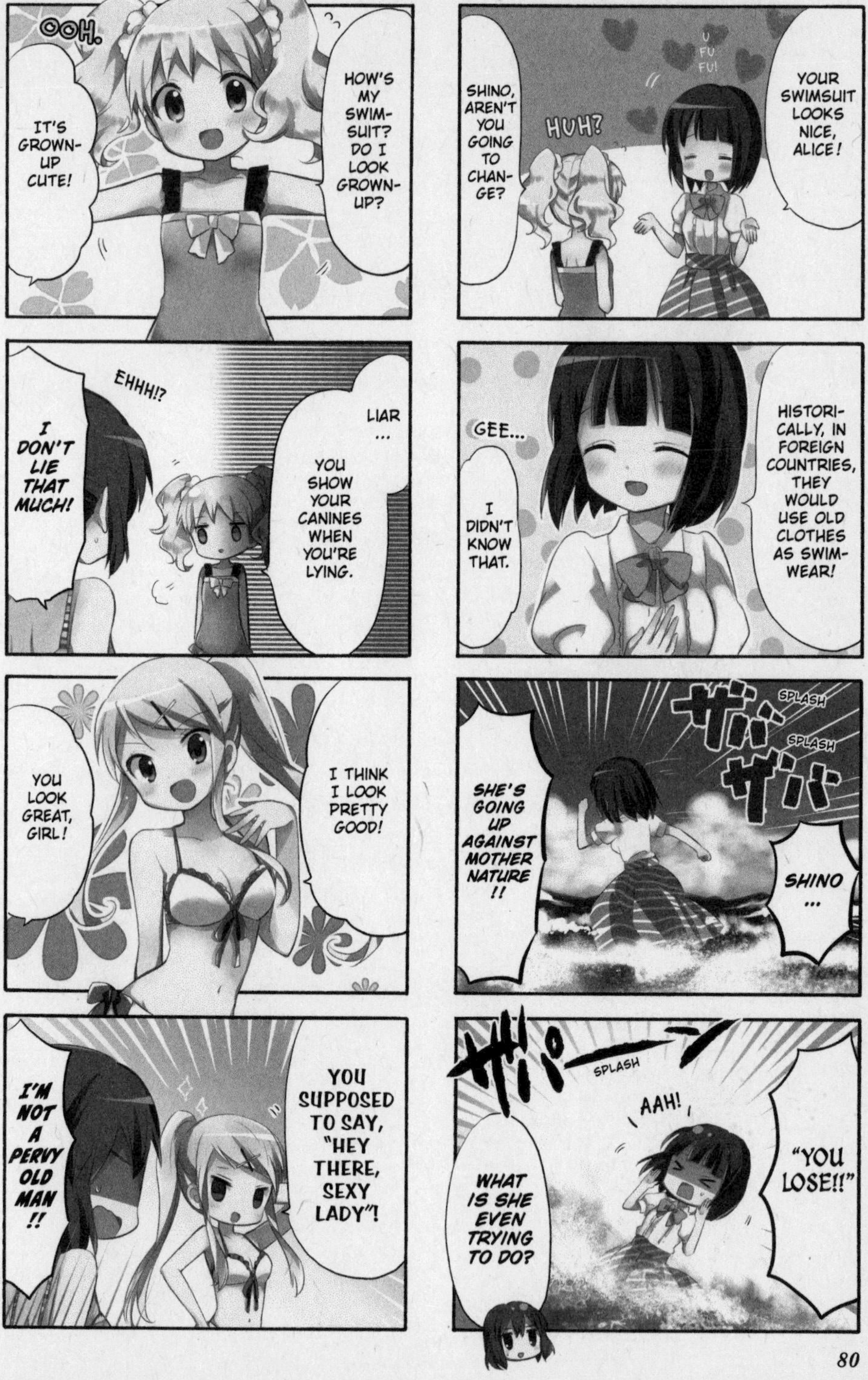
YOUR SWIMSUIT LOOKS NICE, ALICE!
UFUFU!
HUH?
SHINO, AREN'T YOU GOING TO CHANGE?
HOW'S MY SWIMSUIT? DO I LOOK GROWN-UP?
OOH.
IT'S GROWN-UP CUTE!
HISTORICALLY, IN FOREIGN COUNTRIES, THEY WOULD USE OLD CLOTHES AS SWIMWEAR!
GEE...
I DIDN'T KNOW THAT.
LIAR...
YOU SHOW YOUR CANINES WHEN YOU'RE LYING.
EHHH!?
I DON'T LIE THAT MUCH!
ザバ
SPLASH
ザバ
SPLASH
SHINO...
SHE'S GOING UP AGAINST MOTHER NATURE!!
I THINK I LOOK PRETTY GOOD!
YOU LOOK GREAT, GIRL!
ザパーー
SPLASH
"YOU LOSE!!"
AAH!
WHAT IS SHE EVEN TRYING TO DO?
YOU SUPPOSED TO SAY, "HEY THERE, SEXY LADY"!
I'M NOT A PERVY OLD MAN!!

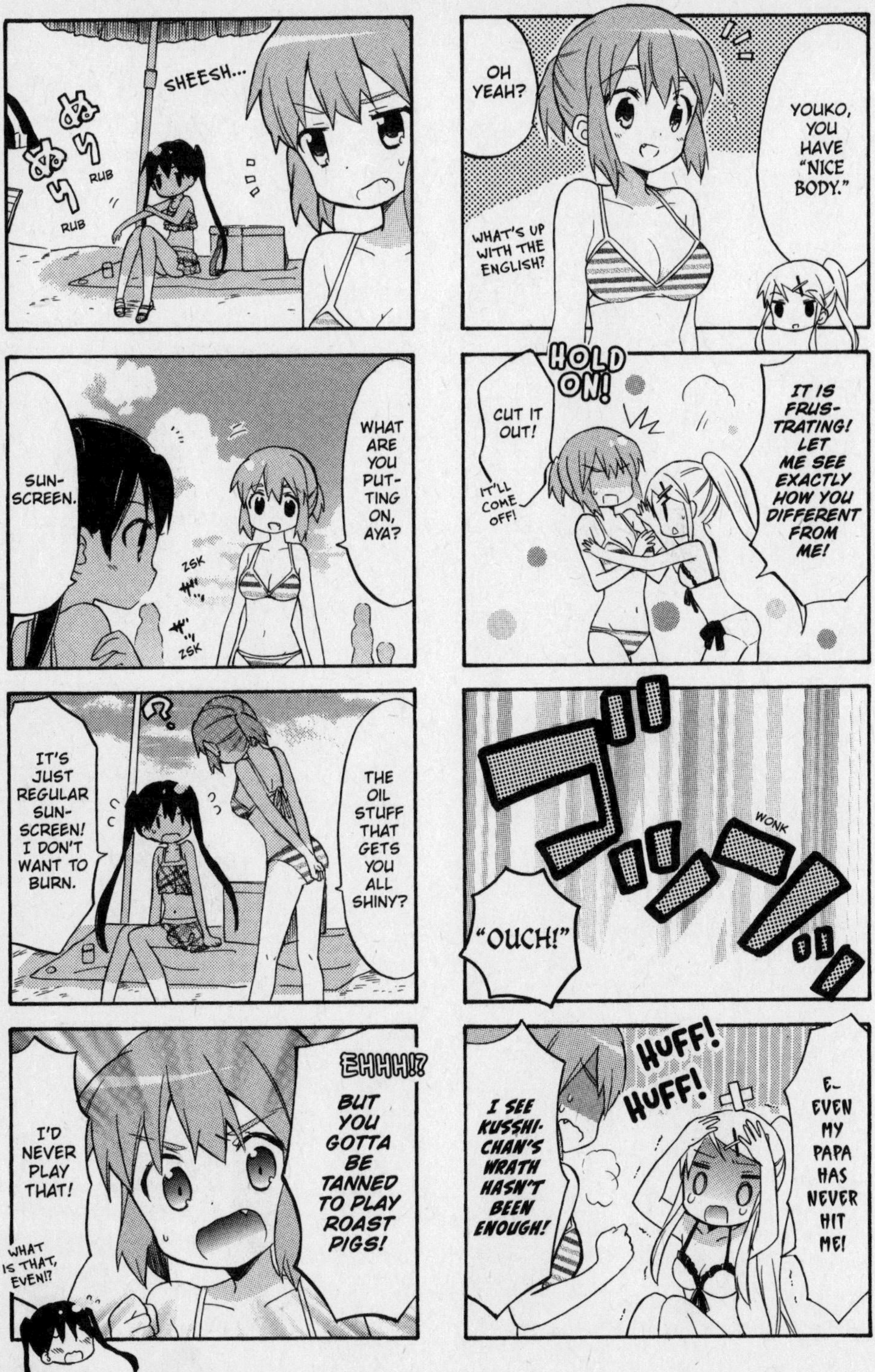
YOUKO, YOU HAVE "NICE BODY."
OH YEAH?
WHAT'S UP WITH THE ENGLISH?
IT IS FRUS-TRATING! LET ME SEE EXACTLY HOW YOU DIFFERENT FROM ME!
HOLD ON!
CUT IT OUT!
IT'LL COME OFF!
WONK
"OUCH!"
HUFF! HUFF!
E-EVEN MY PAPA HAS NEVER HIT ME!
I SEE KUSSHI-CHAN'S WRATH HASN'T BEEN ENOUGH!
SHEESH...
ぬりぬり
RUB
RUB
WHAT ARE YOU PUTTING ON, AYA?
SUN-SCREEN.
ZSK
ZSK
THE OIL STUFF THAT GETS YOU ALL SHINY?
IT'S JUST REGULAR SUN-SCREEN! I DON'T WANT TO BURN.
EHHH!?
BUT YOU GOTTA BE TANNED TO PLAY ROAST PIGS!
I'D NEVER PLAY THAT!
WHAT IS THAT, EVEN!?

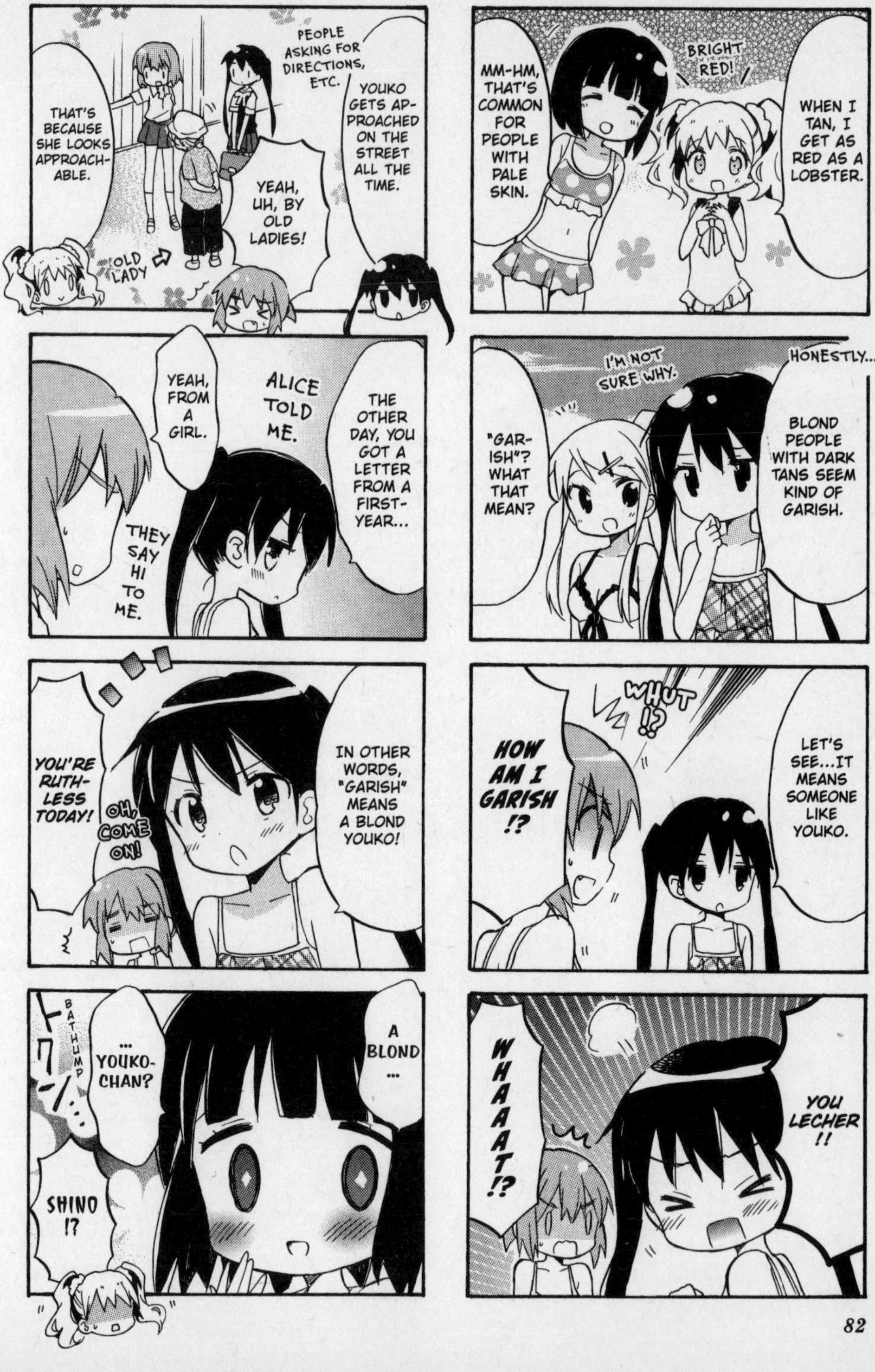

WHEN I TAN, I GET AS RED AS A LOBSTER.
BRIGHT RED!
MM-HM, THAT'S COMMON FOR PEOPLE WITH PALE SKIN.
HONESTLY...
BLOND PEOPLE WITH DARK TANS SEEM KIND OF GARISH.
I'M NOT SURE WHY.
"GAR-ISH"? WHAT THAT MEAN?
LET'S SEE...IT MEANS SOMEONE LIKE YOUKO.
WHUT !?
HOW AM I GARISH !?
YOU LECHER !!
WHAAAAT!?
PEOPLE ASKING FOR DIRECTIONS, ETC.
YOUKO GETS AP-PROACHED ON THE STREET ALL THE TIME.
YEAH, UH, BY OLD LADIES!
THAT'S BECAUSE SHE LOOKS APPROACH-ABLE.
OLD LADY
THE OTHER DAY, YOU GOT A LETTER FROM A FIRST-YEAR...
ALICE TOLD ME.
YEAH, FROM A GIRL.
THEY SAY HI TO ME.
IN OTHER WORDS, "GARISH" MEANS A BLOND YOUKO!
YOU'RE RUTH-LESS TODAY!
OH, COME ON!
A BLOND ...
... YOUKO-CHAN?
BATHUMP
SHINO !?

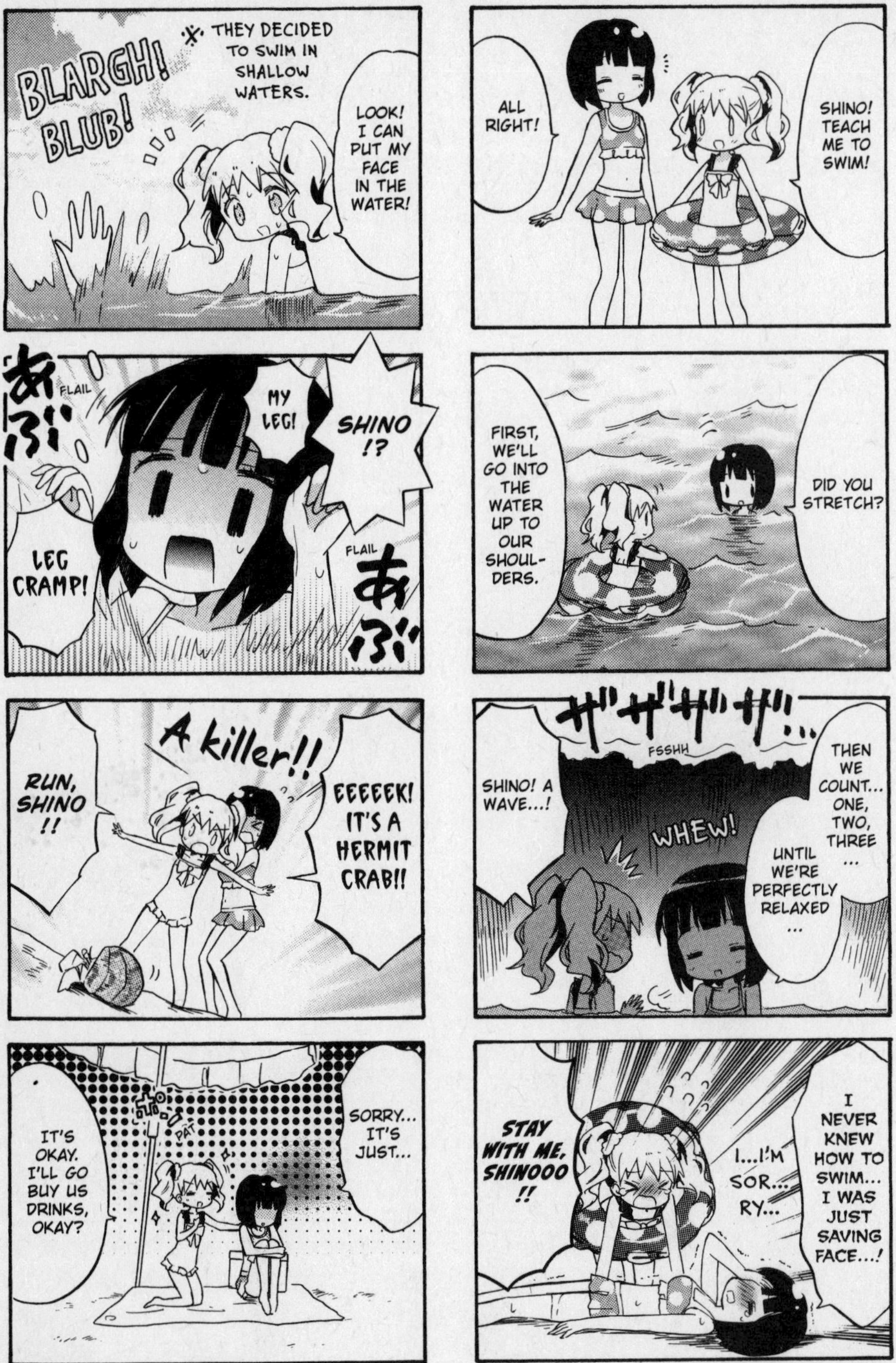

SHINO! TEACH ME TO SWIM!
ALL RIGHT!
DID YOU STRETCH?
FIRST, WE'LL GO INTO THE WATER UP TO OUR SHOULDERS.
ザザザザ…
FSSHH
THEN WE COUNT... ONE, TWO, THREE ...
UNTIL WE'RE PERFECTLY RELAXED ...
WHEW!
SHINO! A WAVE...!
I NEVER KNEW HOW TO SWIM... I WAS JUST SAVING FACE...!
I...I'M SOR... RY...
STAY WITH ME, SHINOOO !!
LOOK! I CAN PUT MY FACE IN THE WATER!
※ THEY DECIDED TO SWIM IN SHALLOW WATERS.
BLARGH! BLUB!
SHINO !?
MY LEG!
あぶ
FLAIL
あぶ
FLAIL
LEG CRAMP!
EEEEEK! IT'S A HERMIT CRAB!!
A killer!!
RUN, SHINO !!
SORRY... IT'S JUST...
PAT
IT'S OKAY. I'LL GO BUY US DRINKS, OKAY?

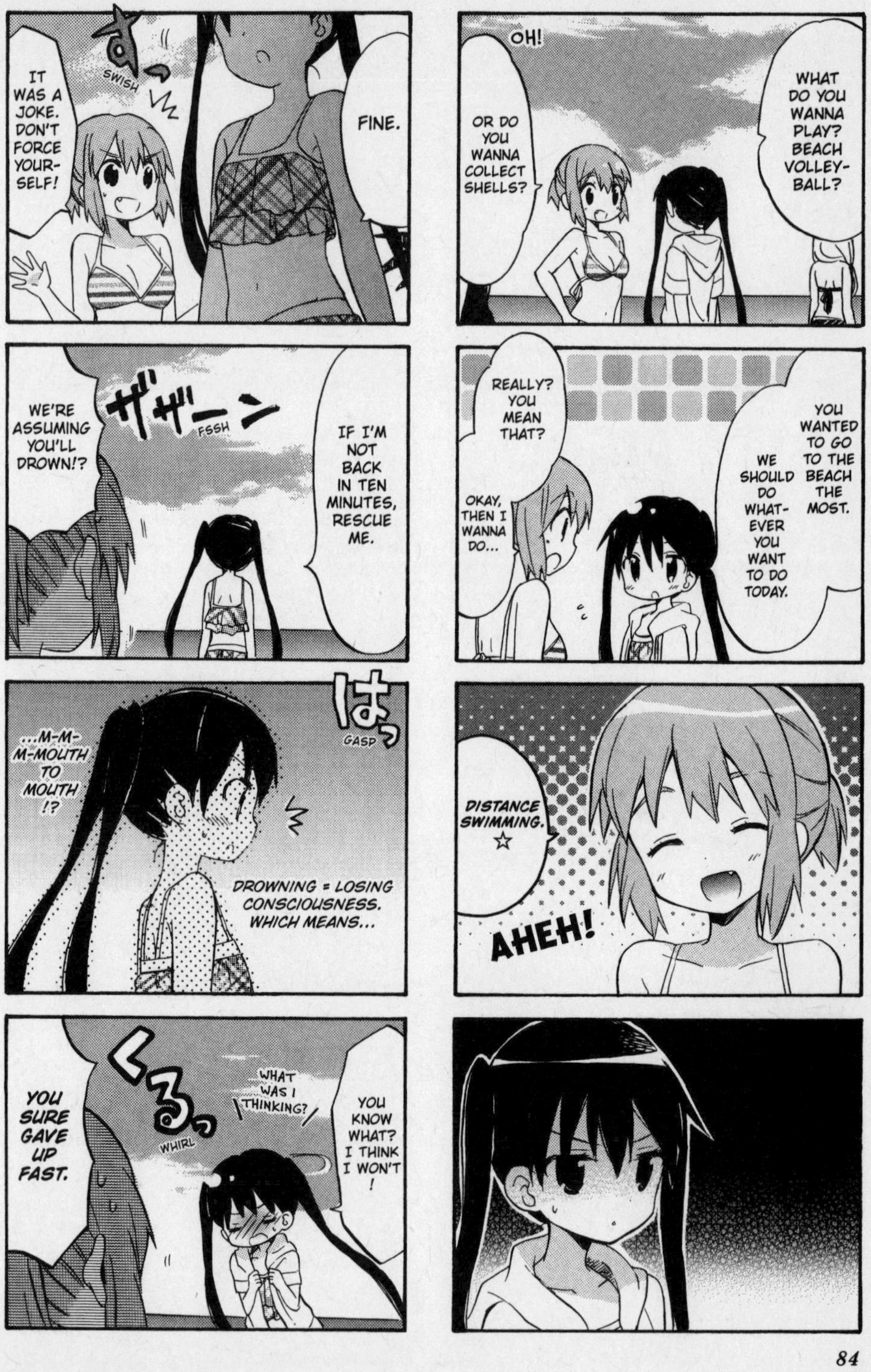
WHAT DO YOU WANNA PLAY? BEACH VOLLEY-BALL?
OH!
OR DO YOU WANNA COLLECT SHELLS?
YOU WANTED TO GO TO THE BEACH THE MOST.
WE SHOULD DO WHAT-EVER YOU WANT TO DO TODAY.
REALLY? YOU MEAN THAT?
OKAY, THEN I WANNA DO...
DISTANCE SWIMMING. ☆
AHEH!
FINE.
すっ
SWISH
IT WAS A JOKE. DON'T FORCE YOUR-SELF!
IF I'M NOT BACK IN TEN MINUTES, RESCUE ME.
ザザーン
FSSH
WE'RE ASSUMING YOU'LL DROWN!?
はっ
GASP
...M-M-M-MOUTH TO MOUTH !?
DROWNING = LOSING CONSCIOUSNESS. WHICH MEANS...
YOU KNOW WHAT? I THINK I WON'T !
WHAT WAS I THINKING?
くるっ
WHIRL
YOU SURE GAVE UP FAST.

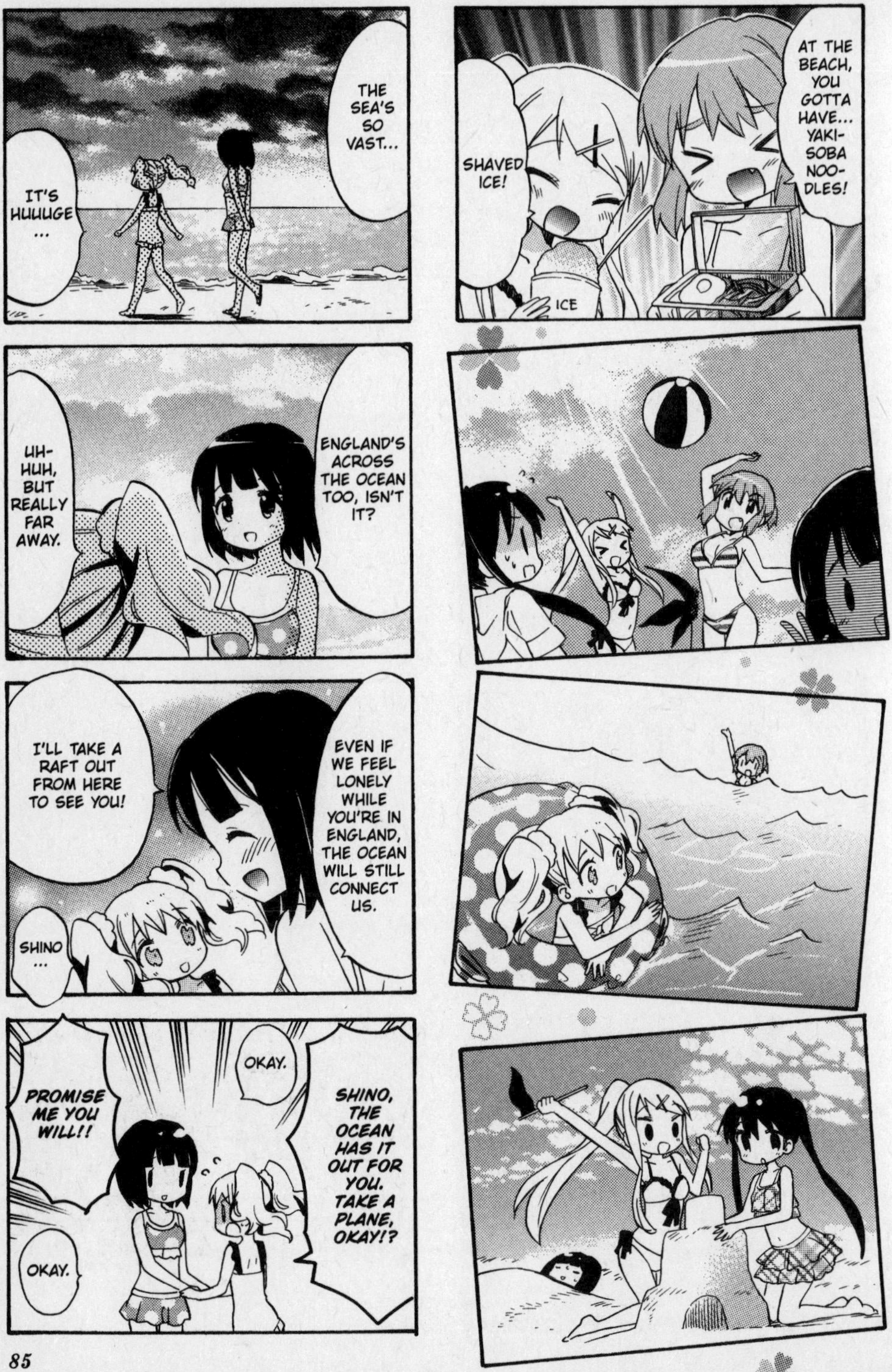

AT THE BEACH, YOU GOTTA HAVE... YAKI-SOBA NOODLES!
SHAVED ICE!
ICE
THE SEA'S SO VAST...
IT'S HUUUGE ...
ENGLAND'S ACROSS THE OCEAN TOO, ISN'T IT?
UH-HUH, BUT REALLY FAR AWAY.
EVEN IF WE FEEL LONELY WHILE YOU'RE IN ENGLAND, THE OCEAN WILL STILL CONNECT US.
I'LL TAKE A RAFT OUT FROM HERE TO SEE YOU!
SHINO ...
SHINO, THE OCEAN HAS IT OUT FOR YOU. TAKE A PLANE, OKAY!?
OKAY.
PROMISE ME YOU WILL!!
OKAY.

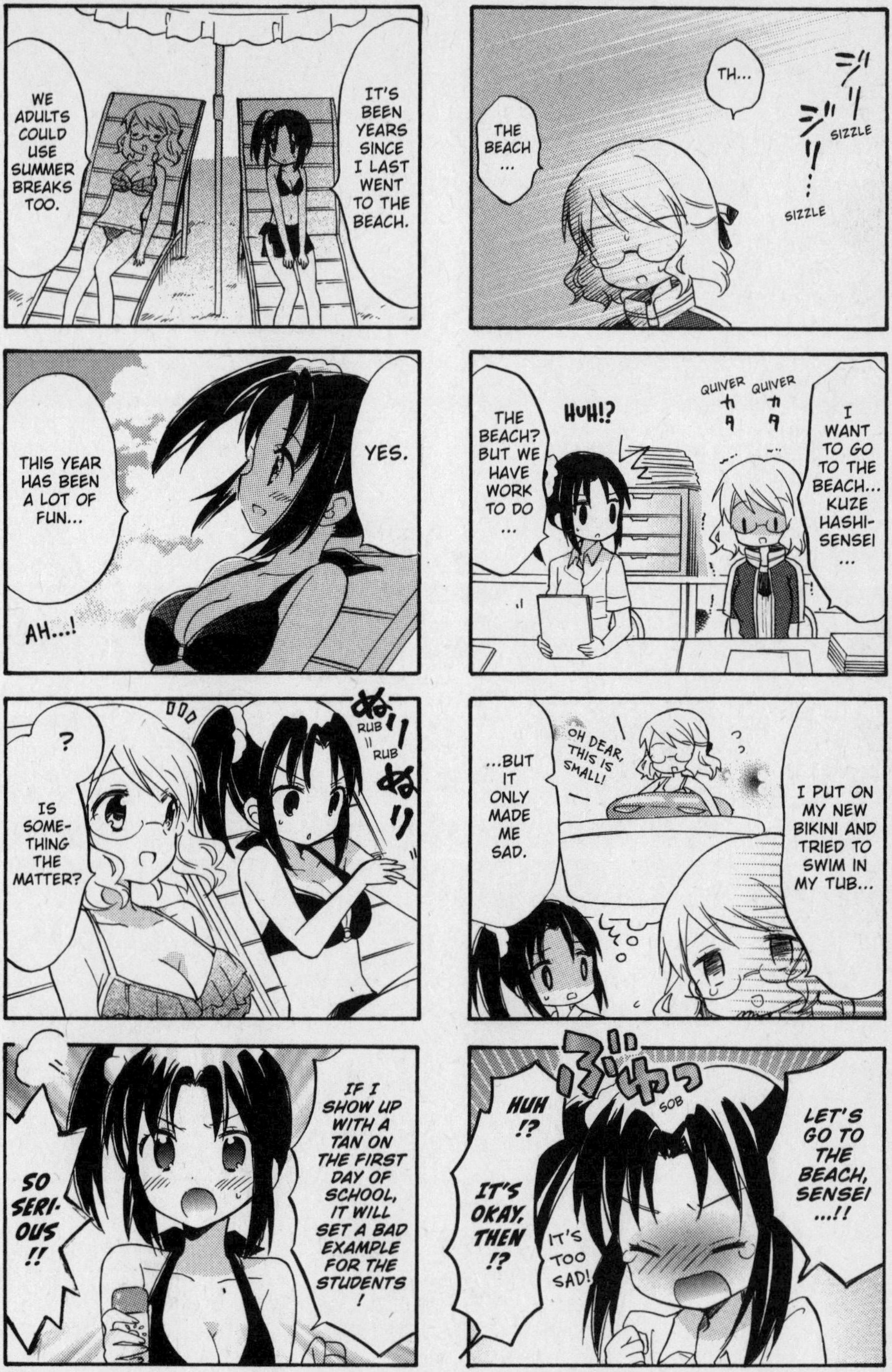
TH...
THE BEACH...
SIZZLE
SIZZLE
I WANT TO GO TO THE BEACH... KUZE HASHI-SENSEI...
QUIVER
QUIVER
HUH!?
THE BEACH? BUT WE HAVE WORK TO DO...
I PUT ON MY NEW BIKINI AND TRIED TO SWIM IN MY TUB...
OH DEAR, THIS IS SMALL!
...BUT IT ONLY MADE ME SAD.
LET'S GO TO THE BEACH, SENSEI...!!
SOB
HUH!?
IT'S OKAY, THEN!?
IT'S TOO SAD!
IT'S BEEN YEARS SINCE I LAST WENT TO THE BEACH.
WE ADULTS COULD USE SUMMER BREAKS TOO.
YES.
THIS YEAR HAS BEEN A LOT OF FUN...
AH...!
RUB
RUB
?
IS SOMETHING THE MATTER?
IF I SHOW UP WITH A TAN ON THE FIRST DAY OF SCHOOL, IT WILL SET A BAD EXAMPLE FOR THE STUDENTS!
SO SERIOUS!!

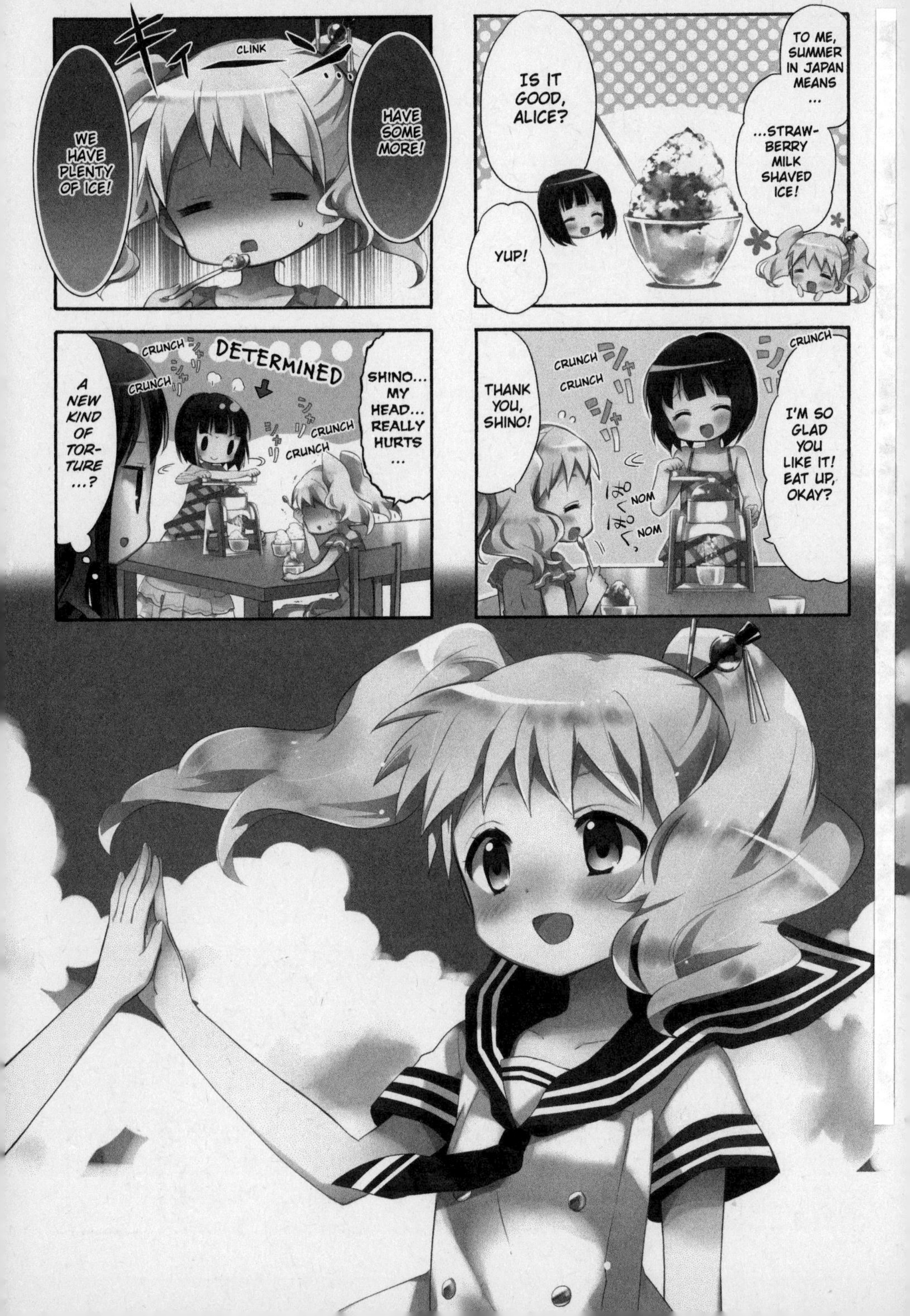
TO ME, SUMMER IN JAPAN MEANS ...
...STRAWBERRY MILK SHAVED ICE!
IS IT GOOD, ALICE?
YUP!
CLINK
HAVE SOME MORE!
WE HAVE PLENTY OF ICE!
CRUNCH
I'M SO GLAD YOU LIKE IT! EAT UP, OKAY?
CRUNCH
CRUNCH
THANK YOU, SHINO!
NOM
NOM
SHINO... MY HEAD... REALLY HURTS ...
CRUNCH
CRUNCH
DETERMINED
CRUNCH
CRUNCH
A NEW KIND OF TORTURE ...?

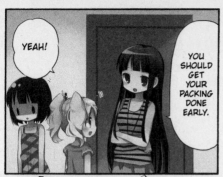

8 August
TUE WED THU FRI SAT
キュッ
SQUEAK
WITH EACH PASSING DAY...
...OUR SUMMER VACATION IS FLYING BY, HMM?
YUP!
OH?
THAT STAR MARK...
DO WE HAVE SPECIAL PLANS FOR THE DAY AFTER TOMORROW?
THAT'S THE DAY I LEAVE FOR ENGLAND!
WE TALKED ABOUT IT, REMEMBER?
YOU SHOULD GET YOUR PACKING DONE EARLY.
YEAH!
WHERE IS MY BAG?
UM, SHINO!?
PLEASE TAKE ME WITH YOU!
BAM
EHHHHHHHH!?
I'LL MISS YOU TOO MUCH, ALICE...
SHINO!
YOU'RE MAKING IT HARD FOR ME TOO!
OKAY! YOU'RE COMING WITH ME!!
ぎゅうぎゅう
PUSH PUSH
ALICE! MY NECK! MY NECK!

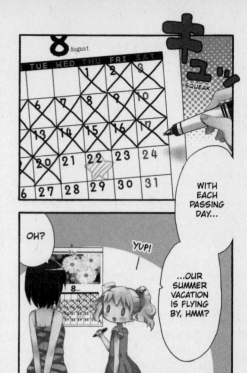

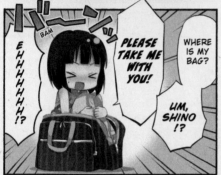

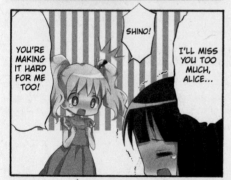

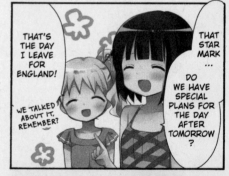

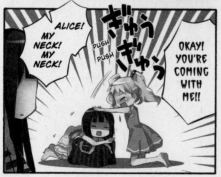

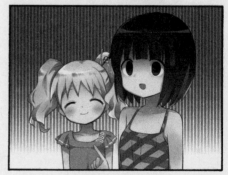

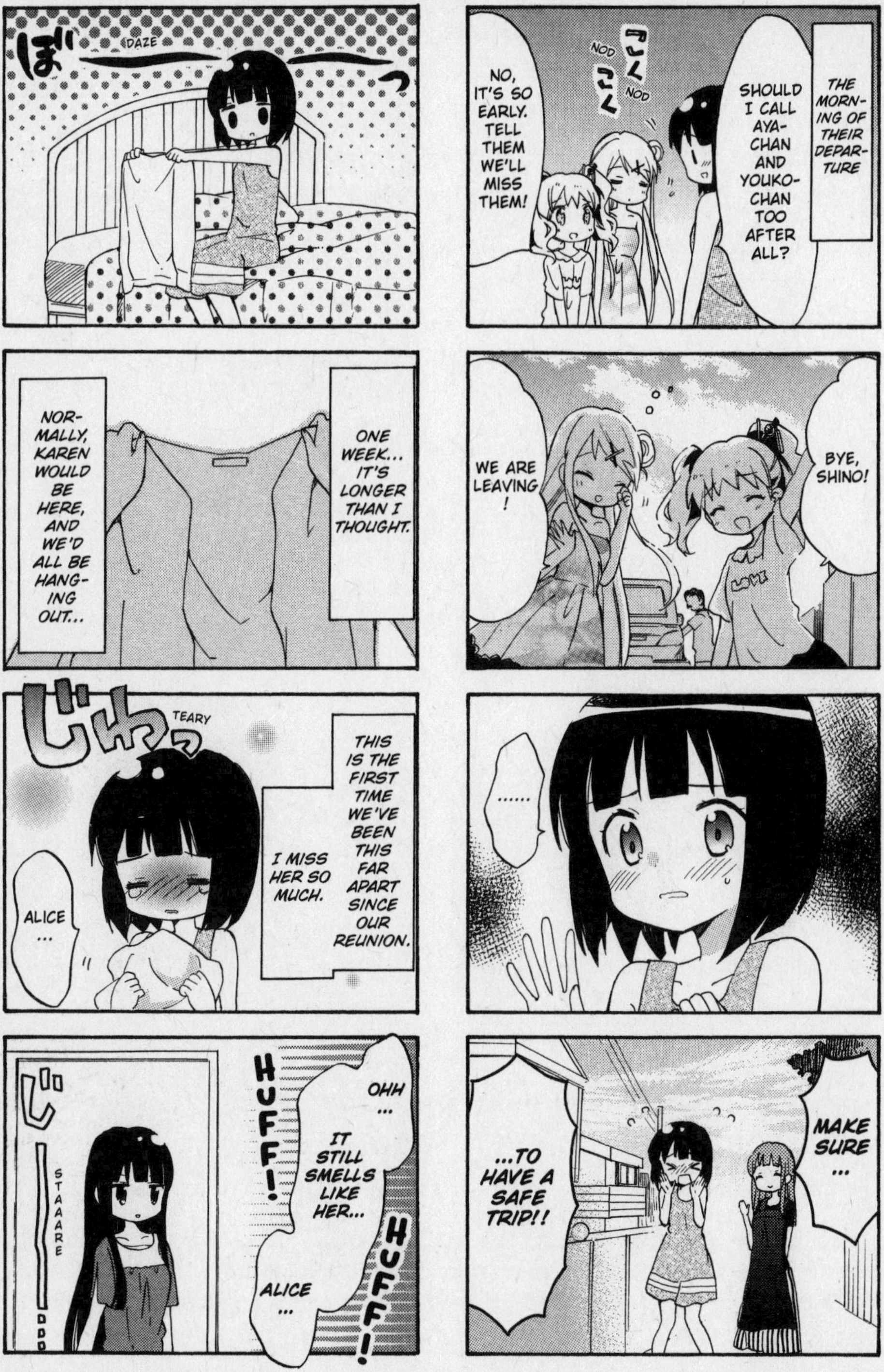
THE MORNING OF THEIR DEPARTURE
SHOULD I CALL AYA-CHAN AND YOUKO-CHAN TOO AFTER ALL?
NOD NOD
NO, IT'S SO EARLY. TELL THEM WE'LL MISS THEM!
DAZE
BYE, SHINO!
WE ARE LEAVING!
ONE WEEK... IT'S LONGER THAN I THOUGHT.
NORMALLY, KAREN WOULD BE HERE, AND WE'D ALL BE HANGING OUT...
......
TEARY
THIS IS THE FIRST TIME WE'VE BEEN THIS FAR APART SINCE OUR REUNION.
I MISS HER SO MUCH.
ALICE...
MAKE SURE...
...TO HAVE A SAFE TRIP!!
OHH... IT STILL SMELLS LIKE HER...
HUFF! HUFF!
ALICE...
STAAARE

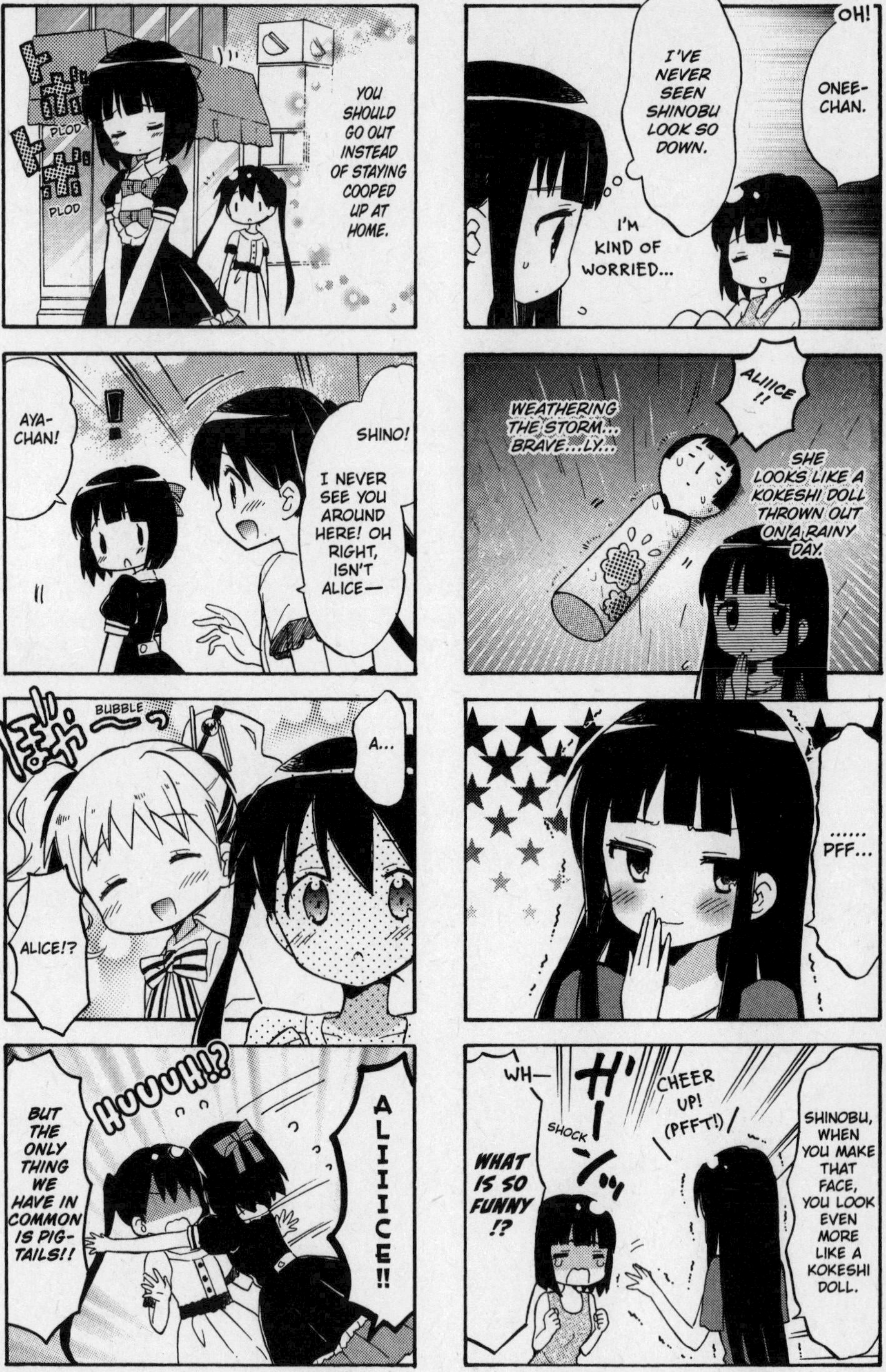
OH!
ONEE-CHAN.
I'VE NEVER SEEN SHINOBU LOOK SO DOWN.
I'M KIND OF WORRIED...
YOU SHOULD GO OUT INSTEAD OF STAYING COOPED UP AT HOME.
PLOD
PLOD
ALIIICE!!
WEATHERING THE STORM... BRAVE...LY...
SHE LOOKS LIKE A KOKESHI DOLL THROWN OUT ON A RAINY DAY.
SHINO!
I NEVER SEE YOU AROUND HERE! OH RIGHT, ISN'T ALICE—
AYA-CHAN!
......PFF...
A...
BUBBLE
ALICE!?
SHINOBU, WHEN YOU MAKE THAT FACE, YOU LOOK EVEN MORE LIKE A KOKESHI DOLL.
CHEER UP! (PFFT!)
SHOCK
WH—
WHAT IS SO FUNNY!?
ALIIICE!!
HUUUH!?
BUT THE ONLY THING WE HAVE IN COMMON IS PIG-TAILS!!

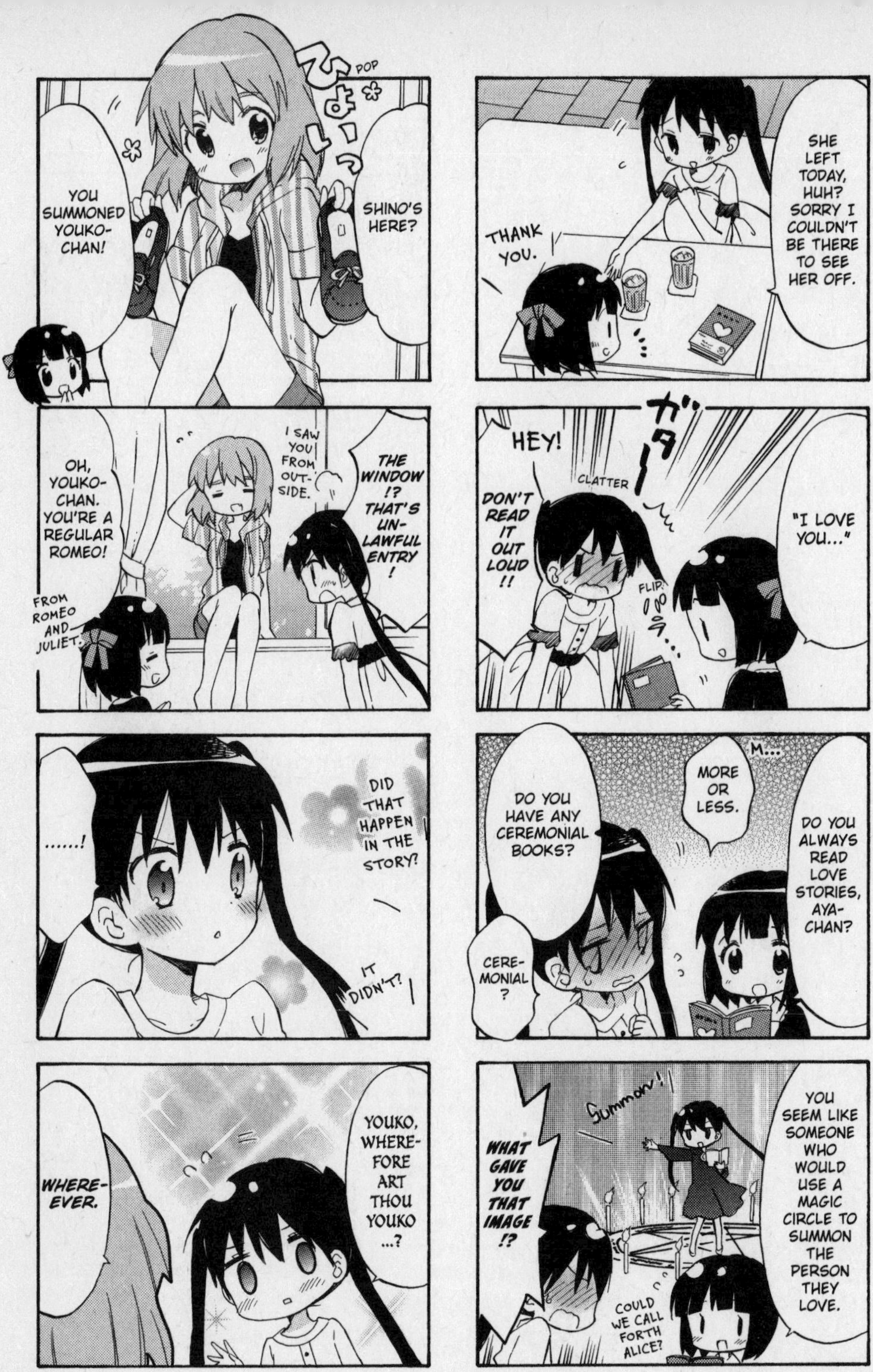
SHE LEFT TODAY, HUH? SORRY I COULDN'T BE THERE TO SEE HER OFF.
THANK YOU.
"I LOVE YOU..."
ガタ
CLATTER
HEY!
DON'T READ IT OUT LOUD!!
FLIP
DO YOU ALWAYS READ LOVE STORIES, AYA-CHAN?
M...
MORE OR LESS.
DO YOU HAVE ANY CEREMONIAL BOOKS?
CEREMONIAL?
YOU SEEM LIKE SOMEONE WHO WOULD USE A MAGIC CIRCLE TO SUMMON THE PERSON THEY LOVE.
Summon!
WHAT GAVE YOU THAT IMAGE!?
COULD WE CALL FORTH ALICE?
ひょこっ
POP
SHINO'S HERE?
YOU SUMMONED YOUKO-CHAN!
THE WINDOW!? THAT'S UNLAWFUL ENTRY!
I SAW YOU FROM OUTSIDE.
OH, YOUKO-CHAN. YOU'RE A REGULAR ROMEO!
FROM ROMEO AND JULIET.
DID THAT HAPPEN IN THE STORY?
IT DIDN'T?
......!
YOUKO, WHEREFORE ART THOU YOUKO...?
WHEREEVER.

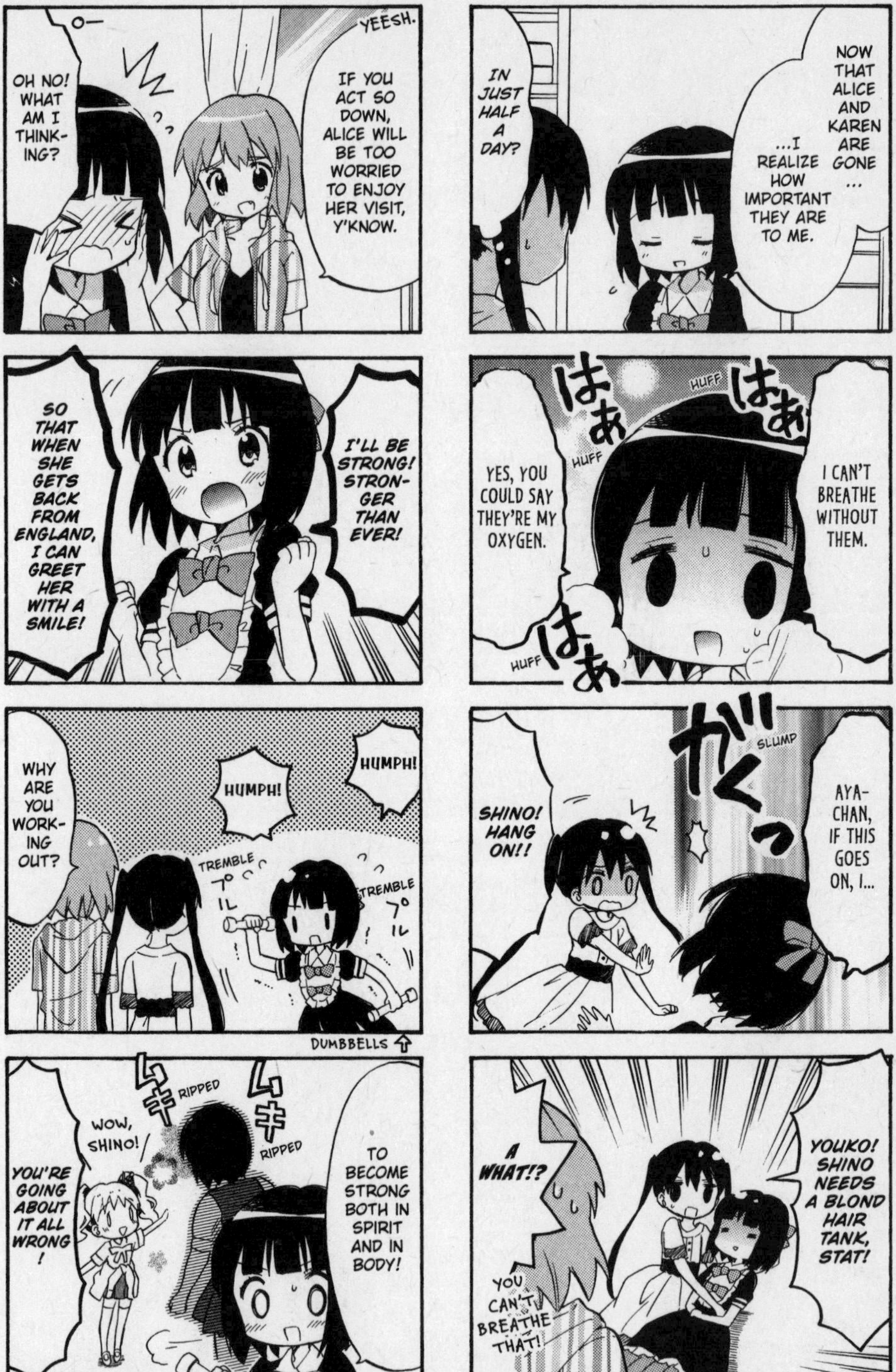
NOW THAT ALICE AND KAREN ARE GONE...
...I REALIZE HOW IMPORTANT THEY ARE TO ME.
IN JUST HALF A DAY?
はぁ
HUFF
はぁ
HUFF
I CAN'T BREATHE WITHOUT THEM.
YES, YOU COULD SAY THEY'RE MY OXYGEN.
はぁ
HUFF
がくっ
SLUMP
AYA-CHAN, IF THIS GOES ON, I...
SHINO! HANG ON!!
YOUKO! SHINO NEEDS A BLOND HAIR TANK, STAT!
A WHAT!?
YOU CAN'T BREATHE THAT!
YEESH.
IF YOU ACT SO DOWN, ALICE WILL BE TOO WORRIED TO ENJOY HER VISIT, Y'KNOW.
O—
OH NO! WHAT AM I THINKING?
I'LL BE STRONG! STRONGER THAN EVER!
SO THAT WHEN SHE GETS BACK FROM ENGLAND, I CAN GREET HER WITH A SMILE!
HUMPH!
HUMPH!
TREMBLE
プル
TREMBLE
プル
WHY ARE YOU WORKING OUT?
DUMBBELLS
ムキ
RIPPED
ムキ
RIPPED
TO BECOME STRONG BOTH IN SPIRIT AND IN BODY!
WOW, SHINO!
YOU'RE GOING ABOUT IT ALL WRONG!

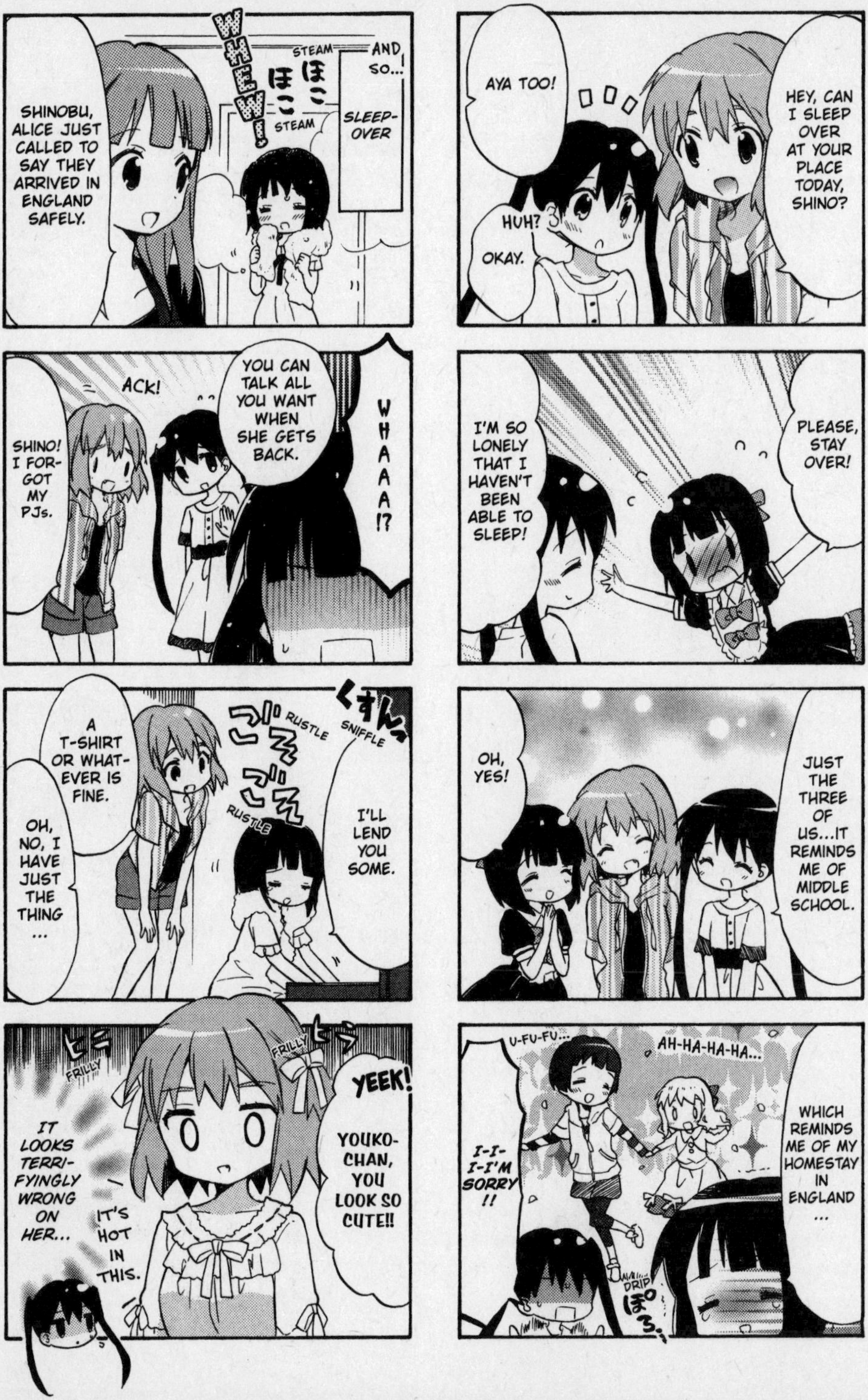
HEY, CAN I SLEEP OVER AT YOUR PLACE TODAY, SHINO?
AYA TOO!
HUH?
OKAY.
AND SO... SLEEP-OVER
STEAM ほこ ほこ STEAM
WHEW!
SHINOBU, ALICE JUST CALLED TO SAY THEY ARRIVED IN ENGLAND SAFELY.
PLEASE, STAY OVER!
I'M SO LONELY THAT I HAVEN'T BEEN ABLE TO SLEEP!
WHAAAA!?
YOU CAN TALK ALL YOU WANT WHEN SHE GETS BACK.
ACK!
SHINO! I FOR-GOT MY PJs.
JUST THE THREE OF US...IT REMINDS ME OF MIDDLE SCHOOL.
OH, YES!
くすん SNIFFLE
I'LL LEND YOU SOME.
ごそごそ RUSTLE RUSTLE
A T-SHIRT OR WHAT-EVER IS FINE.
OH, NO, I HAVE JUST THE THING...
WHICH REMINDS ME OF MY HOMESTAY IN ENGLAND...
AH-HA-HA-HA...
U-FU-FU...
I-I-I-I'M SORRY!!
DRIP ぽろ...
YEEK!
YOUKO-CHAN, YOU LOOK SO CUTE!!
ヒラ FRILLY
ヒラ FRILLY
IT'S HOT IN THIS.
IT LOOKS TERRI-FYINGLY WRONG ON HER...

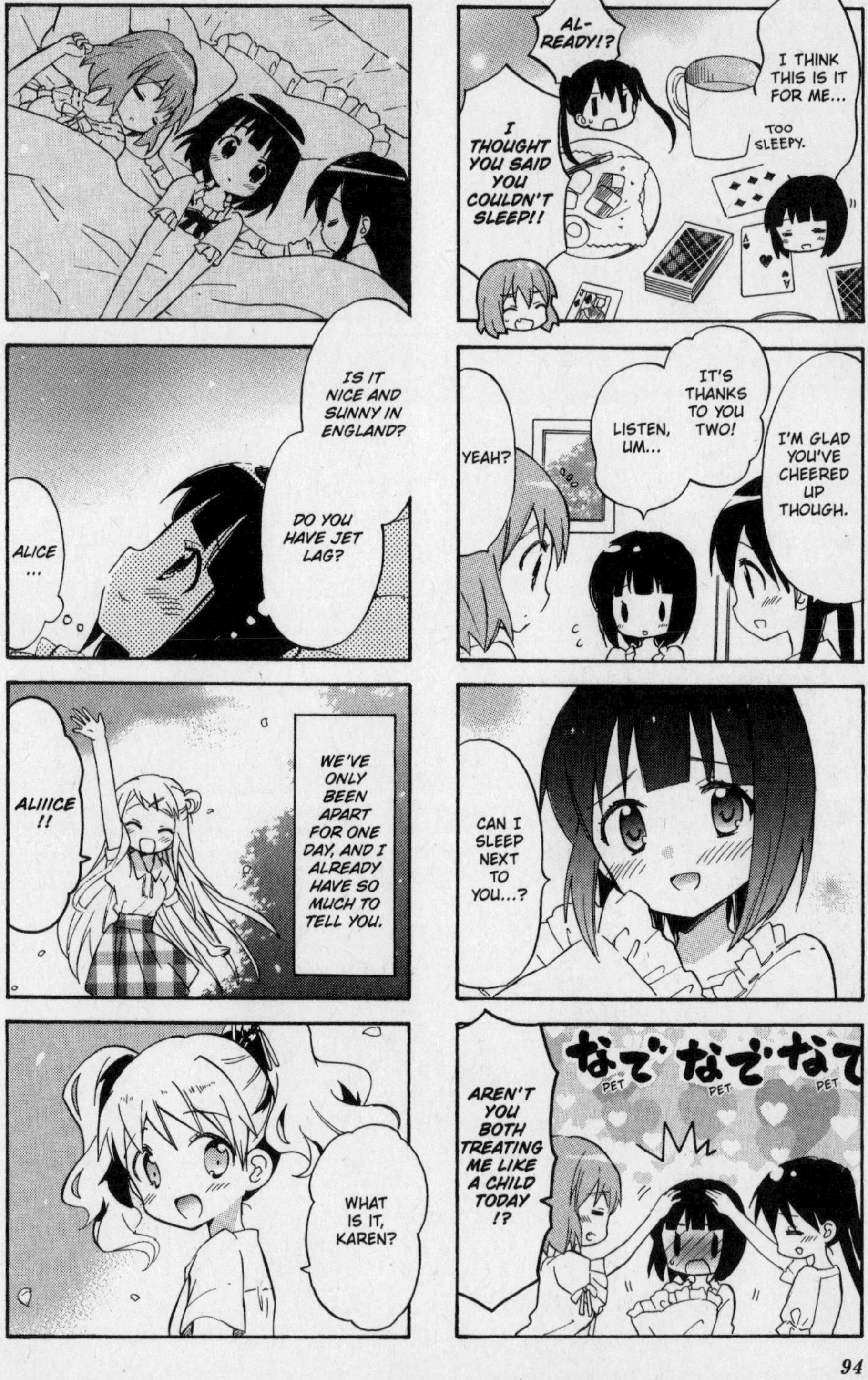
I THINK THIS IS IT FOR ME...
TOO SLEEPY.
AL-READY!?
I THOUGHT YOU SAID YOU COULDN'T SLEEP!!
I'M GLAD YOU'VE CHEERED UP THOUGH.
IT'S THANKS TO YOU TWO!
LISTEN, UM...
YEAH?
IS IT NICE AND SUNNY IN ENGLAND?
DO YOU HAVE JET LAG?
ALICE ...
CAN I SLEEP NEXT TO YOU...?
WE'VE ONLY BEEN APART FOR ONE DAY, AND I ALREADY HAVE SO MUCH TO TELL YOU.
ALIIICE !!
なでなでなで
PET PET PET
AREN'T YOU BOTH TREATING ME LIKE A CHILD TODAY !?
WHAT IS IT, KAREN?

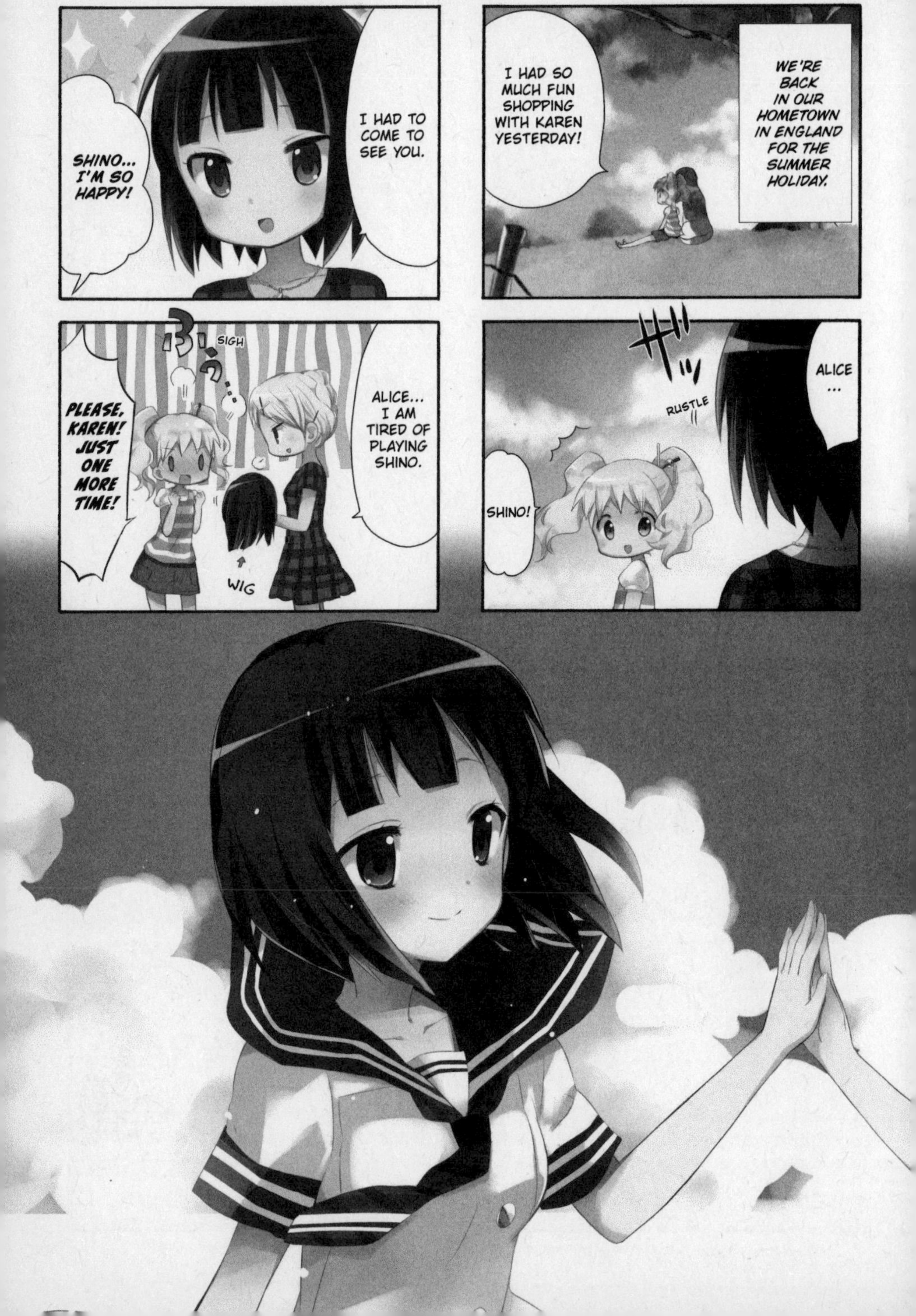
WE'RE BACK IN OUR HOMETOWN IN ENGLAND FOR THE SUMMER HOLIDAY.
I HAD SO MUCH FUN SHOPPING WITH KAREN YESTERDAY!
I HAD TO COME TO SEE YOU.
SHINO... I'M SO HAPPY!
ALICE ...
RUSTLE
SHINO!
ALICE... I AM TIRED OF PLAYING SHINO.
SIGH
PLEASE, KAREN! JUST ONE MORE TIME!
WIG

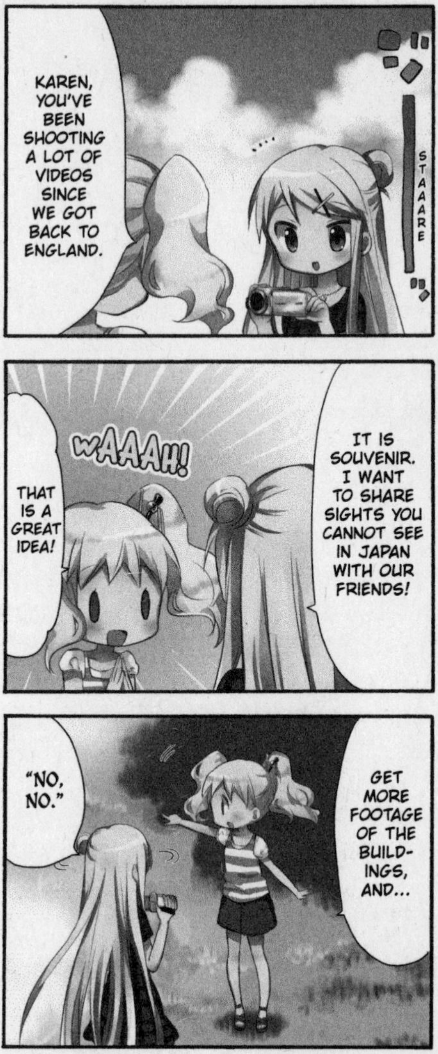
KAREN, YOU'VE BEEN SHOOTING A LOT OF VIDEOS SINCE WE GOT BACK TO ENGLAND.
....
STAAARE
IT IS SOUVENIR. I WANT TO SHARE SIGHTS YOU CANNOT SEE IN JAPAN WITH OUR FRIENDS!
WAAAH!
THAT IS A GREAT IDEA!
GET MORE FOOTAGE OF THE BUILDINGS, AND...
"NO, NO."
THIS IS FOR THE "SAD ALICE MISSES SHINO COLLECTION"!
WHAT IS THAT!?
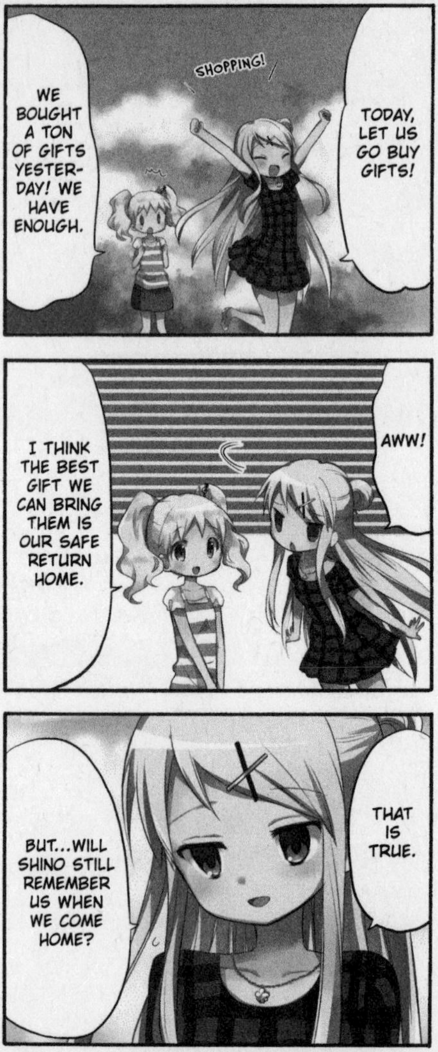
TODAY, LET US GO BUY GIFTS!
SHOPPING!
WE BOUGHT A TON OF GIFTS YESTERDAY! WE HAVE ENOUGH.
AWW!
I THINK THE BEST GIFT WE CAN BRING THEM IS OUR SAFE RETURN HOME.
THAT IS TRUE.
BUT...WILL SHINO STILL REMEMBER US WHEN WE COME HOME?
IT MAY BE TOO LATE...

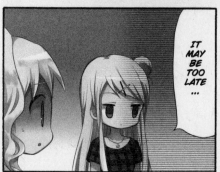

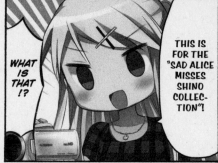

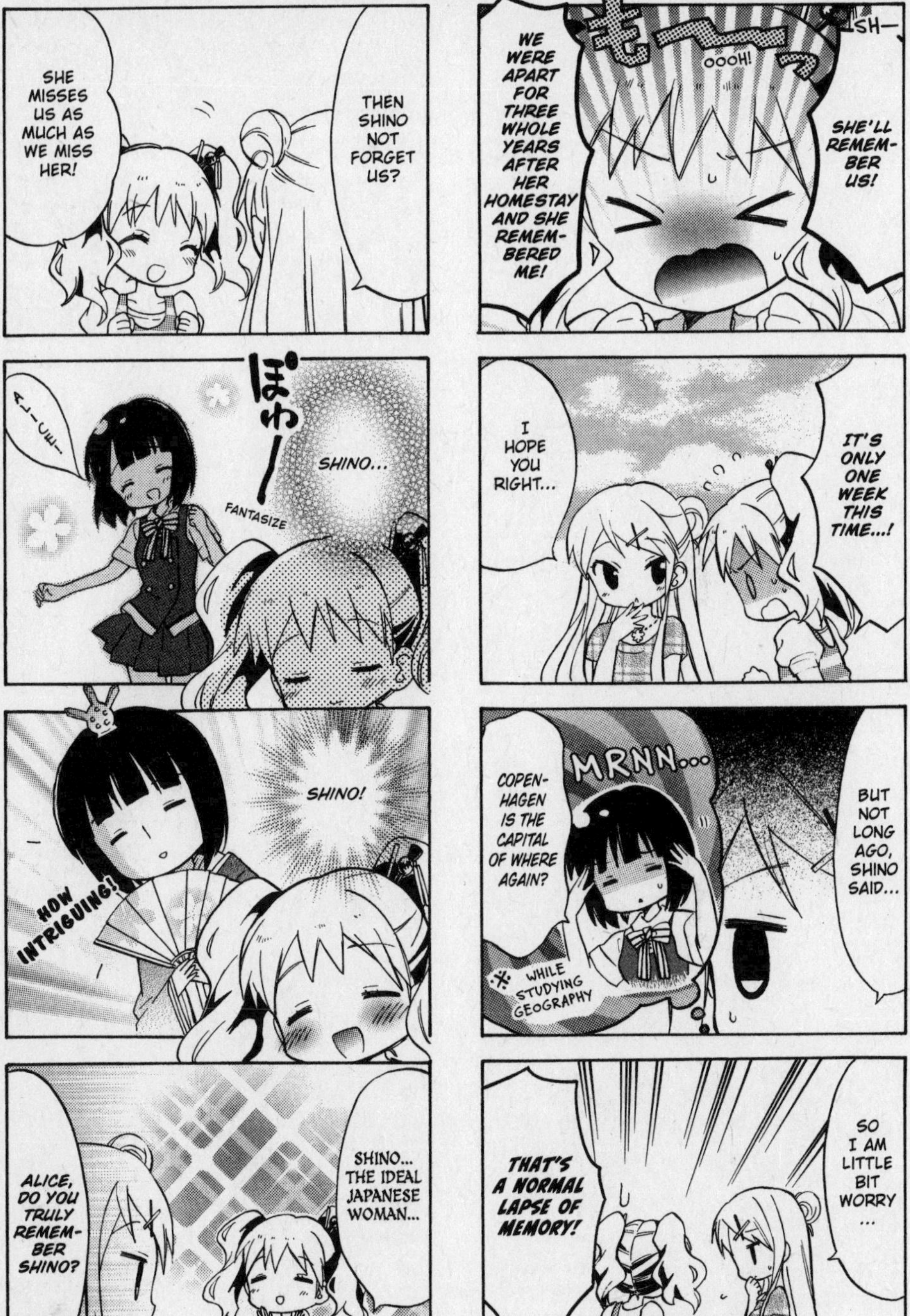

SH—
OOOH!
SHE'LL REMEMBER US!
WE WERE APART FOR THREE WHOLE YEARS AFTER HER HOMESTAY AND SHE REMEMBERED ME!
IT'S ONLY ONE WEEK THIS TIME...!
I HOPE YOU RIGHT...
BUT NOT LONG AGO, SHINO SAID...
MRNN...
COPENHAGEN IS THE CAPITAL OF WHERE AGAIN?
※ WHILE STUDYING GEOGRAPHY
SO I AM LITTLE BIT WORRY ...
THAT'S A NORMAL LAPSE OF MEMORY!
THEN SHINO NOT FORGET US?
SHE MISSES US AS MUCH AS WE MISS HER!
ぽわー
FANTASIZE
SHINO...
A—LICE—
SHINO!
HOW INTRIGUING!
SHINO... THE IDEAL JAPANESE WOMAN...
ALICE, DO YOU TRULY REMEMBER SHINO?

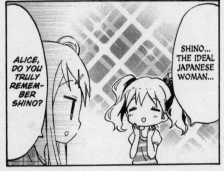

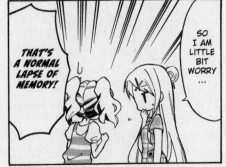

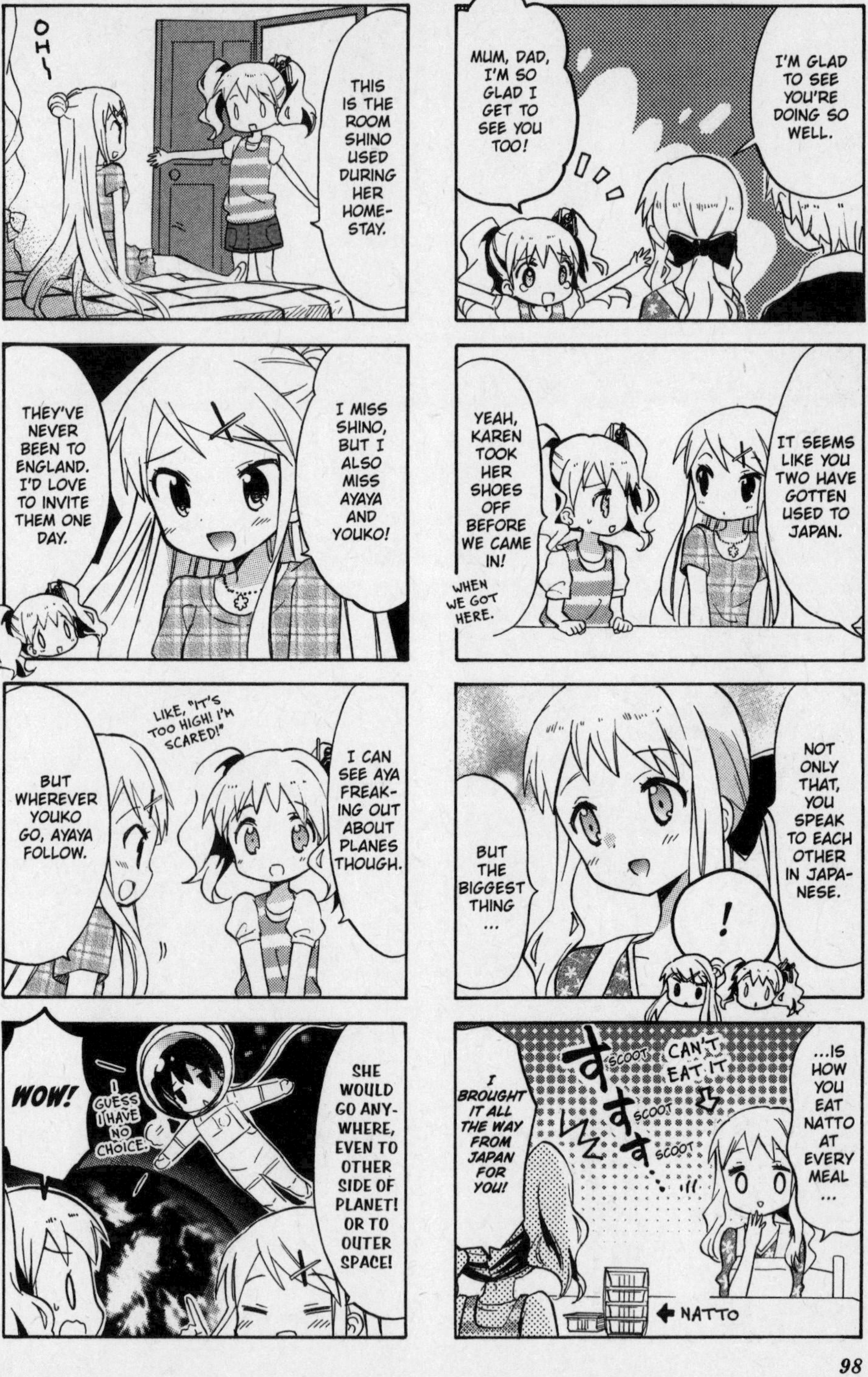
I'M GLAD TO SEE YOU'RE DOING SO WELL.
MUM, DAD, I'M SO GLAD I GET TO SEE YOU TOO!
IT SEEMS LIKE YOU TWO HAVE GOTTEN USED TO JAPAN.
YEAH, KAREN TOOK HER SHOES OFF BEFORE WE CAME IN!
WHEN WE GOT HERE.
NOT ONLY THAT, YOU SPEAK TO EACH OTHER IN JAPANESE.
!
BUT THE BIGGEST THING...
...IS HOW YOU EAT NATTO AT EVERY MEAL...
CAN'T EAT IT
SCOOT
SCOOT
SCOOT
I BROUGHT IT ALL THE WAY FROM JAPAN FOR YOU!
NATTO
THIS IS THE ROOM SHINO USED DURING HER HOME-STAY.
OH~
I MISS SHINO, BUT I ALSO MISS AYAYA AND YOUKO!
THEY'VE NEVER BEEN TO ENGLAND. I'D LOVE TO INVITE THEM ONE DAY.
I CAN SEE AYA FREAKING OUT ABOUT PLANES THOUGH.
LIKE, "IT'S TOO HIGH! I'M SCARED!"
BUT WHEREVER YOUKO GO, AYAYA FOLLOW.
SHE WOULD GO ANYWHERE, EVEN TO OTHER SIDE OF PLANET! OR TO OUTER SPACE!
I GUESS I HAVE NO CHOICE.
WOW!

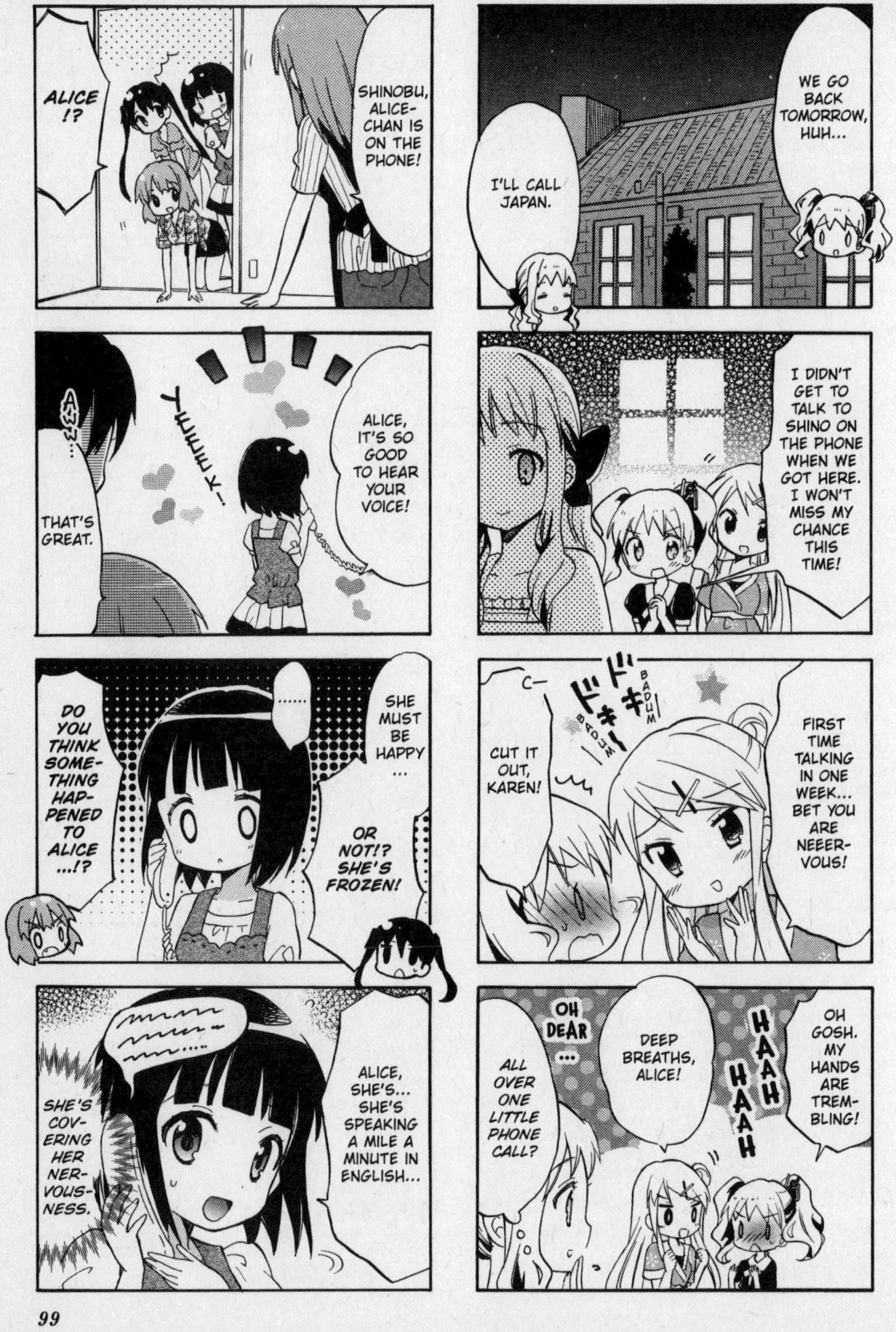

WE GO BACK TOMORROW, HUH...
I'LL CALL JAPAN.
I DIDN'T GET TO TALK TO SHINO ON THE PHONE WHEN WE GOT HERE. I WON'T MISS MY CHANCE THIS TIME!
FIRST TIME TALKING IN ONE WEEK... BET YOU ARE NEEER-VOUS!
ドキ ドキ
BADUM BADUM
C—
CUT IT OUT, KAREN!
OH GOSH. MY HANDS ARE TREMBLING!
HAAH HAAH
DEEP BREATHS, ALICE!
OH DEAR ...
ALL OVER ONE LITTLE PHONE CALL?
SHINOBU, ALICE-CHAN IS ON THE PHONE!
ALICE !?
ALICE, IT'S SO GOOD TO HEAR YOUR VOICE!
TEEEEK!
AWW... THAT'S GREAT.
SHE MUST BE HAPPY ...
......
OR NOT!? SHE'S FROZEN!
DO YOU THINK SOMETHING HAPPENED TO ALICE ...!?
ALICE, SHE'S... SHE'S SPEAKING A MILE A MINUTE IN ENGLISH...
SHE'S COVERING HER NERVOUSNESS.

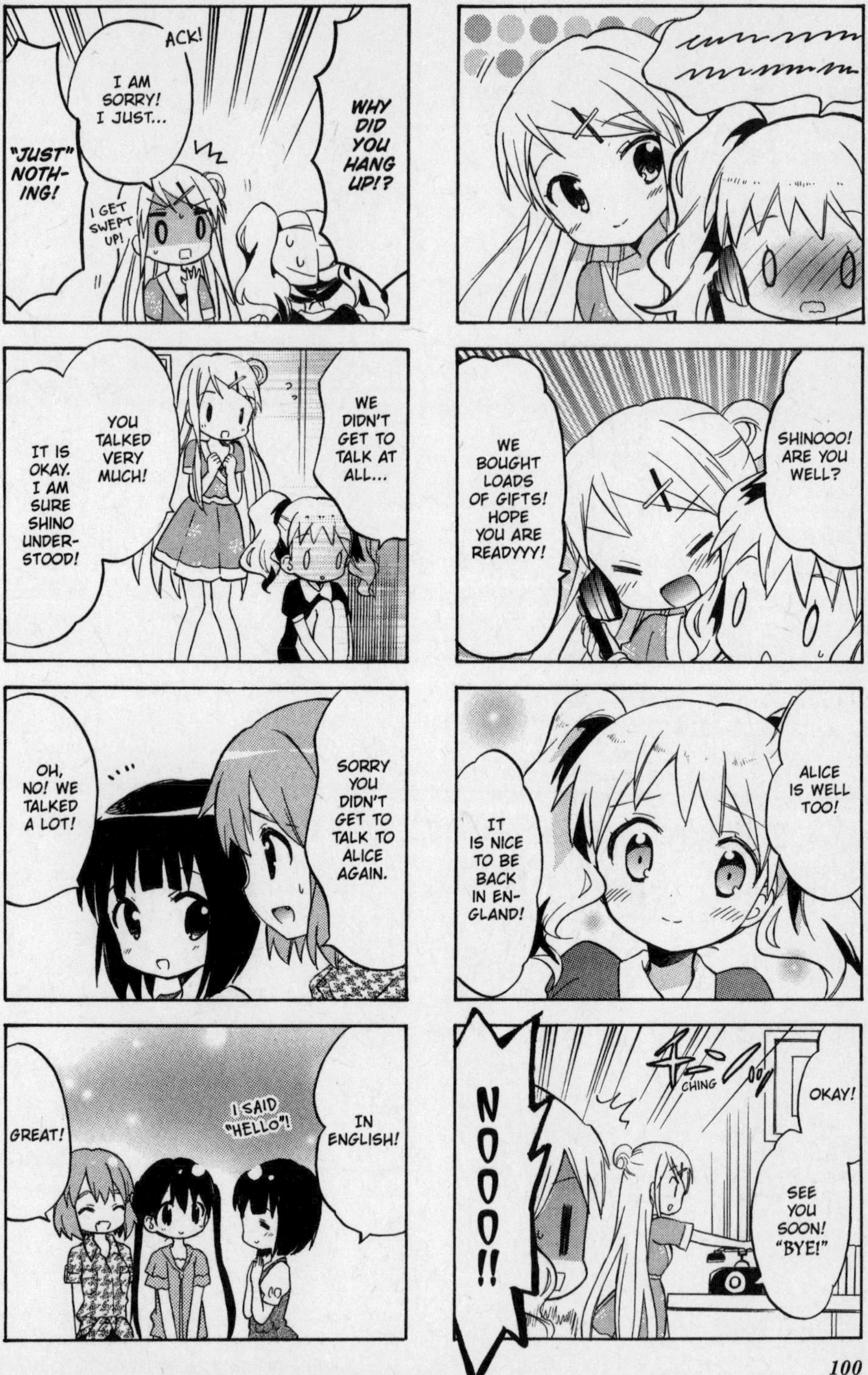
SHINOOO! ARE YOU WELL?
WE BOUGHT LOADS OF GIFTS! HOPE YOU ARE READYYY!
ALICE IS WELL TOO!
IT IS NICE TO BE BACK IN ENGLAND!
CHING
OKAY!
SEE YOU SOON! "BYE!"
NOOOO!!
WHY DID YOU HANG UP!?
ACK!
I AM SORRY! I JUST...
I GET SWEPT UP!
"JUST" NOTHING!
WE DIDN'T GET TO TALK AT ALL...
YOU TALKED VERY MUCH!
IT IS OKAY. I AM SURE SHINO UNDERSTOOD!
SORRY YOU DIDN'T GET TO TALK TO ALICE AGAIN.
OH, NO! WE TALKED A LOT!
IN ENGLISH!
I SAID "HELLO"!
GREAT!

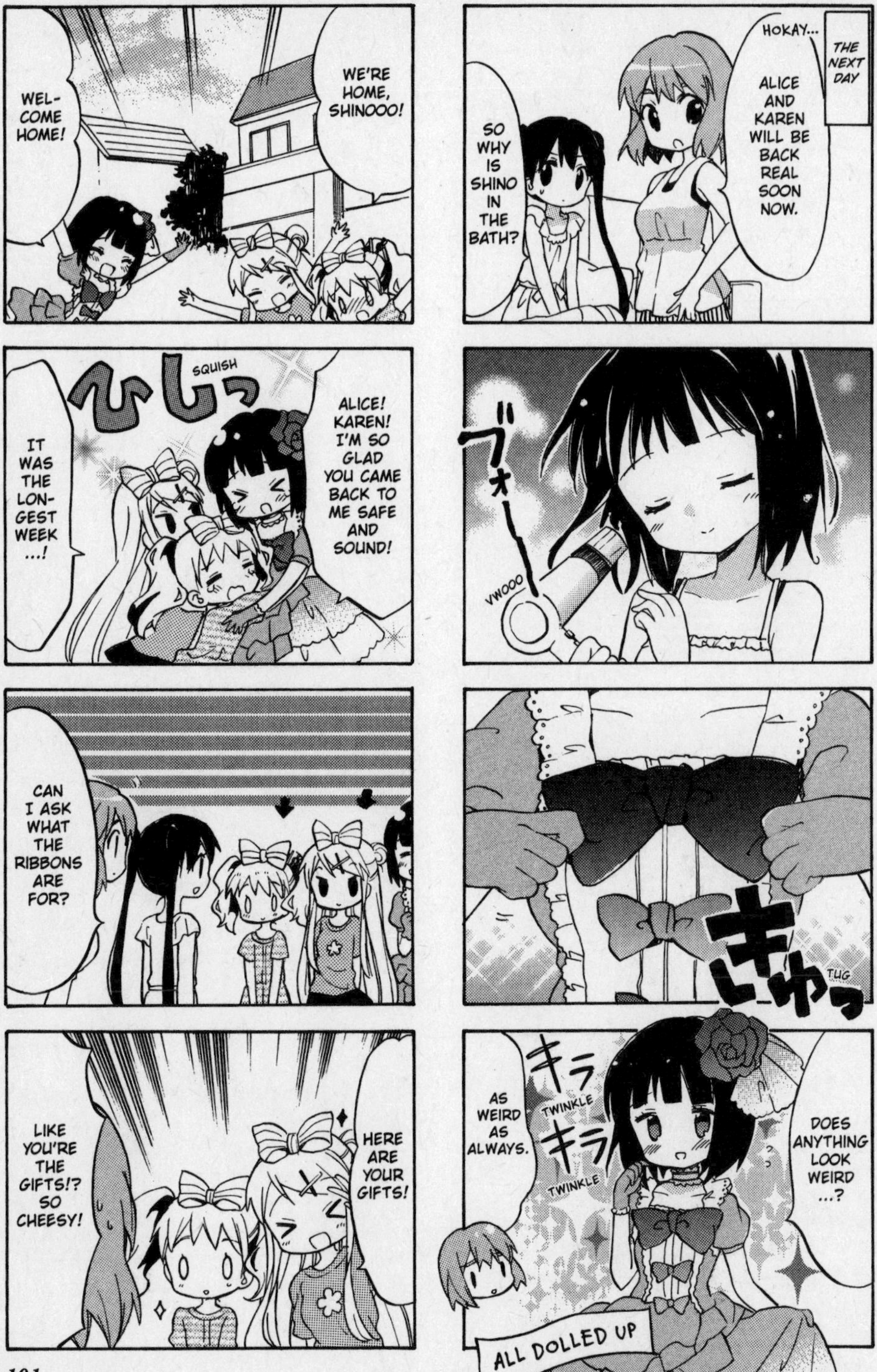
THE NEXT DAY
HOKAY... ALICE AND KAREN WILL BE BACK REAL SOON NOW.
SO WHY IS SHINO IN THE BATH?
ブォー
VWOOO
きゅっ
TUG
DOES ANYTHING LOOK WEIRD ...?
キラ
TWINKLE
キラ
TWINKLE
AS WEIRD AS ALWAYS.
ALL DOLLED UP
WE'RE HOME, SHINOOO!
WEL-COME HOME!
ALICE! KAREN! I'M SO GLAD YOU CAME BACK TO ME SAFE AND SOUND!
ひしっ
SQUISH
IT WAS THE LON-GEST WEEK ...!
CAN I ASK WHAT THE RIBBONS ARE FOR?
HERE ARE YOUR GIFTS!
LIKE YOU'RE THE GIFTS!? SO CHEESY!

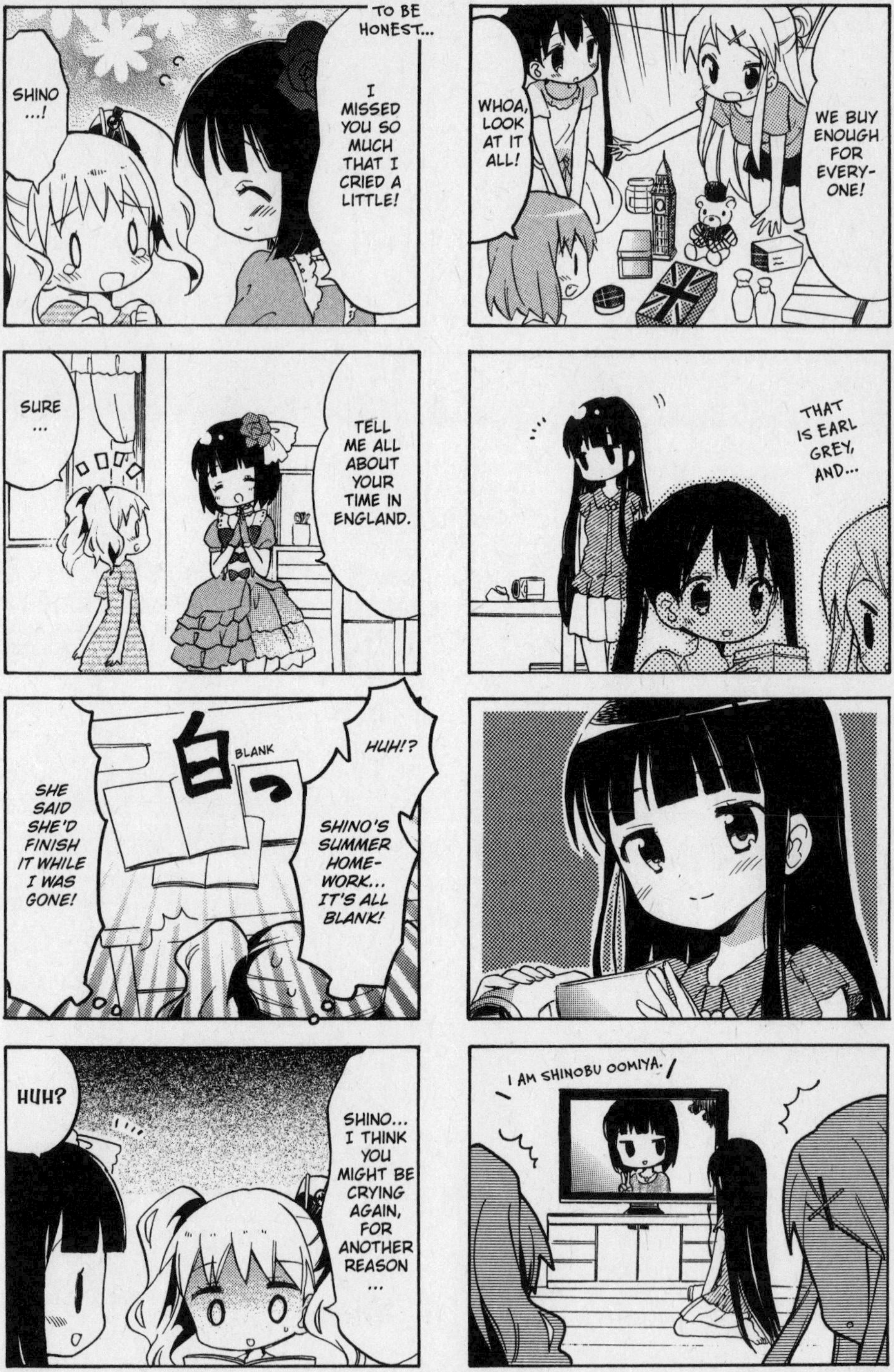
WE BUY ENOUGH FOR EVERY-ONE!
WHOA, LOOK AT IT ALL!
TO BE HONEST...
I MISSED YOU SO MUCH THAT I CRIED A LITTLE!
SHINO ...!
THAT IS EARL GREY, AND...
TELL ME ALL ABOUT YOUR TIME IN ENGLAND.
SURE ...
白っ
BLANK
HUH!?
SHINO'S SUMMER HOME-WORK... IT'S ALL BLANK!
SHE SAID SHE'D FINISH IT WHILE I WAS GONE!
I AM SHINOBU OOMIYA.
SHINO... I THINK YOU MIGHT BE CRYING AGAIN, FOR ANOTHER REASON ...
HUH?

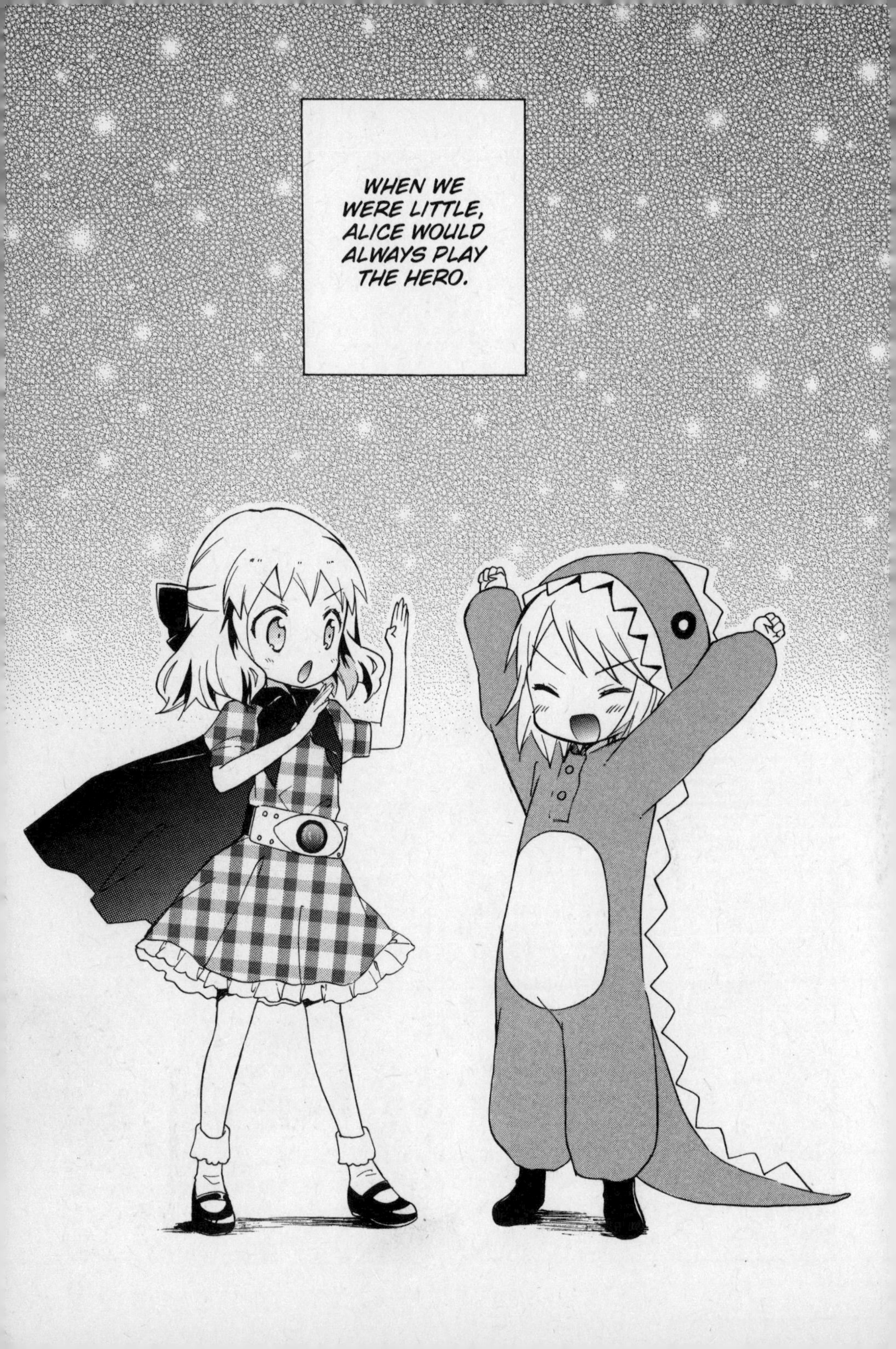
WHEN WE WERE LITTLE, ALICE WOULD ALWAYS PLAY THE HERO.

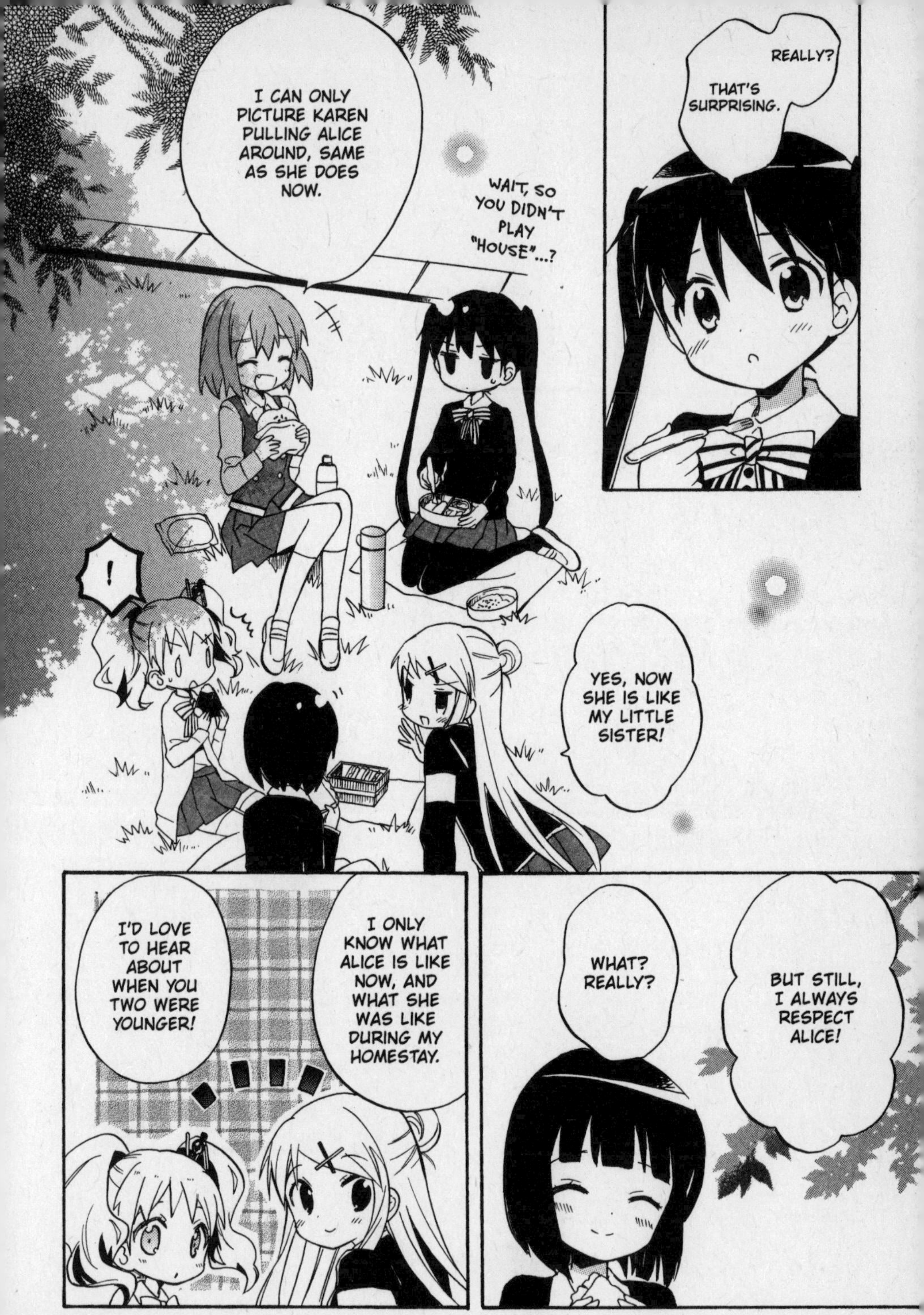
REALLY?
THAT'S SURPRISING.
WAIT, SO YOU DIDN'T PLAY "HOUSE"...?
I CAN ONLY PICTURE KAREN PULLING ALICE AROUND, SAME AS SHE DOES NOW.
!
YES, NOW SHE IS LIKE MY LITTLE SISTER!
BUT STILL, I ALWAYS RESPECT ALICE!
WHAT? REALLY?
I ONLY KNOW WHAT ALICE IS LIKE NOW, AND WHAT SHE WAS LIKE DURING MY HOMESTAY.
I'D LOVE TO HEAR ABOUT WHEN YOU TWO WERE YOUNGER!

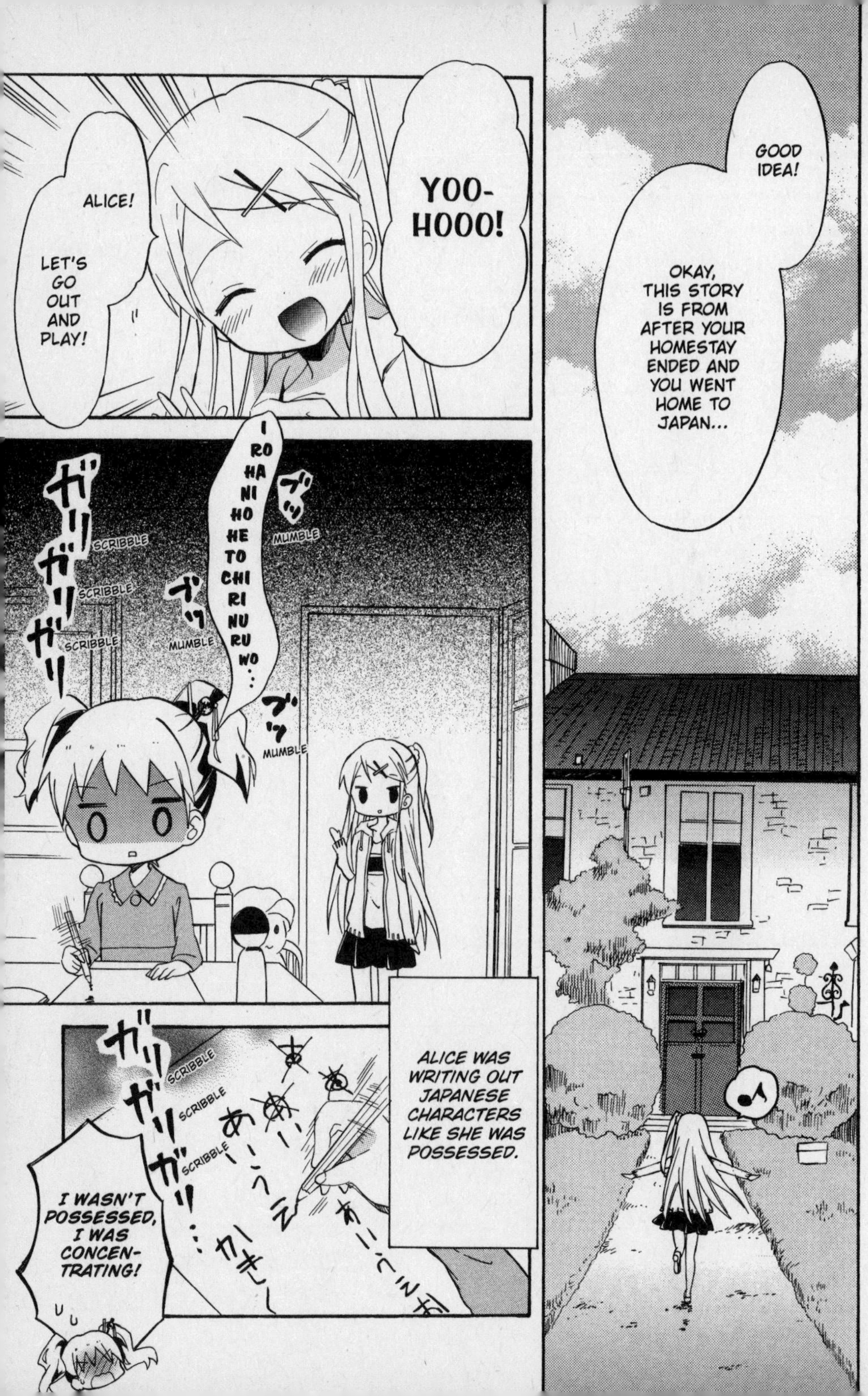
GOOD IDEA!
OKAY, THIS STORY IS FROM AFTER YOUR HOMESTAY ENDED AND YOU WENT HOME TO JAPAN...
YOO-HOOO!
ALICE!
LET'S GO OUT AND PLAY!
I RO HA NI HO HE TO CHI RI NU RU WO...
MUMBLE
MUMBLE
MUMBLE
SCRIBBLE
SCRIBBLE
SCRIBBLE
ALICE WAS WRITING OUT JAPANESE CHARACTERS LIKE SHE WAS POSSESSED.
SCRIBBLE
SCRIBBLE
SCRIBBLE
I WASN'T POSSESSED, I WAS CONCEN-TRATING!

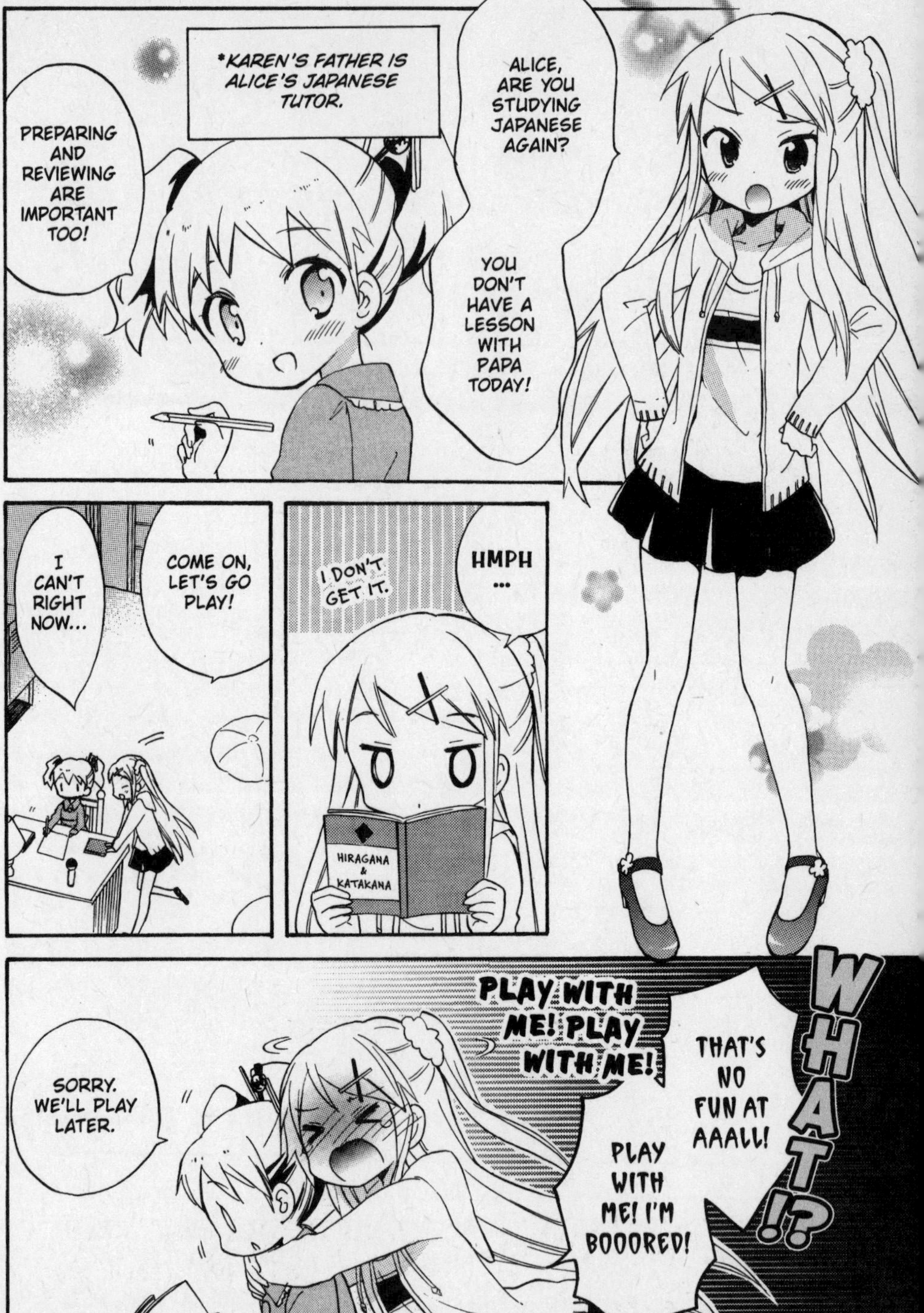
ALICE, ARE YOU STUDYING JAPANESE AGAIN?
YOU DON'T HAVE A LESSON WITH PAPA TODAY!
*KAREN'S FATHER IS ALICE'S JAPANESE TUTOR.
PREPARING AND REVIEWING ARE IMPORTANT TOO!
HMPH ...
I DON'T GET IT.
HIRAGANA & KATAKANA
COME ON, LET'S GO PLAY!
I CAN'T RIGHT NOW...
WHAT!?
THAT'S NO FUN AT AAALL!
PLAY WITH ME! I'M BOOORED!
PLAY WITH ME! PLAY WITH ME!
SORRY. WE'LL PLAY LATER.

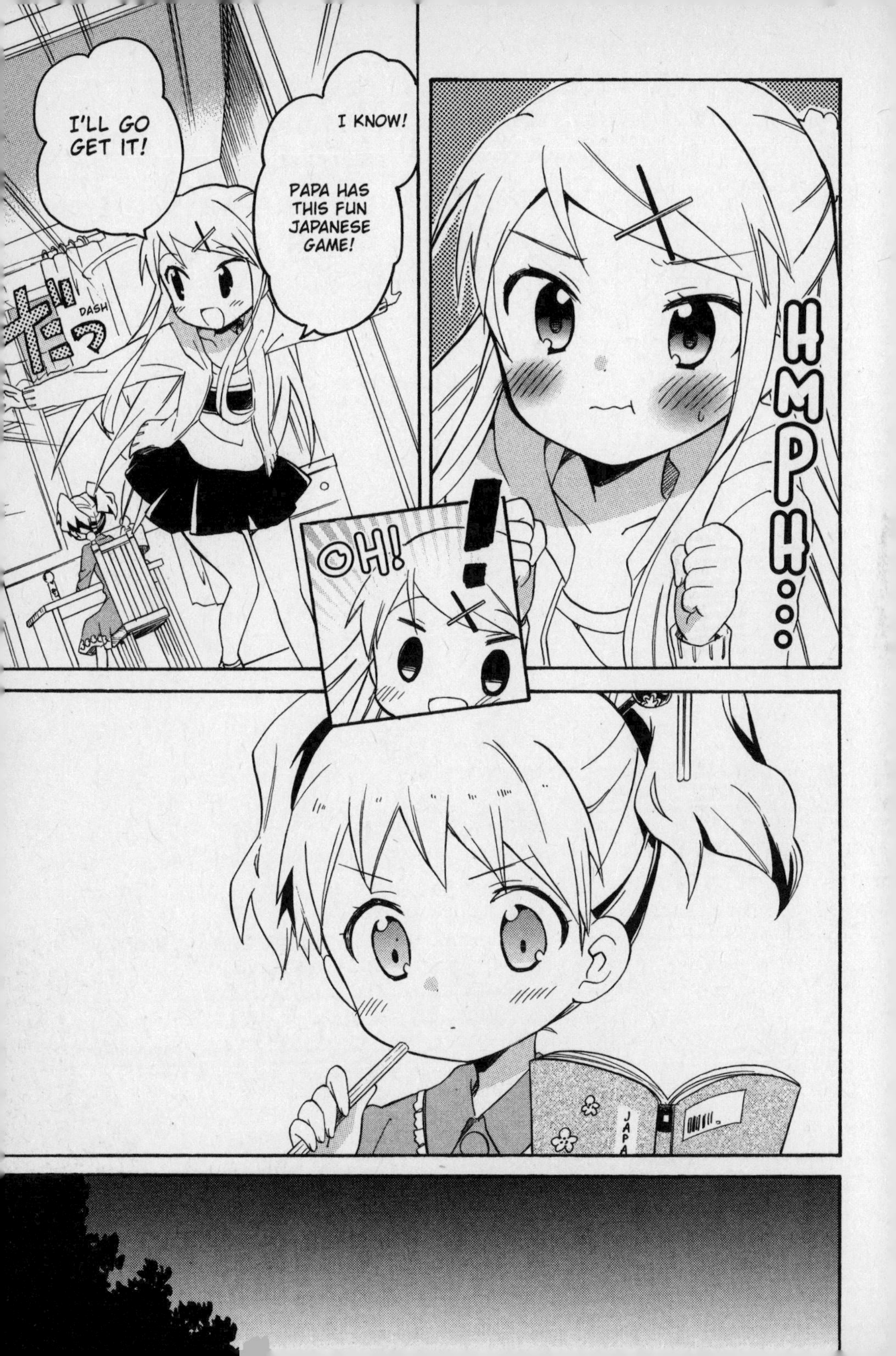
HMPH...
I KNOW!
PAPA HAS THIS FUN JAPANESE GAME!
I'LL GO GET IT!
ダッ
DASH
OH!
!

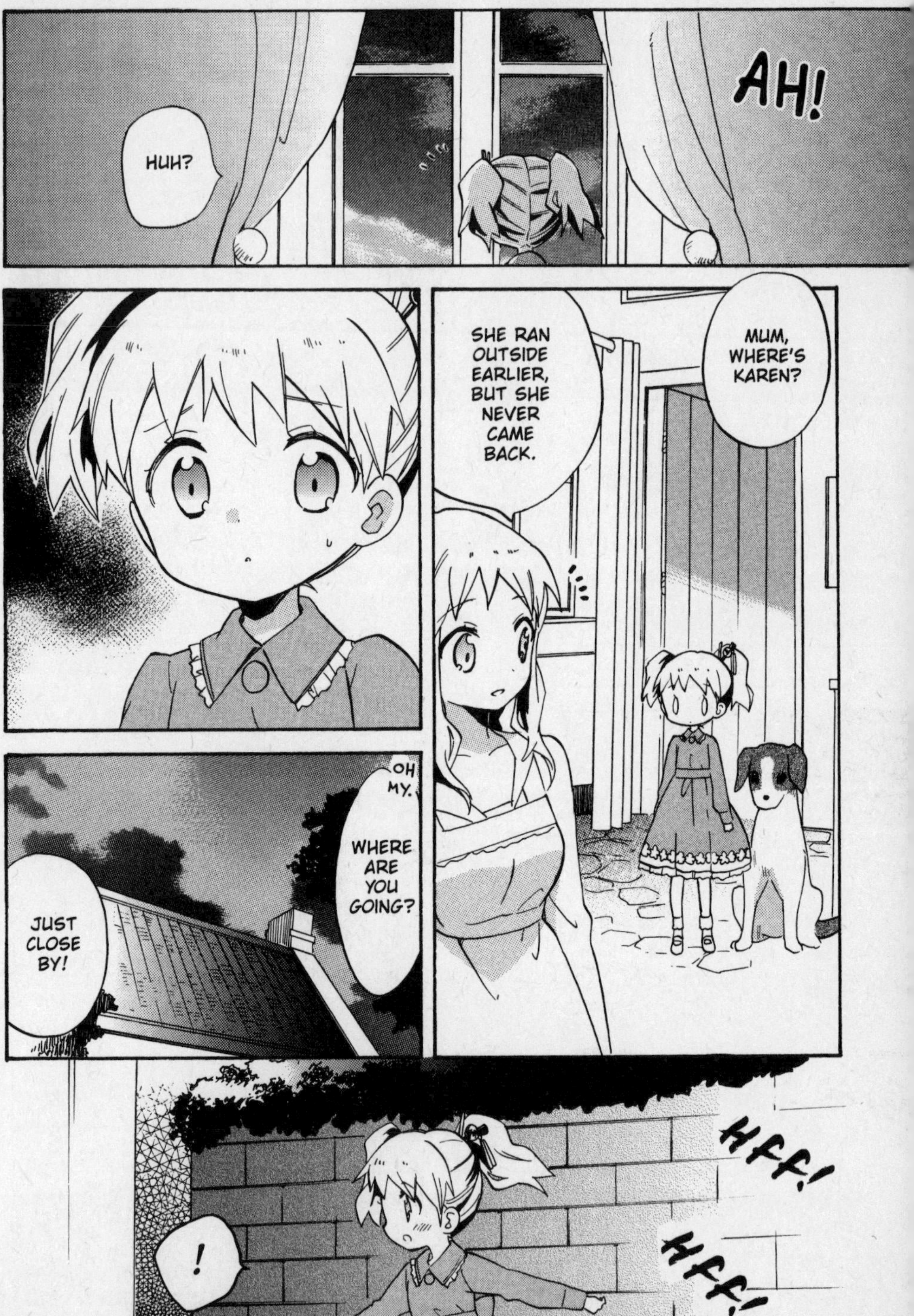
AH!
HUH?
MUM, WHERE'S KAREN?
SHE RAN OUTSIDE EARLIER, BUT SHE NEVER CAME BACK.
OH MY.
WHERE ARE YOU GOING?
JUST CLOSE BY!
HFF!
HFF!
!

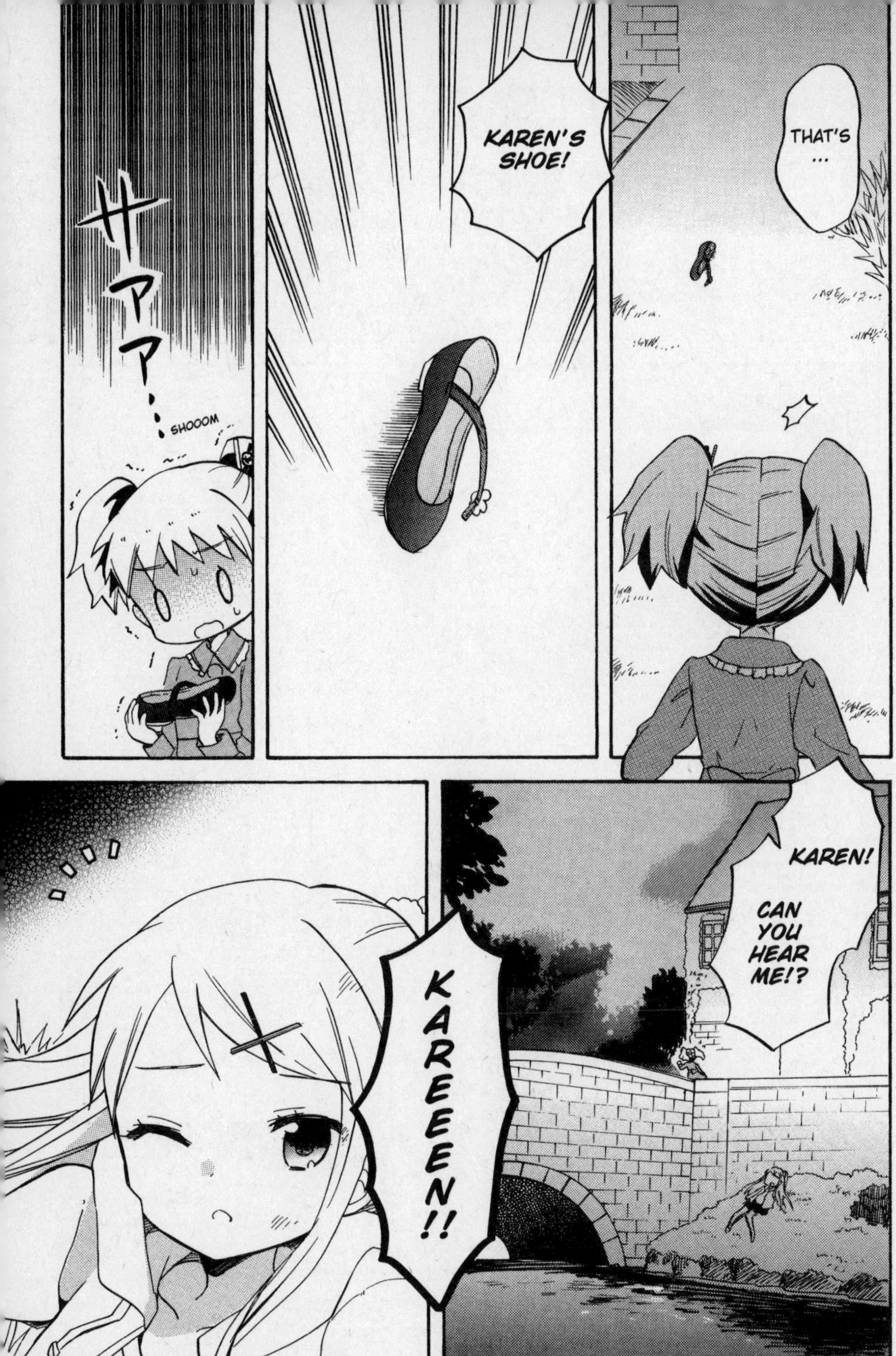
THAT'S ...
KAREN'S SHOE!
サァア...
SHOOOM
KAREN!
CAN YOU HEAR ME!?
KAREEEEN!!

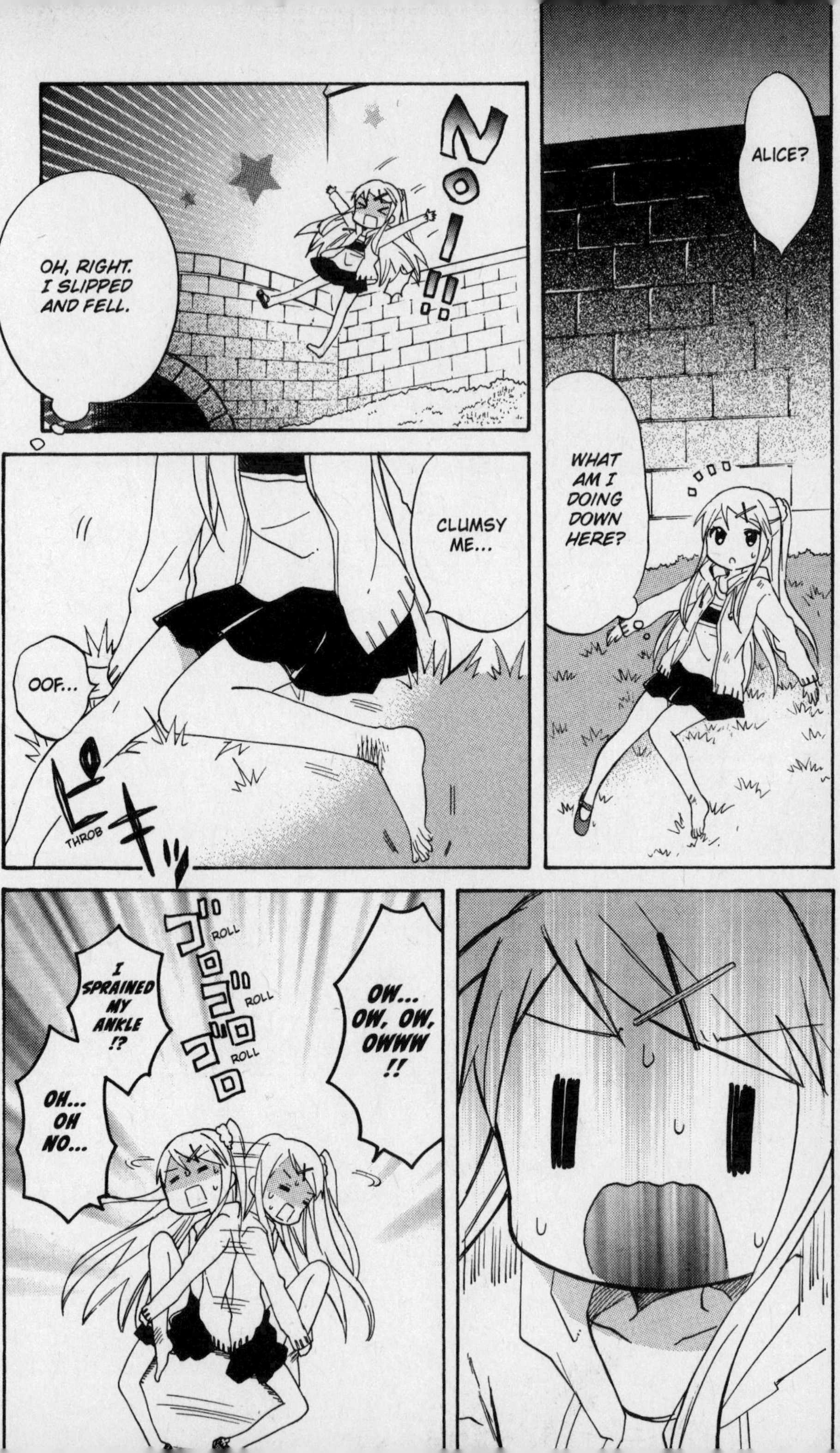
ALICE?
WHAT AM I DOING DOWN HERE?
OH, RIGHT. I SLIPPED AND FELL.
CLUMSY ME...
OOF...
THROB
OW... OW, OW, OWWW!!
I SPRAINED MY ANKLE!?
ROLL
ROLL
ROLL
OH... OH NO...

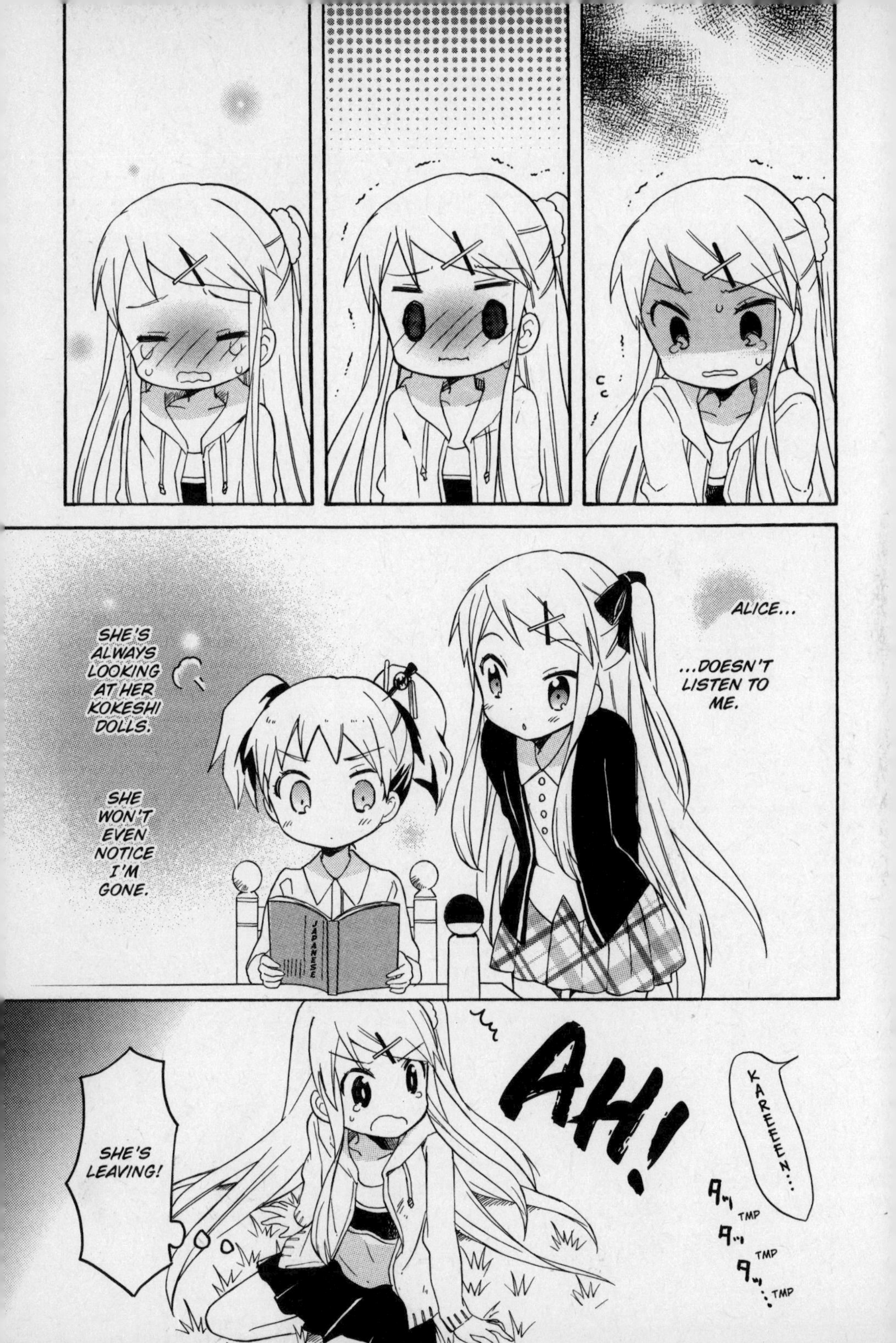
ALICE...
...DOESN'T LISTEN TO ME.
SHE'S ALWAYS LOOKING AT HER KOKESHI DOLLS.
SHE WON'T EVEN NOTICE I'M GONE.
KAREEEN...
TMP
TMP
TMP
AH!
SHE'S LEAVING!

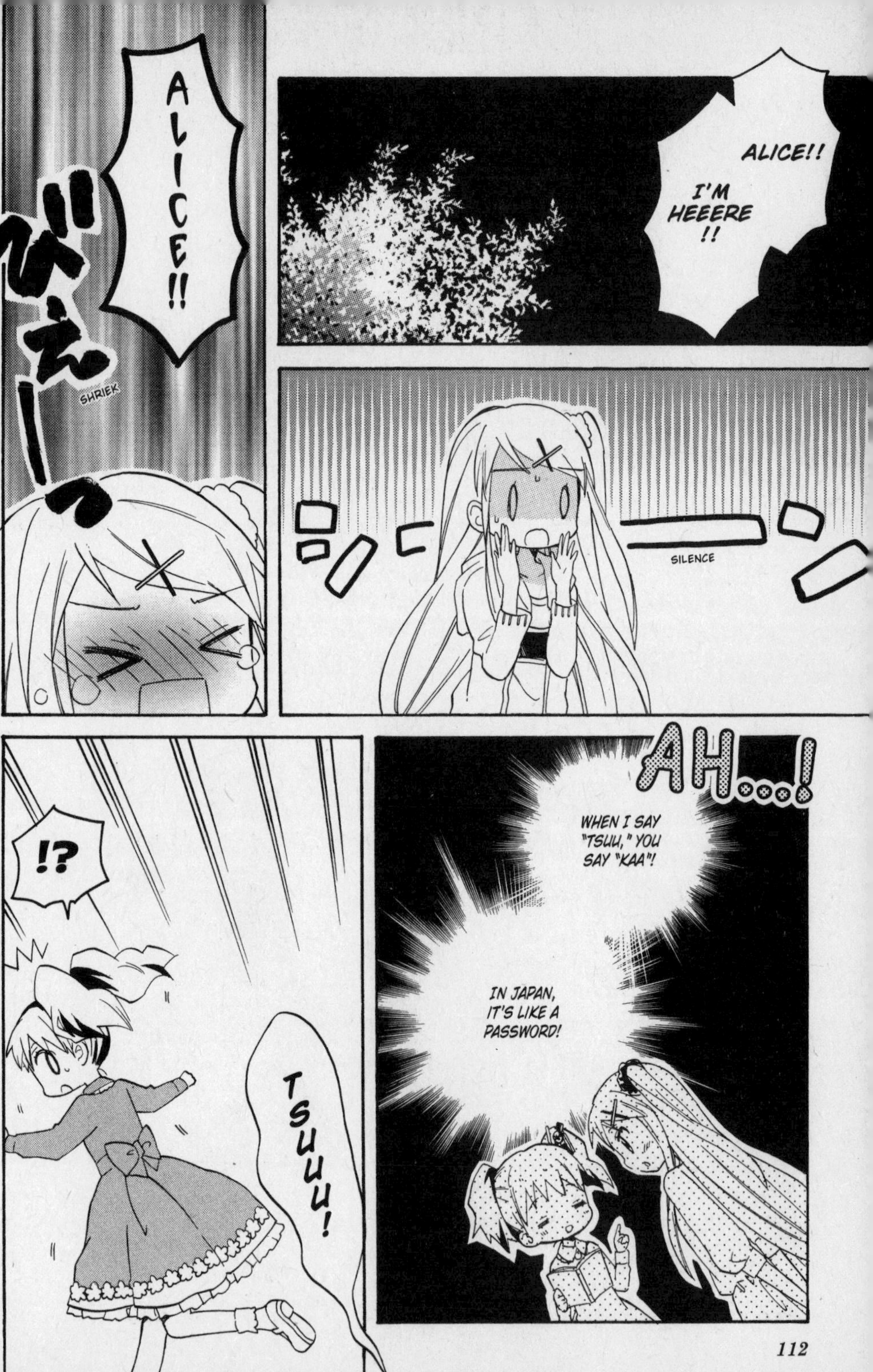
ALICE!!
I'M HEEERE!!
SILENCE
ALICE!!
びえーっ
SHRIEK
AH...!
WHEN I SAY "TSUU," YOU SAY "KAA"!
IN JAPAN, IT'S LIKE A PASSWORD!
!?
TSUUU!

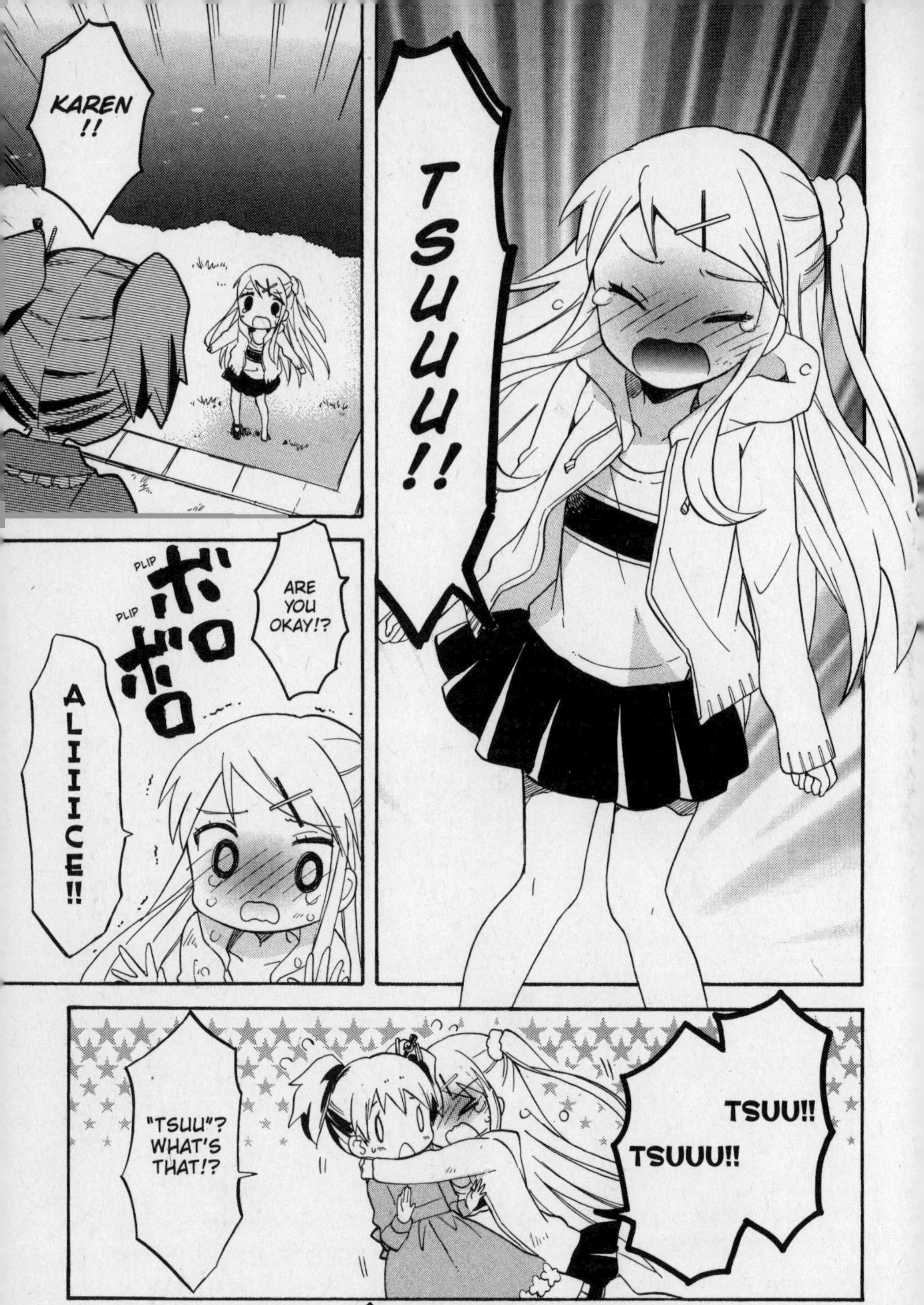
TSUUU!!
KAREN!!
ARE YOU OKAY!?
PLIP PLIP
ボロボロ
ALIIIICE!!
TSUU!!
TSUUU!!
"TSUU"? WHAT'S THAT!?

⇧ FORGOT ABOUT THAT

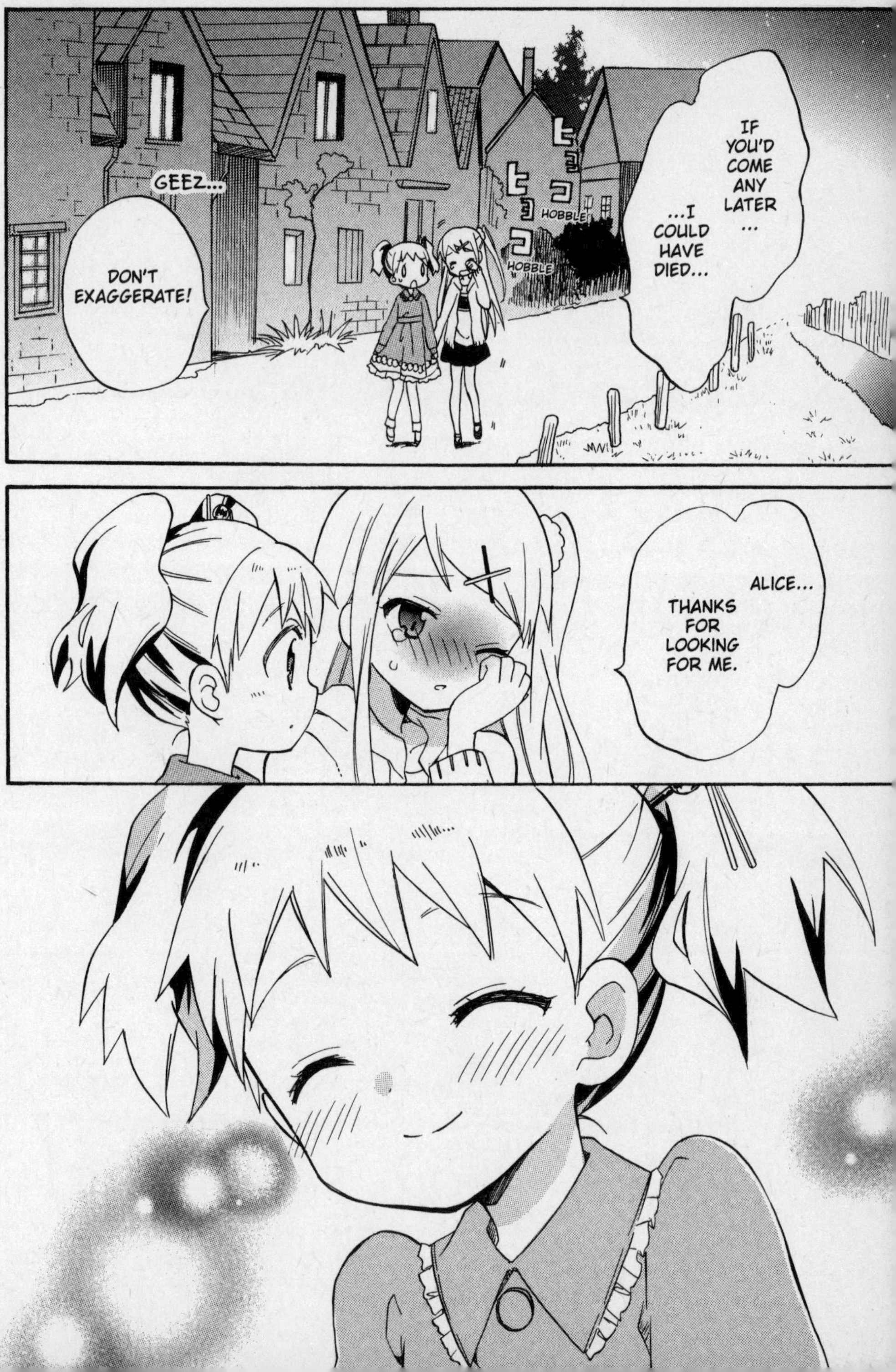
IF YOU'D COME ANY LATER...
...I COULD HAVE DIED...
HOBBLE
HOBBLE
GEEZ...
DON'T EXAGGERATE!
ALICE... THANKS FOR LOOKING FOR ME.

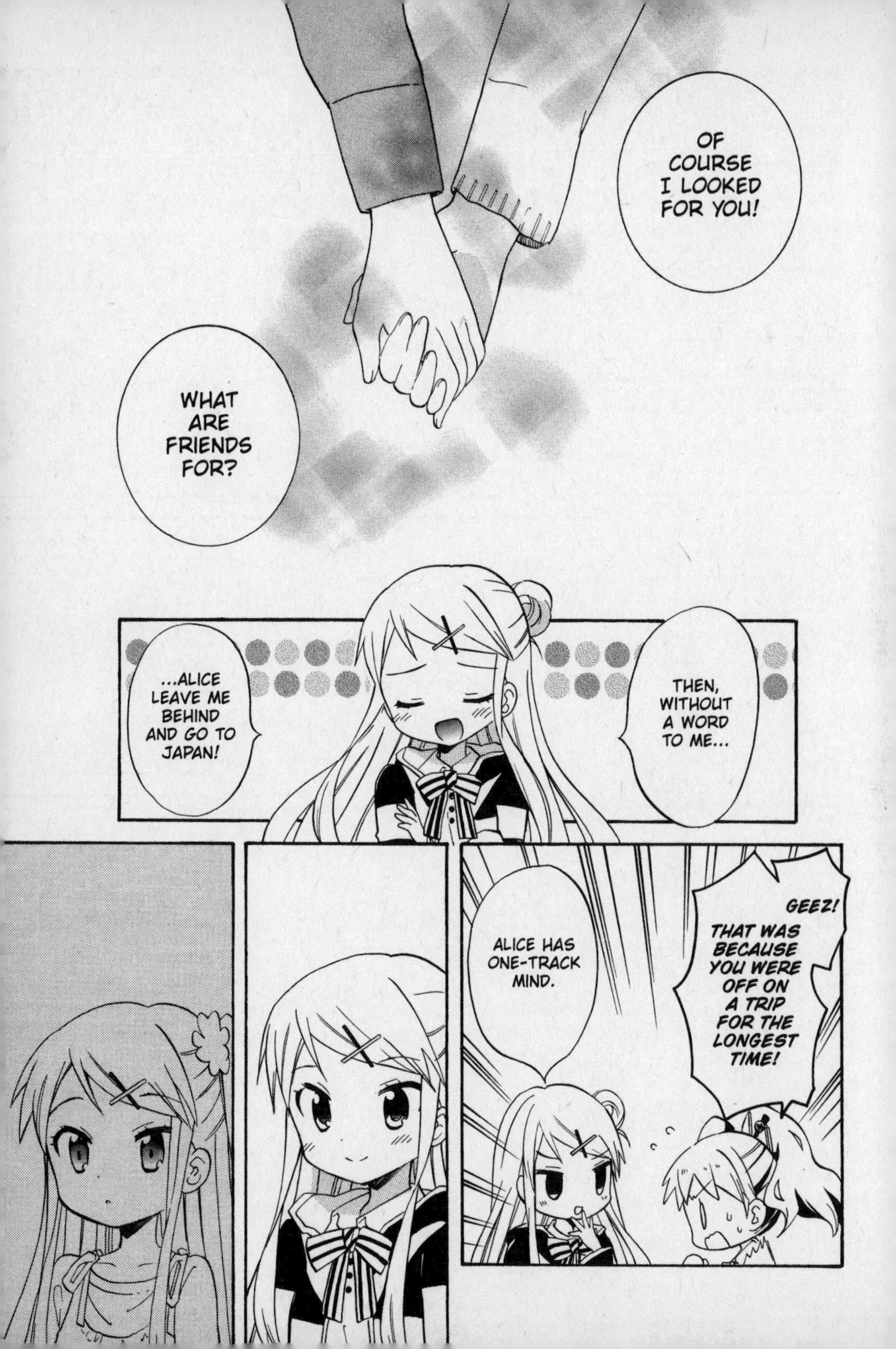
OF COURSE I LOOKED FOR YOU!
WHAT ARE FRIENDS FOR?
THEN, WITHOUT A WORD TO ME...
...ALICE LEAVE ME BEHIND AND GO TO JAPAN!
GEEZ! THAT WAS BECAUSE YOU WERE OFF ON A TRIP FOR THE LONGEST TIME!
ALICE HAS ONE-TRACK MIND.

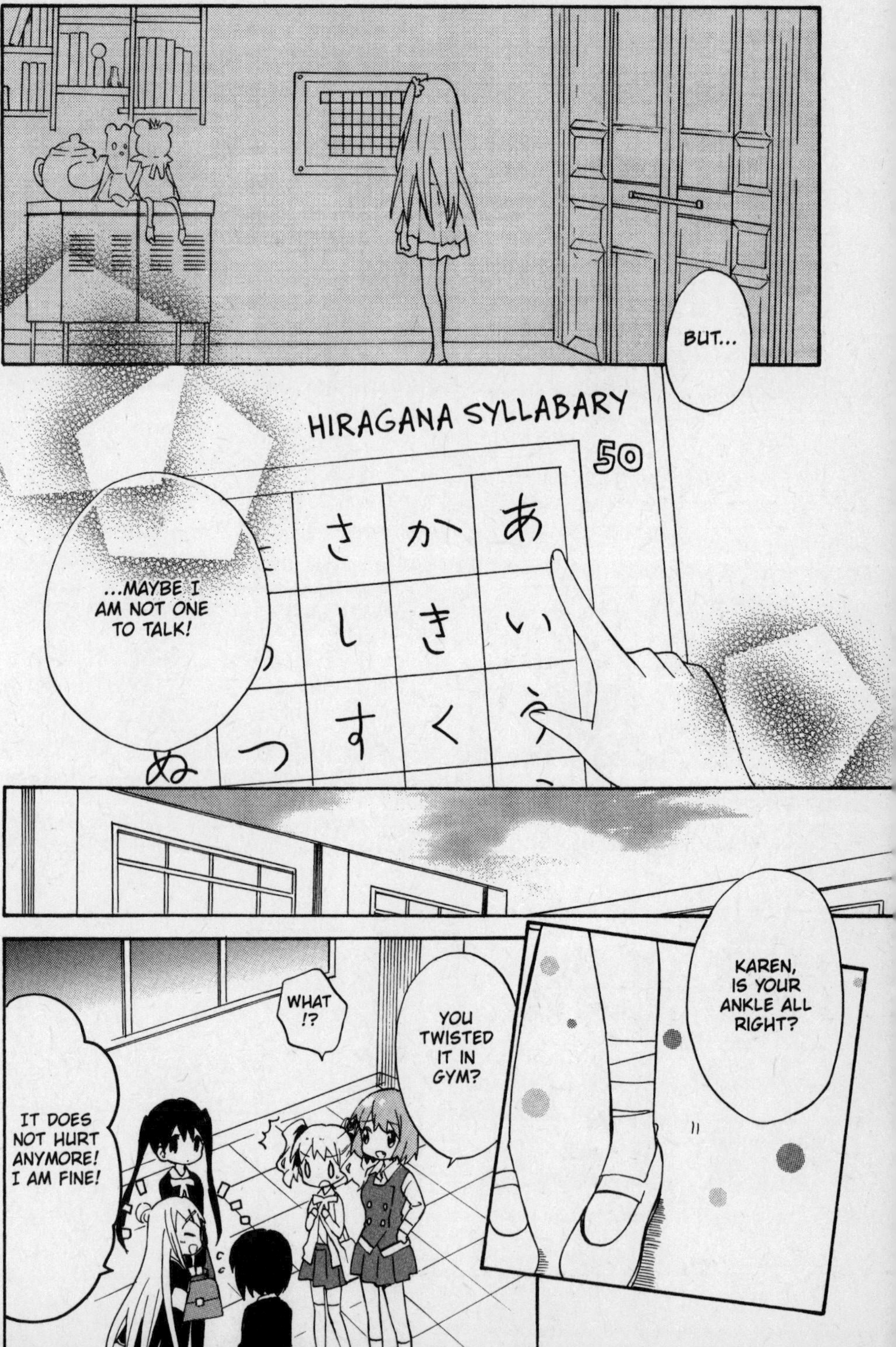
BUT...
HIRAGANA SYLLABARY
50
さ か あ
し き い
ぬ つ す く
...MAYBE I AM NOT ONE TO TALK!
KAREN, IS YOUR ANKLE ALL RIGHT?
YOU TWISTED IT IN GYM?
WHAT !?
IT DOES NOT HURT ANYMORE! I AM FINE!

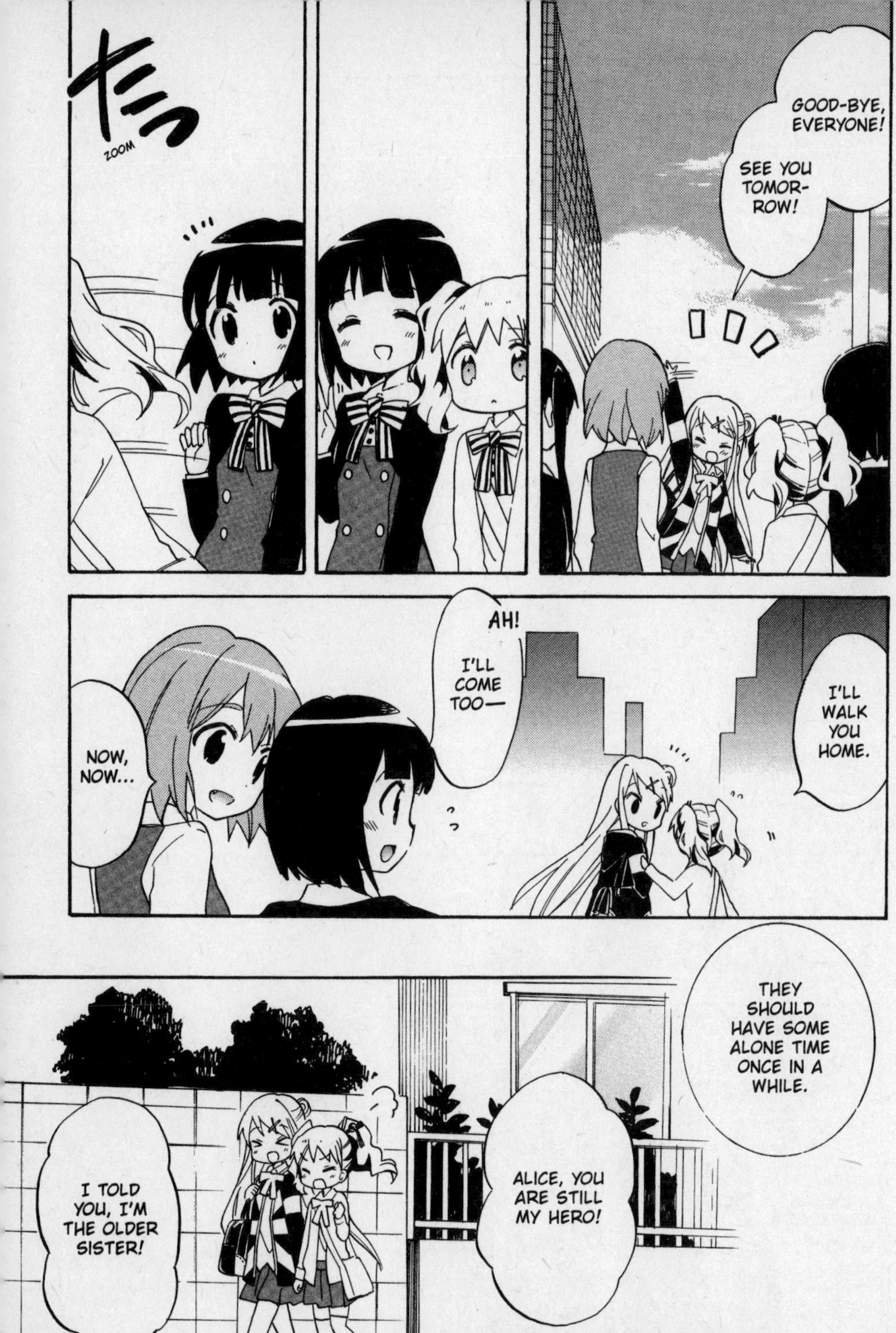
GOOD-BYE, EVERYONE!
SEE YOU TOMORROW!
ZOOM
I'LL WALK YOU HOME.
AH! I'LL COME TOO—
NOW, NOW...
THEY SHOULD HAVE SOME ALONE TIME ONCE IN A WHILE.
ALICE, YOU ARE STILL MY HERO!
I TOLD YOU, I'M THE OLDER SISTER!

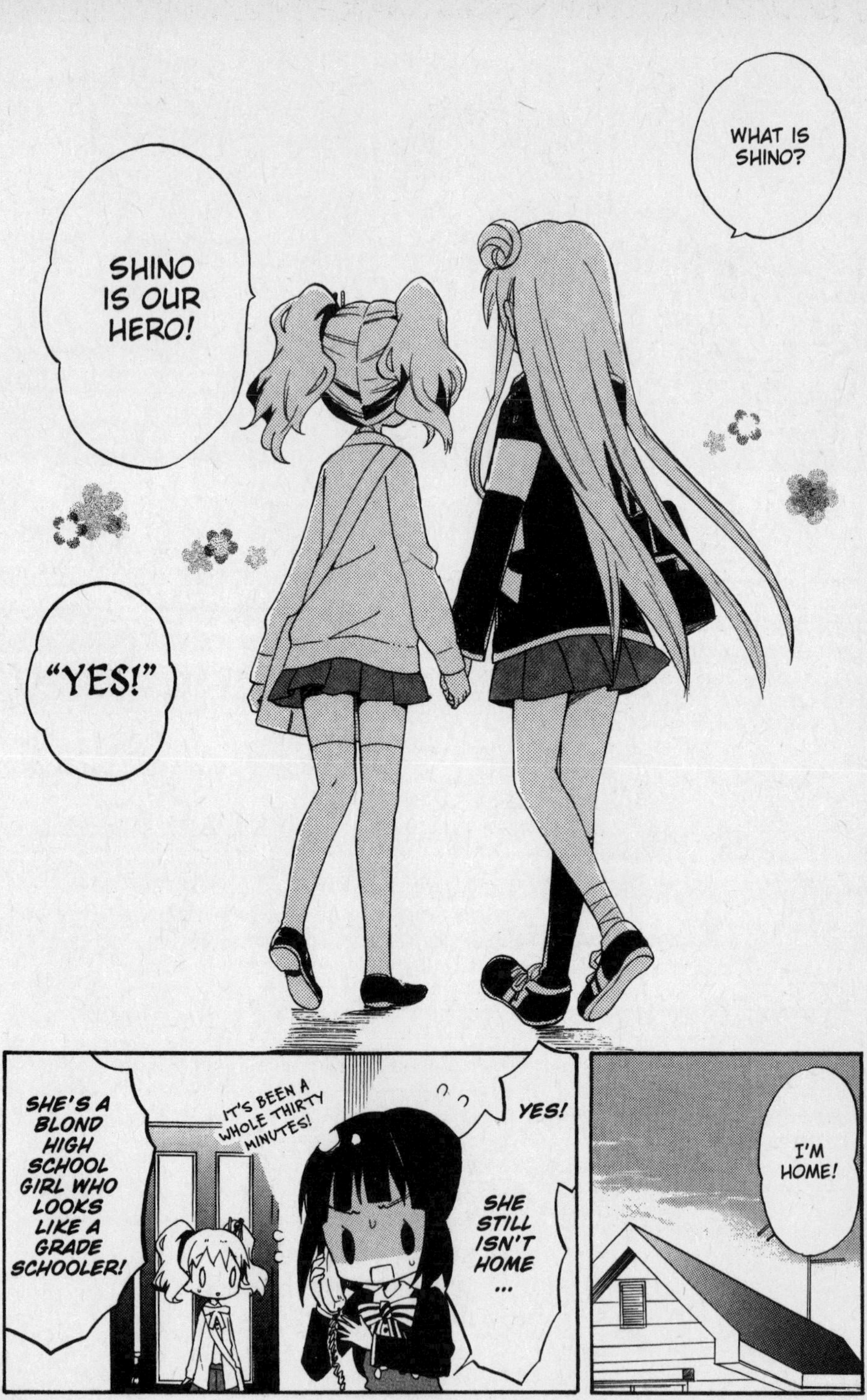
WHAT IS SHINO?
SHINO IS OUR HERO!
"YES!"
I'M HOME!
YES!
IT'S BEEN A WHOLE THIRTY MINUTES!
SHE STILL ISN'T HOME ...
SHE'S A BLOND HIGH SCHOOL GIRL WHO LOOKS LIKE A GRADE SCHOOLER!

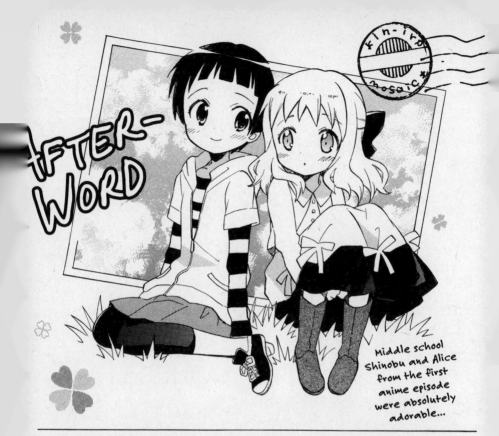

AFTER-WORD

kin-iro mosaic

Middle school Shinobu and Alice from the first anime episode were absolutely adorable...

Thank you for reading *Kiniro Mosaic* volume 4. I'm so grateful that this year two volumes of Kinmoza could be released...!

In both volumes 3 and 4, with the girls moving up a grade and Alice and Karen visiting England, I included some moments of Shinobu and Alice being apart briefly. I hope you could feel how much they care about each other even when they're separated. Now their relationship is even stronger, and I hope you look forward to volume 5!

Many thanks!

My editor: Hideki Satomi-sama
The anime staff and voice cast
All the people who've supported me
All of my readers

Hara Yui

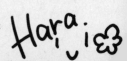

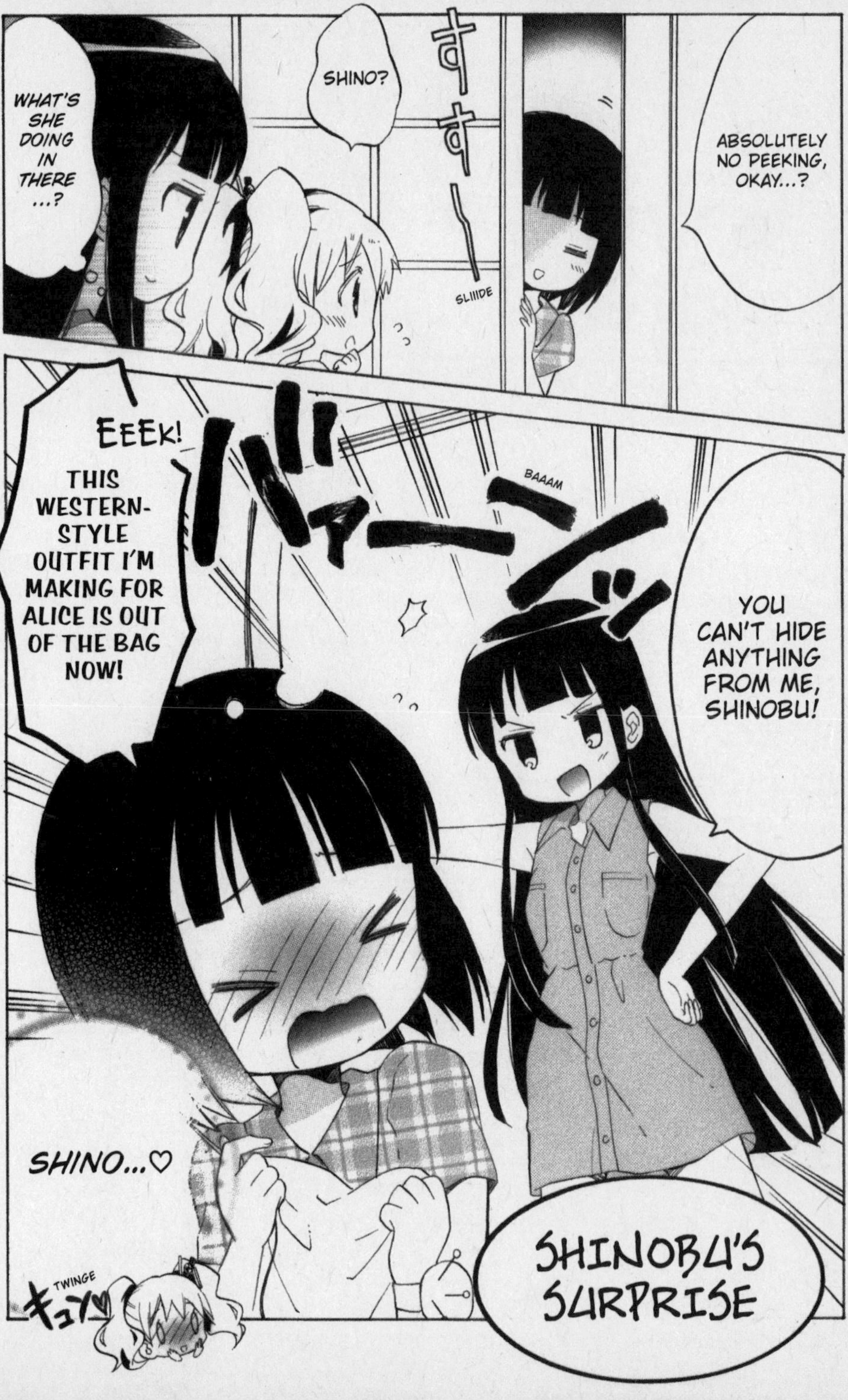
ABSOLUTELY NO PEEKING, OKAY...?
すすー
SLIIIDE
SHINO?
WHAT'S SHE DOING IN THERE ...?
YOU CAN'T HIDE ANYTHING FROM ME, SHINOBU!
バァーン
BAAAM
EEEk!
THIS WESTERN-STYLE OUTFIT I'M MAKING FOR ALICE IS OUT OF THE BAG NOW!
SHINOBU'S SURPRISE
SHINO...♡
キュン♡
TWINGE

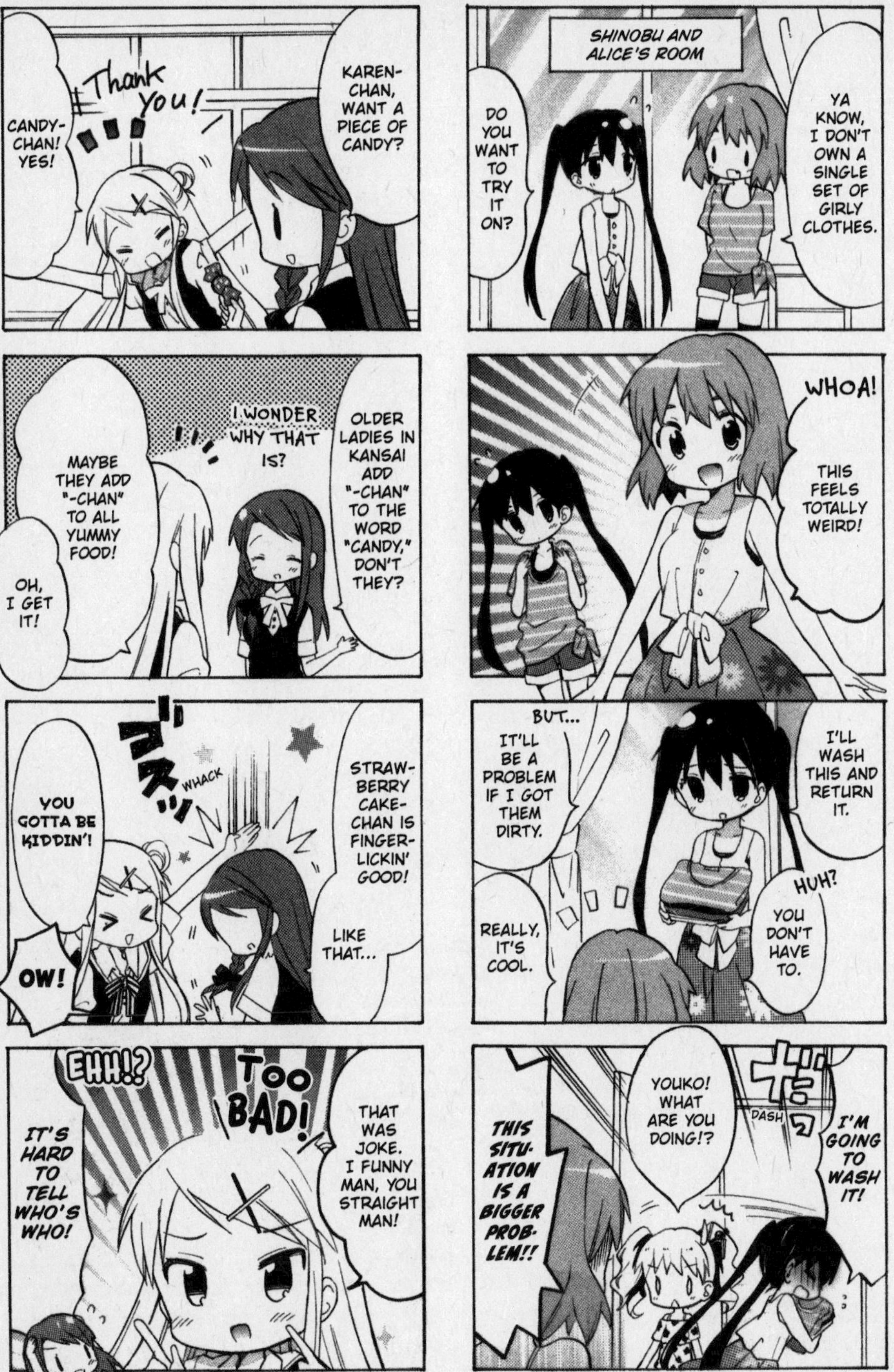
SHINOBU AND ALICE'S ROOM
YA KNOW, I DON'T OWN A SINGLE SET OF GIRLY CLOTHES.
DO YOU WANT TO TRY IT ON?
WHOA!
THIS FEELS TOTALLY WEIRD!
I'LL WASH THIS AND RETURN IT.
BUT... IT'LL BE A PROBLEM IF I GOT THEM DIRTY.
HUH? YOU DON'T HAVE TO.
REALLY, IT'S COOL.
DASH
I'M GOING TO WASH IT!
YOUKO! WHAT ARE YOU DOING!?
THIS SITUATION IS A BIGGER PROBLEM!!
KAREN-CHAN, WANT A PIECE OF CANDY?
Thank You!
CANDY-CHAN! YES!
OLDER LADIES IN KANSAI ADD "-CHAN" TO THE WORD "CANDY," DON'T THEY?
I WONDER WHY THAT IS?
MAYBE THEY ADD "-CHAN" TO ALL YUMMY FOOD!
OH, I GET IT!
STRAWBERRY CAKE-CHAN IS FINGER-LICKIN' GOOD!
LIKE THAT...
WHACK
YOU GOTTA BE KIDDIN'!
OW!
THAT WAS JOKE. I FUNNY MAN, YOU STRAIGHT MAN!
TOO BAD!
EHH!?
IT'S HARD TO TELL WHO'S WHO!

kiniro
mosaic

Translation Notes

COMMON HONORIFICS

no honorific: Indicates familiarity or closeness; if used without permission or reason, addressing someone in this manner would constitute an insult.

-san: The Japanese equivalent of Mr./Mrs./Miss. If a situation calls for politeness, this is the fail-safe honorific.

-sama: Conveys great respect; may also indicate that the social status of the speaker is lower than that of the addressee.

-kun: Used most often when referring to boys, this indicates affection or familiarity. Occasionally used by older men among their peers, but it may also be used by anyone referring to a person of lower standing.

-chan (also -tan): An affectionate honorific indicating familiarity used mostly in reference to girls; also used in reference to cute persons or animals of either gender.

-senpai: An honorific used to address upperclassmen or more experienced coworkers.

-sensei: A respectful honorific for teachers, artists, or high-level professionals.

PAGE 5

The Japanese term used for **emoting** was originally *kidoairaku*, which literally means "joy, anger, pathos, humor."

PAGE 9

"I'm more about food than flowers!", or *hana yori dango*, is a Japanese proverb describing people who prefer practical gifts over beautiful ones.

PAGE 14
The **King of Hell**, known as King Enma in Japanese, is the judge of the underworld who determines whether the dead will reincarnate into pleasant lives or terrible ones. The idea of Enma came to Japan through China.

PAGE 21
Onee-chan means "big sister."

PAGE 27
A **stomach band**, or *haramaki*, is a Japanese clothing accessory meant to keep a person's midsection warm. It is generally considered a very old-fashioned and unfashionable garment.

PAGE 32
One Japanese suffix for club is *bu*, so **Shino-bu** is a pun on Shinobu's name that literally means "Shino Club."

PAGE 33
To **split one's guts** in Japanese is to drop all pretense and have everything out in the open.

PAGE 38
"The air feel so gud!" in the Japanese-language version was *"Kuuki ga oi-C desu!"* This is a play on words between the word *oishii* ("tasty") and the English letter C.

PAGE 40
In Japanese mythology, **heavenly sages**, or *sennin*, are immortal beings capable of riding clouds and sustaining themselves on a diet of mist. This is due to their detachment from worldly desires.

PAGE 47
In Japanese, the words for **money** and **gold** are pronounced differently (*kane* and *kin*, respectively) but are both written with the same Japanese kanji.

PAGE 48
The **kokeshi doll** is a traditional wooden doll with no arms or legs.

PAGE 50
10,000 yen is roughly equivalent to $100 USD.

PAGE 54
The **moral of "The Straw Millionaire"** is supposed to be that selfless actions can potentially lead to greater rewards than expected.

PAGE 58
In the Japanese-language version, wearing **lighter clothes** is expressed through the term "cool biz," which is a move by the Japanese Ministry of the Environment to reduce energy usage. This involves encouraging office workers to wear lighter clothing and for offices to limit air conditioner use.

PAGE 61
The Japanese-language version of the **waistline/ fishing line** misunderstanding involves Alice wondering if *kubire* ("waist") is a type of *hire* ("fin").

PAGE 62

In Japan, it's traditional to give **summer gifts** of gratitude (*ochuugen*) around July.

Wind, forest, fire, mountain, or *fuurinkazan*, is an abbreviated version of a battle standard used by Japanese Sengoku warlord Shingen Takeda. Derived from Sun Tzu's *Art of War*, the phrase in full means "be as swift as wind, as gentle as the forest, as fierce as fire, and as immoveable as the mountain."

PAGE 68

Shiritori **word chain** is a game in which players must come up with a word that begins with the last syllable of the previous word in the chain. If they can't think of one in time, or think up a word ending in the syllable *n* (which never starts a word in Japanese), they lose the game. The original Japanese is *natsu* (summer), *tsumiki* (toy brick), *kitsutsuki* (woodpecker), *kinoko* (mushroom), and koala.

PAGE 69

Dosukoi is an exclamation used by sumo wrestlers, generally used to show their spirit. It derives from the Japanese word *dokkoi*, which roughly means "heave-ho."

PAGE 72

Nagashi-soumen is a fun, summery way of eating *soumen*, a type of thin wheat noodle. The noodles are sent down a bamboo slide in a stream of water, and diners have to catch them with their chopsticks.

PAGE 73
Fireball Smash is a fictional tennis move most commonly associated with the *Tokimeki Memorial* dating sim series. In those games, it's a technique used by the members of the Habataki Private High School Tennis Club.

Page 81
"E-even my papa has never hit me!" is a play on a famous line uttered by Amuro Ray, the main character of the anime *Mobile Suit Gundam*. Amuro, a civilian who is thrust into war and unused to military structure, is responding to being slapped by his commanding officer Bright Noa for acting out of line.

Page 85
Yakisoba is a stir-fried noodle dish commonly made with meat or seafood, vegetables (cabbage, carrots, onions), bonito flakes, and a savory sauce. Yakisoba is a "use whatever's available" type of food, so there is no set ingredients list for it.

Page 97
The concept of the **ideal Japanese woman**, known as *yamato nadeshiko*, gained prominence during World War II. Women were to be demure on the outside, strong on the inside, and fiercely loyal to their husbands and country. In time, the term has come to mean a "classic beauty."

Page 98
Natto is a sticky, fermented soybean snack. Because of its powerful smell, taste, and texture, it can be a love-it-or-hate-it food.

PAGE 105
Alice is reciting **"Iroha,"** a classic poem that uses every character of the Japanese syllabary only once. Japanese children are taught to recite the "Iroha" in the same way that American children are taught the alphabet.

PAGE 112
Tsuu and *kaa* come from a Japanese phrase that states when someone says *"tsuu,"* a *"kaa"* will soon follow. It refers to two people who are so connected to each other that they can practically finish each other's thoughts.

PAGE 121
Karen and Honoka are behaving like a ***manzai* duo**. This is a form of Japanese comedy popular in the Kansai region that involves having one performer play the fool (*boke*) while the other acts as the straight man (*tsukkomi*). The fool will usually say something wrong or utterly ridiculous, and then get corrected by the straight man.

Two girls, a new school, and the beginning of a beautiful friendship.

Volumes 1-3 available now

1
Kiss & White Lily for My Dearest Girl
CANNO

Kiss & White Lily for My Dearest Girl

In middle school, Ayaka Shiramine was the perfect student: hard-working, with excellent grades and a great personality to match. As Ayaka enters high school she expects to still be on top, but one thing she didn't account for is her new classmate, the lazy yet genuine genius Yurine Kurosawa. What's in store for Ayaka and Yurine as they go through high school...together?

Yen Press

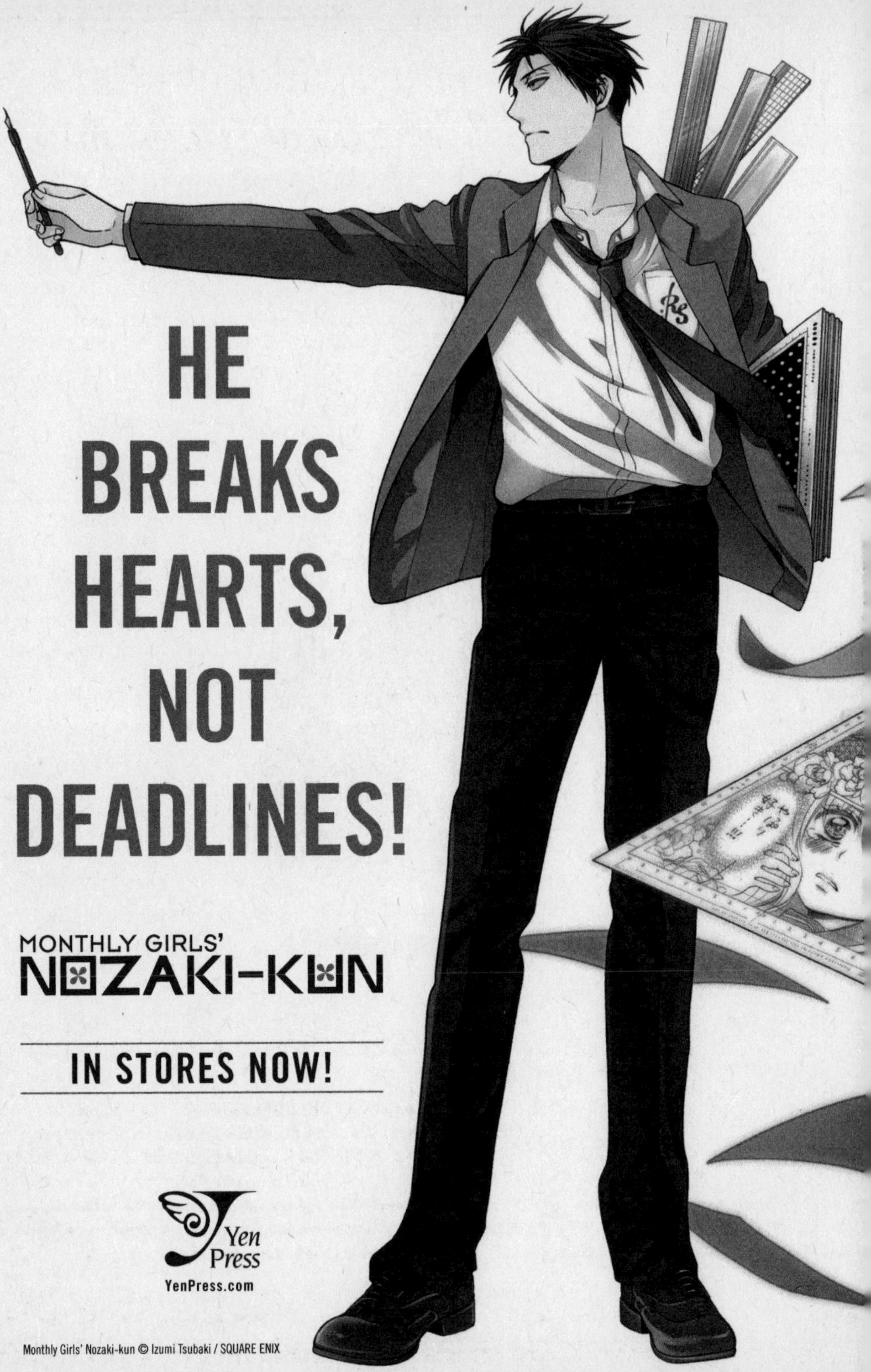